CONFLICT IN ASIA

D1738711

CONFLICT IN ASIA

Korea, China-Taiwan, and India-Pakistan

EDITED BY UK HEO AND SHALE A. HOROWITZ

Westport, Connecticut
London

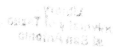

Library of Congress Cataloging-in-Publication Data

Conflict in Asia : Korea, China-Taiwan, and India-Pakistan / edited by Uk Heo and Shale A. Horowitz.
    p.   cm.
    Includes bibliographical references and index.
    ISBN 0–275–97779–X (alk. paper)—ISBN: 0–275–97791–9 (pbk.: alk. paper)
    1. Korea (South)—Foreign relations—Korea (North) 2. Korea (North)—Foreign relations—Korea (South) 3. India—Foreign relations—Pakistan. 4. Pakistan—Foreign relations—India. 5. China—Foreign relations—Taiwan. 6. Taiwan—Foreign relations—China. 7. World politics—1989–
    I.   Heo, Uk, 1962–   II. Horowitz, Shale Asher.
DS910.2.K7 C66   2003
327′.095—dc21   2002067300

British Library Cataloguing in Publication Data is available.

Library of Congress Catalog Card Number: 2002067300
ISBN: 0–275–97779–X
        0–275–97791–9 (pbk.)

First published in 2003

Praeger Publishers, 88 Post Road West, Westport, CT 06881
An imprint of Greenwood Publishing Group, Inc.
www.praeger.com

Printed in the United States of America

The paper used in this book complies with the Permanent Paper Standard issued by the National Information Standards Organization (Z39.48–1984).

10 9 8 7 6 5 4 3 2 1

Contents

Illustrations

Acknowledgments

This book is based on papers presented at a conference held at the University of Wisconsin-Milwaukee in April, 2000. We would like to thank Patrice Petro and the Center for International Education for generously supporting the conference. We also thank Peter Finn for his help in typesetting the final version of the book.

Introduction and Review of Findings

Uk Heo and Shale Horowitz

With the end of the Cold War, the focus of world politics has moved from "high," military affairs, to "low," economic affairs, in many parts of the world. However, many Cold War-era geopolitical conflicts are not yet resolved in Asia. This is particularly true for those conflicts with ethnic and territorial components. Although the end of the Cold War has largely eliminated the threat of Soviet expansionism, as well as Soviet support for client states such as Vietnam and North Korea, there are still three main epicenters of potential conflict: (1) China-Taiwan; (2) North Korea-South Korea; and (3) India-Pakistan.

In terms of war likelihood, a number of scholars argue that the most war-prone regions during the 1945-76 period were the Middle East and Asia.[1] This remains true in the twenty-first century. The Middle East has been struggling toward a peace settlement between Israel, the Palestinian Liberation Organization (PLO), and a number of Arab states. Long-lasting US sanctions on Iraq and the response to the September 11, 2001, attack on the US make the situation in the region even more complicated and volatile.

Asia has also been volatile due to enduring rivalries and conflicts.[2] The power vacuum left by the demise of the Soviet Union has been partially filled by an economically resurgent and increasingly assertive China. As Taiwan has democratized and forged a strong indigenous identity, Chinese threats to use force to reintegrate Taiwan have increased. China has also become more aggressive about asserting territorial possession of much of the South China Sea, particularly in the Spratly Islands. Moreover, Chinese diplomacy, often linked with economic initiatives, is increasingly active in Asia.

On the Korean peninsula, where huge, heavily armed forces still face each other across the demilitarized zone, South Korea's "sunshine" policy toward North Korea has eased tensions. However, lingering food shortages in North

Korea have led her leaders to continue to play a survival game by developing nuclear weapons and long-range missiles. The North Korean regime remains highly unpredictable. North Korea has recently improved ties with Russia and China, joining them in an attempt to forestall US efforts to develop a missile defense system.

The India-Pakistan rivalry has been ongoing since the postcolonial partition. The recent nuclear arms race and a succession of bloody clashes in Kashmir indicate a rising level of tension and conflict. Since the end of the Cold War, India's rival China has developed closer relations with Pakistan. At the same time, the US has largely abandoned its loose Cold War alliance with Pakistan, and has increasingly tilted toward India. With the September 11 terrorist attack on the US, the US-Pakistan relationship has improved as Pakistan supports the US retaliatory efforts in Afghanistan. At the same time, Pakistani support for more militant secessionist groups in Kashmir, which have conducted increasingly bold terrorist attacks against prominent Indian targets, has brought India and Pakistan to the brink of war. The US and India are trying to force Pakistan to retreat into providing more passive support to local, less extreme Kashmiri separatist groups, and particularly to uproot the more extreme fundamentalist groups. The latter have been financed and organized by Pakistani military intelligence, from bases in both Pakistan and Afghanistan, and they are largely constituted of Pakistanis and volunteers from various other Islamic countries or regions.

In this book, we attempt to assess the post-Cold War changes and future prospects of the Asian security system by looking at these three conflicting dyads—China-Taiwan, North Korea-South Korea, and India-Pakistan. To this end we employ all three major theoretical perspectives in international relations theory: neo-realism, neo-liberalism and constructivism. The characteristic insights of all three approaches are found to be necessary to understanding the three Asian conflicts. Through case studies using these theoretical approaches, we attempt to explain the evolution of each country's security policy and changing mix of alliances. We also analyze US interests, and discuss how the likely character of US intervention affects the strategies of the conflicting states. The reason is that the US is likely to become involved in any escalation of the Korean and China-Taiwan conflicts. The India-Pakistan conflict could also involve the US, particularly if hostilities escalate toward a nuclear exchange, or if internal instability in Pakistan risks putting its nuclear weapons into the hands of extremists. In any event, the chances for peaceful resolution of all three conflicts will depend strongly on the role played by the US. Thus, this book will not only help us better understand the security relationship between these three pairs of rivals, but will also provide a larger picture of how the conflicts interact within the overall Asian security system.

We now summarize the findings of the chapters. In Chapter 1, Shale Horowitz discusses three major theoretical approaches in international relations theory and briefly applies them to the three conflicts covered in the book. He argues that constructivism adds strong contributions to the traditional insights of the neo-realist and neo-liberal theoretical approaches. Constructivism focuses on national and state identities and their impacts on preferences and strategies, and on how the resulting international strategic interactions can feed back to influence the evolution of national and state identities. For the China-Taiwan conflict, constructivism calls attention to China's presently vague state identity, and to how strategic interaction with China's legitimacy-oriented Communist Party elites is likely to accelerate the development of Taiwan's "islander" national identity. For the Korean conflict, on the other hand, the stability and strength of a united Korean identity in both North and South facilitates the South's conciliatory stabilizing policy toward the North's insecure elites. For India and Pakistan, constructivism casts light on the way both states' identities, objectives, and strategies have been shaped by the history of the conflict since independence. In particular, Pakistani national and state identity has arrived at a momentous crossroads. Down one road lies militant Islamism and a risky intensification of conflict with India. Down the other is the East Asian economic development model, which emphasizes internal economic growth, political stability, and a more cautious foreign policy.

In Chapter 2, Jing Huang discusses China's military policy toward Taiwan. Within the context of the one-China principle, according to them, Beijing's policy toward Taiwan has undergone significant changes in the past five decades. It evolved from one of "liberating" Taiwan using military force in 1950-79, to the "sunshine" policy of 1979-95, to the present policy of military coercion with more flexibility and incentives. In this chapter, Huang examines how and why these policies were adopted, given the internal and external environments at the time, and the implications of the policies for cross-strait relations. The analysis highlights the policy dilemma faced by Chinese leaders and assesses the policy choices available to them. This dilemma involves related issues of regime survival and redefinition of China's national identity.

In Chapter 3, Alexander C. Tan asks what shapes Taiwan's national security policy decision making, and how Taiwan has conducted its foreign policy to ensure that the island can remain relatively secure in the face of the constraints it faces in the international arena. Tan seeks to answer these questions by showing how Taiwan uses trade, foreign investment, foreign aid, and a growing need for guest workers to integrate with the world economy and consequently to increase its national security by tying the fate of other countries to its own. He also discusses the issue of Taiwan's national identity. As the relative power of Beijing grew and made an invasion increasingly feasible, Taiwan's will to resist and to maintain its independence has come to depend increasingly on the development of an "islander" identity distinct from the "mainlander" identity of Taiwan's early authoritarian elites.

In Chapter 4, A. Cooper Drury investigates the role of the US in the China-Taiwan conflict. The US policy toward the region has been rather ambiguous. According to Drury, this American policy aims to maintain the status quo until some form of unification between Beijing and Taipei is mutually acceptable. This policy appears to have gradually evolved over the past fifty years, and it appears quite stable. Yet the policy has not in fact gradually evolved, and its stability is questionable. Instead, US policy toward the region has developed through a series of ad hoc, nonrational decisions. Close examination of several watershed decisions reveals that the policy was driven by domestic politics, international lobbying, divided presidential administrations, and ideology, rather than by a consistent strategic principle. Further, the current policy is contested by many in the US who call for a stronger orientation toward either China or Taiwan. Drury traces several watershed events, showing that US policy has been based on ad hoc decision making, and that American resolve toward both Taiwan's security and relations with China has never been put to a hard test such as an open conflict. Therefore, the president, and future presidents do not have a guiding doctrine or unequivocal public support on which to draw, and as such, their decisions will continue to be ad hoc. This lack of guidance makes it difficult to predict future decisions and suggests a paradoxical conclusion: US policy toward the Strait is only stable as long as the Strait itself is stable. These findings highlight the importance of neo-liberalism and constructivism as supplements to neo-realist explanations.

In Chapter 5, Terence Roehrig studies the evolution of North Korea's defense policy through the North-South summit meeting in June 2000. According to him, the summit between Kim Dae Jung and Kim Jong Il was a groundbreaking event that brought hope for further reconciliation between the two Koreas. Yet, while North Korean policy preferences appear to have changed, the North remains a heavily armed state whose intentions are not always entirely clear. Certainly, the incoming Bush administration has thought so, as "skepticism" in dealing with the North Korean regime has chilled the enthusiasm for improving relations on the peninsula. Has North Korea altered its policy preferences? The North seems to be in the process of reshaping its policy preferences in light of changing circumstances and continued engagement. The North is not moving as quickly to implement change as some maintain it should. However, North Korea will need some time to reshape a domestic environment that for many years has not been open to reform.

In Chapter 6, Uk Heo and Chong-Min Hyun review the history of South Korean policy toward the North and then analyze Seoul's recent "sunshine policy." Since Kim Dae Jung took office as president in 1998, South Korea's approach toward North Korea has changed dramatically, from a hard-line policy based on a Cold War mentality to a sunshine policy emphasizing engagement. Under the sunshine policy, South Korea has provided a lot of economic aid, but the North has not reciprocated with a reduction in military preparations. In order to analyze why the North has not responded positively, the authors revisit the history of inter-Korean relations and employ a game-theoretic model. Based on this analysis, the authors suggest that the Seoul government use more pressure in coordination with the US, rather than rushing to increase unilateral aid to Pyongyang. Although neo-liberalism and constructivism have some relevance to the Korean conflict, the strength of a unified Korean identity and the nature of the North Korean regime make a neo-realist approach most useful in explaining South Korean preferences and strategies.

In Chapter 7, Karl DeRouen Jr. and David J. Jackson investigate the role of the US, particularly the current administration, in the inter-Korean relationship.

According to the authors, American foreign policy plays the key role in maintaining peace in the region. To maintain peace, President George W. Bush and his foreign policy team have an important choice to make. They can proceed cautiously by honoring the 1994 Agreed Framework, maintaining the current trade status, supplying North Korea with food aid, and conducting four-way talks with China, South Korea, and North Korea. President Bush could also be more risk-acceptant. Apart from narrow national security considerations, domestic politics could result in a policy that sees the US pursuing Theater Missile Defense and pushing South Korea on trade issues. A review of the history of US involvement on the peninsula provides evidence that domestic political institutions and norms—i.e., neoliberalism and constructivism—also play an important role in forming the more detailed outlines of US national security policies.

In Chapter 8, Kanishkan Sathasivam and Sahar Shafqat start by telling the story of Pakistan's independence and describing the historical and geographical settings. The authors move on to discuss the role of the military in Pakistani politics. Pakistan has been under military rule for half its history. The reason is that Pakistan inherited weak civilian political institutions from British colonialism. The military has characterized itself as the only real guarantor of Pakistani national security. In many crises, it has stepped in to take political control. Even when the military did not hold power directly, it exerted enormous influence on policymaking, particularly on security policy. In Pakistan's security policy, the Arab world and China have played significant roles. With Arab financial assistance and Chinese technical help, Pakistan was able to develop nuclear weapons. Having stated the effect of foreign assistance and the role of the military, the most important factor in Pakistan's security policymaking is the Indian threat. Based on a review of the Indian threat and the Pakistani response, the authors conclude that India's overwhelming superiority in conventional military forces is the primary cause of Pakistan's security fears.

In Chapter 9, Timothy D. Hoyt looks at India's approach to dealing with Pakistan. According to him, India has attempted for decades to follow an independent path in the international system. Its foreign policy has been convoluted, and sometimes apparently contradictory: Seeking security, it has avoided close alliances. A state born of non-violence, it has waged aggressive wars and prepared robust military forces. A leader in the quest for nuclear disarmament, it has rejected international treaties on nuclear proliferation and weapons tests—including a treaty that India itself initially proposed. In this chapter, Hoyt examines three areas of Indian foreign policy: non-alignment, the use of military force, and nuclear weapons policy. Each demonstrates the importance of different levels of analysis. The roles of individuals, of domestic political change and pressure groups, and of broader systemic pressures are all crucial to understanding continuity and change. Indian foreign policy has strong elements of realism (pursuit of autarky, military power, and prestige) and of liberalism and constructivism (support for international cooperation and establishment of new behavioral norms). The study of Indian foreign policy strongly indicates the importance of perception and misperception, and of broad and narrow concepts of security, in the development of an increasingly prominent and powerful regional actor.

In Chapter 10, Christopher Sprecher and Sungho Park discuss the role of the US in the India-Pakistan relationship. Since the two countries became independent in 1947, the United States has played a major role in the region. In an attempt to promote peace and stability between these two contentious rivals, the US has supplied both states with vast amounts of foreign aid, both economic and military. The US has had two major goals in the region. First, during the Cold War, to prevent the spread of Soviet influence in South Asia, the US routinely supplied the region with assistance. Second, the US sought to spread democracy in the region and promote peaceful relations between India and Pakistan. At times, therefore, the US penalized India and Pakistan for their actions through the use of sanctions. In this chapter, Sprecher and Park review the roots of the India-Pakistan conflict and discuss the rationale for American involvement in the region. They also discuss the impact that US aid has had on the two countries, and how the US has attempted to reduce tensions between these two rivals.

NOTES

1. Michale Brecher (1984), "International Crises and Protracted Conflicts," *International Interactions* 11, 2, pp. 237-97; Michael Brecher and Jonathan Wilkenfeld (1982), "Crises in World Politics," *World Politics* 34, 2, pp. 380-417; William Eckhardt and Edward Azar (1978), "Major World Conflicts and Interventions 1945-1975," *International Interactions* 5, 1, pp. 75-110; Istavan Kende (1978), "Wars of Ten Years, 1967-1976," *Journal of Peace Research* 15, 2, pp. 227-41.

2. According to Goertz and Diehl, long-term rivals are responsible for almost half of the wars and military disputes over the last two centuries. See Gary Goertz and Paul F. Diehl (1992), "The Empirical Importance of Enduring Rivalries," *International Interactions* 18, 2, pp. 151-63; Gary Goertz and Paul F. Diehl (1993), "Enduring Rivalries: Theoretical Constructs and Empirical Patterns," *International Studies Quarterly* 35, 2, pp. 195-209.

Conflict in Asia after the Cold War: Identity, Regime Types, and Strategic Interaction

Shale Horowitz

What does international relations theory tell us about the conflicts between China and Taiwan, North and South Korea, and India and Pakistan? This is a useful question to ask before plunging into the intricacies of the conflicts. There are three major theoretical schools in international relations, the traditional ones of neorealism and neoliberalism, and a more radical variant of neoliberalism, constructivism. In a framework of rational choice and strategic interaction, it will be shown that these schools tend to focus on different sources of change and conflict. The insights of all the frameworks will then be applied to the China-Taiwan, Korean and India-Pakistan conflicts. The focus will be on explaining recent developments, especially after the Cold War, and on constructing plausible scenarios of future developments. It will be seen that constructivism has much to add to the more familiar insights of neorealism and neoliberalism.

Neorealism tends to view identities and preferences as relatively similar and unchanging, and to emphasize how objective conditions, such as military power, influence states' foreign policy strategies. Neoliberalism places more emphasis on diversity of identities and preferences, which it views as strongly influenced by political regime type. This diversity is taken to explain much variation in foreign policy strategies. Like neoliberalism, constructivism focuses on national and state identities and their impacts on preferences and strategies. But it argues that such identities are mutable, and emphasizes how international strategic interactions of states' foreign policies can feed back to influence the evolution of national and state identities. The causal impacts are taken to be simultaneous. National and state identities influence choices of objectives and strategies, and the associated strategic policy choices in turn influence stability or change in national and state identities.

For the China-Taiwan case, constructivism calls attention to China's presently vague state identity, and to how strategic interaction with China's legitimacy-oriented Communist Party elites is likely to accelerate the development of Taiwan's "islander" national identity. The inflammatory rhetoric of Communist

Party elites indicates that factional struggles and regime survival have taken precedence over Chinese national interests. By further firing islander identity in Taiwan, this almost guarantees that Taiwan will be willing and able to defend itself before Chinese economic growth delivers a "war dividend" sufficient to successfully invade the island.

For the Korean conflict, on the other hand, the stability and strength of a united Korean identity in both North and South facilitates the South's concilia-tory stabilizing policy toward the North's insecure elites.

In the conflict between India and Pakistan, Pakistani identity has come to an important crossroads. On the one side, adopting a more radical Islamist iden-tity will deepen Pakistan's low-intensity "jihadi" strategy in Kashmir and else-where in India, under the shelter of Pakistan's nuclear deterrent. On the other side, East Asian developmental nationalism, looking to build national strength and political consensus over the long run, targets rapid economic growth and eschews risky foreign policy adventures. This choice will determine whether the India-Pakistan conflict will worsen—increasing the risk of a nuclear ex-change—or whether it will revert to a more stable, if still chronically unsettled, hostility.

THREE THEORETICAL APPROACHES AND THEIR IMPLICATIONS FOR EAST ASIAN GEOPOLITICS

Consider first stylized versions of the neorealist, neoliberal, and construc-tivist frameworks. These are used to advance a series of questions and hypothe-ses about the China-Taiwan, Korean, and India-Pakistan conflicts. Again, all the frameworks are here taken to involve rational choice in a strategic context. Choice is taken to be rational in the sense that actors make choices to maximize the likelihood of achieving their objectives. And this rational choice is taken to be strategic in the sense that multiple rational actors are acting more or less si-multaneously, so that the optimal choice of a given actor at a given time will usually depend on the choices made by other actors.[1]

Neorealism

Neorealism assumes that the interaction of states in the international system imposes similar pressures and threats on all states. Regardless of other differ-ences in their makeups and objectives, all states face threats to their integrity and survival. They can never be entirely certain where threats may arise. There-fore, they have to take seriously all potential threats and deter them by arming and attracting allies. Thus, the common environment of the international system tends to confront different types of states with relatively homogeneous predica-ments, and to elicit relatively homogeneous responses. International systems, and the situations of particular states in any given system, are thus characterized by two primary variables: the number of states in the international system, and the distribution of military power between them.[2]

In this framework, the primary mechanism for preventing war, and hence for assuring territorial integrity and survival of states, is the balance of power. Threats exist from any state or coalition of states with enough military power to have a chance of defeating another state and its allies. A successful balance of power exists where all such threats can be successfully deterred by adaptations in states' arming and alliance strategies. The balance of power may fail to deter war for a variety of reasons. In the neorealist framework, uncertainty about military capabilities is usually the most important reason. States may significantly over-assess their own or their allies' military capabilities, or underassess enemy capabilities, such that a level of preparations sufficient to deter war in the presence of accurate assessments no longer suffices. On the other hand, uncertainty about preferences of other states is not usually taken to be similarly destabilizing. This is because cautionary countermeasures are more easily taken to hedge against the risk of uncertainty about preferences. Theoretically, if a country hitherto perceived to be an ally or a neutral becomes a threat, arms and alliances can be used to deter such a threat just as readily as they can be used to deter threats from states that are more certainly enemies.[3]

In the contemporary Asian context, the neorealist framework thus implies a focus on whether or not the expected alliance constellations for each conflict are likely to deter both sides from launching a war. For Korea, will North Korea continue to be deterred by South Korean preparations in conjunction with its ally, the United States (US)? Will South Korea and available US forces be deterred by the combination of North Korean preparations and the possibility of Chinese backing? In this analysis, war is most likely to break out if North Korea overassesses its own capabilities, or underassesses South Korean capabilities or US resolve to back South Korea; or if South Korea overassesses its own capabilities, or underassesses North Korean capabilities or China's resolve to back North Korea.[4] A similar analysis applies to the China-Taiwan and India-Pakistan conflicts.[5]

There are a number of salient characteristics of one or more of the three conflicts that are not well explained by the neorealist approach.

1. Salience of conflicts between dyads of similar ethnicity, or over ethnically specific stakes. The China-Taiwan and Korean conflicts are between different regime types ruling over groups sharing a common ethnicity. Within the neorealist approach, there is no necessary reason why this should be so. Territory and resources are desirable as territory and resources, regardless of whether or not the group inhabiting the territory is more or less ethnically related. But this is obviously not the case in the Korean and China-Taiwan conflicts. Whatever the objectives of the states beyond the immediate conflict, unifying the territories of common ethnicity is viewed as the primary foreign policy objective of both Koreas, of the mainland China government, and of the "mainlander" elites that until recently dominated Taiwan. Similarly, by far the most important issue in the India-Pakistan conflict is sovereignty over the disputed territory of Kashmir—most of which has been under Indian control since 1947. Pakistan views Kashmir as rightfully Pakistani, because it is both contiguous to Pakistan and has a majority Muslim population. Maintaining this claim has become a core value of Pakistani national identity.

2. Enduring patterns of objectives, and of alliances and rivalries, associated with differences in regime type. The neorealist framework views defensive objectives as easily sliding over into at least practically offensive objectives, and views alliances and rivalries as logically and practically substitutable. However, this has not been the case in the Korea and China-Taiwan conflicts. Although unification of ethnically similar territories has been widely viewed as desirable, authoritarian regimes in North Korea, China, and Kuomintang (KMT)-ruled Taiwan have been much more serious about mounting offensive military operations to obtain unification. On the other hand, South Korea under a democratic regime and the KMT governments after democratization in Taiwan have typically viewed unification as only to be pursued by peaceful, voluntary means. (However, as the course of the Korean War indicated, neither democratic state would necessarily stop short of achieving unification by force in the event of a total victory in a war begun by the other side.) Similarly, democratic South Korea and democratic Taiwan have been allied with the democratic US, while authoritarian North Korea has relied upon similar regimes in the Soviet Union and China for support. Of course, authoritarian Taiwan and authoritarian South Korea were also allied to the US, and communist regimes have often been at odds.[6] The point is that democracies are more likely to share common threats, and less likely to view each other as threats.

   3. *Rigidities in burden-sharing among allies due to historical memories of Japanese rule.* The last point is also buttressed by the weak but ongoing presence of democratic Japan alongside the US in the alliances with South Korea and Taiwan, but this raises an additional point. Given Japan's strong military interests in preserving democratic regimes in South Korea and Taiwan, why has Japan's participation in the defensive alliances been so weak, not going much beyond providing bases for US forces? The reasons go beyond the usual logic by which larger alliance partners tend to provide a greater share of collective defense goods.[7] Japan is not as populous and wealthy as the US, but a pure collective goods analysis would predict a much greater and more active Japanese contribution. What is preventing this?

   Historical memories of Japan's behavior before and during World War II have created enduring opposition to Japan's assuming a greater share of common defense responsibilities. This opposition exists not only within Japan itself, but also in Korea, Taiwan, and other states that came under Japanese rule. Of course, given that Japan is today a stable democracy, this kind of restraint is a luxury. In the event of a major US military withdrawal from the region, Japan would almost certainly move at least partially into the security vacuum by common consent. But this does not change the fact that historical memories make Japan a less desirable ally than it would be otherwise, thereby having a strong influence on the existing pattern of mobilization and alliances, and by extension on the balance of power.[8]

   These three points have similar theoretical implications. Whether due to ethnicity, regime type, historical memory, or other factors, some alliance and rivalry patterns are much more common and enduring than others; and war is more likely to be launched by particular states within such specific alliance and rivalry constellations. It is not that neorealism ignores such specific patterns of international relations and threats in practice. It is just that there is no good justification for such patterns within the neorealist theoretical framework, and that as a result the patterns are implicitly assumed when the framework is actually applied.

Neoliberalism

The basic tenet of neoliberalism is that state objectives and thus strategies are largely determined by regime type and state identity. State identity includes not only a "civic identity," like democracy and individual rights, but also an "ethnic identity" based upon the state's ethnic composition. States typically reconcile both types of identity into a legitimizing ideology that is at least the nominal basis of representation by political elites. Such legitimizing ideologies can be binding on political elites in two main ways. Institutions can impose electoral, procedural or legal constraints on policymaking. Also, elites themselves may, to varying degrees, internalize legitimizing ideologies or norms as self-imposed constraints and guides for policymaking.[9]

This implies that the units of the international system are viewed as heterogeneous rather than homogeneous, and that international systems are heterogeneous products of their heterogeneous parts. Neoliberal theories about the international system tend to extrapolate the significance of institutions and norms from within states to the international interaction of states. Representative institutions with norms that are perceived as clear, fair, and hence legitimate can make for more harmonious relations between states, just as they can within them. Similarly, whether international interactions take place within formal institutions or in informal diplomatic exchanges, commonly held, self-imposed norms play an important informal role in guiding international relations between similarly inclined state cultures.[10]

Because of this emphasis on the "socialized" character of state interactions, neoliberalism tends to focus on misperception of state preferences as the primary source of conflict. These misperceptions come in two main variants, "hawkish" and "dovish." Hawks misperceive states that are not necessarily hostile as being more inherently so. This creates a self-fulfilling prophecy when hawkish defensive preparations are misperceived as aggressive by the state with a hitherto more indeterminate strategy. The latter state's objectives might have produced a more peaceful strategy if it was faced with a dovish rather than a hawkish counterpart. There is also the opposite, dovish misperception. Doves misperceive more aggressive states as peaceful, and so their inadequate preparations invite war that might have been avoided by more hawkish preparations. Many specific foreign policy debates are over what a particular state's true preferences are, and whether these preferences will produce a more peaceful or a more warlike response to other states' strategies.

In contemporary Asia, these debates typically turn on what strategies are most likely to pacify North Korea, China, and Pakistan. The dovish view is that these regimes are liable to remain peaceful as long as certain of their fundamental interests are not threatened. For North Korea, this means that economic aid and trade and diplomatic recognition are desirable to prevent worsening famine and the possibility of a desperation-driven invasion of the South.[11] For China, it means that declaring and recognizing an independent Taiwan are to be avoided as an affront to the strong national pride of Chinese elites. Such a provocation may lead otherwise cautious leaders to consider more seriously a military solution to the "one China problem."[12] For Pakistan, it means that India can avoid conflict by negotiating with Kashmiri secessionists and increasing regional autonomy. This strategy avoids pushing Pakistan into a corner, where the regime is forced to choose between peace and favorable change in Kashmir.[13]

On the other hand, the hawkish view is that the North Korean, Chinese, and Pakistani regimes are more likely to use violent means to achieve their aggressive unificationist objectives unless they are met with strong and unambiguous deterrence. For North Korea, this means that economic aid and trade make war more likely by strengthening an aggressive foe, and that diplomatic recognition may be misinterpreted as a lack of resolve.[14] For China, it means that the US should better arm Taiwan and make clear that its defensive commitment will be unchanged by a Taiwanese declaration of independence.[15] For Pakistan, it means that India must not reward secessionist violence in Kashmir with concessions, but must rather impose retaliatory costs on Pakistani support for such violence.[16]

Neoliberalism is also inadequate to explaining some important characteristics of the China-Taiwan, Korean, and India-Pakistan conflicts. Neoliberalism tends to take state preferences as given, largely determined by their regime types and state identities. For example, according to nealiberalism, regime types can change and produce dramatic changes in foreign policy preferences. However, it turns out that the relations between given regime types, state identities, and foreign policy preferences are often malleable and contingent.

For example, since 1979 the Chinese communist regime has dropped the distinguishing economic policy features of its ruling ideology. Although lip service is still paid to socialism, the regime has transformed itself into a variant of East Asian developmental authoritarianism. Other than pursuit of Chinese national interests and economic growth, there is little left to legitimize the regime. Yet these vague principles are consistent with a wide range of domestic and foreign policy objectives and strategies, and various tendencies appear to exist within the ruling elite. Many within the ruling elite may be inclined to use Chinese national greatness and economic growth objectives instrumentally, to justify policies that are perceived as more likely to preserve the regime. Other elites may be more concerned with pursuing a purer interpretation of national interests, even at the risk of losing power in the future.

Similarly, democratization in Taiwan has empowered the 80 percent "islander" majority, as opposed to the 20 percent "mainlander" minority. The latter is descended from those who came over in the late 1940s, when the KMT installed itself in power. The islanders have a distinct ethnic or sub-ethnic identity within the larger group of ethnic Chinese, and they are not willing to sacrifice their prosperity, freedom, and independence to a nationalistic authoritarian regime in Beijing. On the other hand, it remains widely debated whether or not these conservative interests go along with independence as an overriding goal in and of itself; and if they do not, whether or not independence is the most effective means of safeguarding a minimum interim autonomy until the possibility of unification no longer poses a serious threat to local living standards and lifestyles.

Since 1947, Pakistan has oscillated between secular nationalist and Islamist identities. The Islamist identity has become stronger over time, particularly after the Soviet invasion of Afghanistan and the end of the Cold War. At a time when India's relative power has been increasing, Pakistan's growing Islamist identity drove a more risky, "jihadi" strategy in Afghanistan and Kashmir. Similarly, India has oscillated between a socialist-internationalist and a Hindu nationalist identity. Again, the end of the Cold War accelerated the rise of the Hindu nationalist identity.

Constructivism

In other words, preferences often appear to be vague and malleable, and hence their relations to choice of foreign policy strategies can be quite loose and debatable. These issues are confronted more directly by a third type of theoretical approach, that of constructivism. In this perspective, regime types, state identities, and hence state preferences do not only strategically interact to produce policies in a systemic context. Such regime types, state identities, and state preferences are also formed and continuously reshaped, in part by the process and outcomes of their interactions with other states.[17] This can be understood as neoliberalism going "general equilibrium," i.e., as neoliberalism in which the heterogeneous preferences of the states are made more fully endogenous. It is not that neoliberals have not recognized the forming and reforming of state preferences, in part through international interactions. It is rather that neoliberals have not typically sought to make preference formation a constant and systematic part of their analysis.

Foreign policy debates in constructivist terms often resemble a radicalized form of the neoliberal debates. Here it is not only that preferences can be misperceived, and the misperception actualized by erroneously conceived policies. It is also that national and state identities and regime types can themselves be shaped by policies. This raises the issue of what the various tendencies of national and state identities are, and how alternative foreign policies can reinforce or counteract the various tendencies.[18] The neoliberal "hawk"-"dove" debates are thus often reprised in constructivist terms. With respect to China, doves often believe that economic policy concessions and respect for the "one China" principle will make ruling elites and mass opinion satisfied with the status quo, and hence more likely to support deepened economic openness and a move toward political openness in the future. On the other hand, hawks believe that such policies may embolden Chinese elites to take risks to achieve early unification, based on a desire to further national interests in a manner consistent with repressing dissent and preserving their own power. Such developments invite open clashes that would mobilize Chinese national identity behind the authoritarian regime and away from norms and institutions associated with a "Western" enemy.[19] Regarding Taiwan, another debate concerns whether strong US military and diplomatic backing will accelerate or slow the emergence of islander identity and its tendency to embrace the independence cause.[20]

A similar debate examines the likely effects of making concessions to North Korea and Pakistan. Will concessions push North Korea toward following China's reform path, or will they merely solidify the existing regime and embolden its more radical elements?[21] Will concessions lead Pakistan to return toward secular nationalism and mutually beneficial political and economic stability, or will they vindicate and thus deepen Islamist identity and the associated "jihadi" methods?[22] To conclude, constructivism has the merit of explicitly addressing the kinds of transformations of state identity and regime type that are now under way in China, Taiwan, Pakistan, and possibly North Korea.

Constructivism should be seen as a complement to the other two theoretical approaches, which continue to yield valuable theoretical insights. Constructivism and neoliberalism emphasize, respectively, the sources of foreign policy preferences and the transforming effects of interaction between states with different foreign policy preferences. Neorealism focuses more on whether or not the balance of power mechanism is effective in the context of a system with units of given preferences and resources. In the following sections, all of these theoretical approaches will be used within an overall framework of strategic interaction between states. Here the treatment will be brief and the focus will be on the core dyads of each conflict—China and Taiwan, North and South Korea, and India and Pakistan. The analysis begins by looking at recent changes and trends in regime types and state identities. This approach implies further changes or possible changes in foreign policy preferences and in the corresponding structure of threats. Alternative strategies and the likely patterns of strategic interaction are then laid out. Finally, the various possible outcomes are mapped back into further changes in regime types, state identities, preferences, and threats. With these consequences or payoffs of different patterns of strategic interaction in view, it is possible to select out a number of more plausible scenarios for the future development of the three conflicts.

THE CHINA-TAIWAN CONFLICT

In examining the present state of the China-Taiwan conflict, we begin with the constructivist question of recent changes and trends in regime types and state identities (see Row 1 of Figure 1.1). Recent decades have seen momentous changes in both China and Taiwan. Since 1979, China has progressively unleashed the private sector, which has grown to the point where it is far larger than the stagnant state sector. The primary issue of economic policy is now how to restructure and shrink the residual state sector without producing a financial crisis and surges of unemployment. This issue has undermined the ideological foundations of Communist Party (CP) rule. The state sector is now merely an important and potentially destabilizing political clientele, rather than the engine of economic transformation and social justice. The regime's legitimacy now rests on continued economic growth, and on progress in restoring China to her historical place at the center of East Asia and the broader world. In this sense, China's regime today has more in common with the regimes of Mahathir Mohamad in Malaysia and Lee Kuan Yew in Singapore—and with the old authoritarian Kuomintang (KMT) regime in Taiwan—than with the regime of Mao Zedong.

China's national interests and the role of the Communist Party (CP) in advancing them have become correspondingly more vague and contestable (Row 2). A much greater variety of internal and foreign policies can be ideologically justified. None of these policies necessarily requires a CP regime. Policy options advanced by more conservative CP elites are often justified with appeals to political stability. But they are more clearly linked to the survival and expansion interests of traditional CP constituencies, such as the People's Liberation

Figure 1.1
China-Taiwan Conflict: Changes in Regime Type and Identity, the Structure of Preferences and Threats, and Strategic Interaction

Solid arrows denote increased probability, *dashed* arrows reduced probability

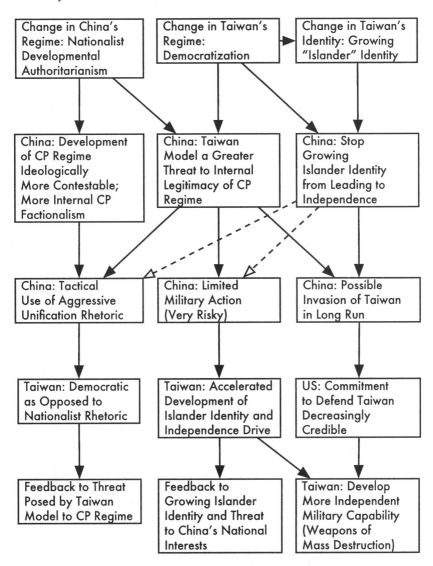

Army (PLA), economic planning ministries, and state enterprise managers, than to the national interests in economic growth and long-term geopolitical and cultural revival. On the other hand, internal reformers are charting a path of dismantling the state sector and depoliticizing the CP, leaving the PLA as the main bulwark of the regime. Such reformers are easily accused of destabilizing the regime; they are vulnerable to PLA pressure and hence need to cultivate PLA support.

Largely in response to the internal economic and political changes in China, Taiwan has also been transformed, albeit in more purely political terms (Row 1 again). In the mid-1980s, the ruling KMT began the process of democratization. A sequence of free elections climaxed in April 2000 with the first democratic transfer of presidential power to an opposition party. In turn, democratization necessarily brought the cleavage between "islanders" and "mainlanders" into the open. The islanders form approximately 80 percent of the population, and they are descended from Chinese who migrated to Taiwan in past centuries. The mainlanders are descended from the political and military elites and refugees who came over in the late 1940s, with the KMT's ouster from the mainland.

The ethnic cleavage has been manifested politically over national and state identity rather than over economic policy. Taiwan's outstanding economic performance has created a consensus in favor of preserving the autonomy of the economic technocrats.[23] There is a certain amount of corruption. Yet the ethnic cleavage is itself largely responsible for what, in the East Asian context, is a conspicuous restraint in state sponsorship of the private sector, and a corresponding paucity of the huge conglomerates so typical of other economies in the region.[24] However, the islander majority is concerned about conserving its hard-won prosperity and freedom. Furthermore, although islander ethnic identity is Chinese, this fact has not been inconsistent with a distinct and growing, sub-ethnic Taiwanese national identity, which is in turn grafted onto the state identity of Taiwan. Once the island became de facto independent, and distinguished itself by its relative economic achievements and cultural enlightenment, this distinct identity was growing stronger beneath the frozen surface of KMT authoritarianism.[25] The process has been accelerated by democratization, which both transferred electoral sovereignty to the islanders and allowed them to openly express, debate, and develop their identity.

Taiwan's democratization and the continued evolution of Taiwanese identity have created a new set of threats to the CP regime on the mainland and to Chinese national interests per se (Row 2). The CP regime, itself increasingly transformed into a developmental authoritarian regime, is now confronted with an ethnic Chinese state on Taiwan that offers an alternative regime type. This alternative not only provides a superior economic development model. It has combined this model with a successful transition to democracy. It is a bit ironic that a democratization process that has moved Taiwan toward advancing a more distinct national and state identity has, from a mainland perspective, made the Taiwanese model all the more alluring. By contrast, the CP regime's heavy-handed repression and more unstable and uncertain economic development path look unnecessary and anachronistic. Not surprisingly, this uncomfortable comparison has led the CP regime to identify all the more strongly with a Chinese national interest in preserving the territorial integrity of China and enhancing its power and prestige. Tibet and Xinjiang are only the most prominent of China's regions likely to look to the Taiwan precedent, and Taiwan's permanent separation from China represents a "loss" of relative economic power and prestige that it will take an extra decade or two of sustained economic growth to make up. The "change of subject" from internal policy and regime type to Taiwanese separatism provides the CP regime with an important mission that genuinely speaks to mainland public opinion.[26]

The effects of changing regime types and state identities on the foreign policy preferences of the CP regime can be summarized as follows. Just as the regime's self-transformation is making its own legitimacy questionable and its future direction more uncertain, Taiwan is moving in a direction that in different ways challenges both the legitimacy of the CP regime and the broader national identity and aspirations of the mainland. This situation creates at least three crucial fronts along which CP elites may pursue objectives. First, the *internal struggles for power* within the CP are increasingly legitimized by rival visions of China's future that appeal to masses as well as elites. Second, the *CP's struggle to maintain its rule* must also be justified in such terms. Third, there is broad support among masses and elites for *keeping Taiwan within China's orbit* in order to protect the state's territorial integrity and use it as a vehicle to raise China's power and prestige as quickly as possible. The main point here is that these three objectives are not clearly prioritized under present conditions, and they are also not necessarily best served by the same strategies. As will become evident, this situation makes it difficult to predict Chinese strategy vis-à-vis Taiwan.

The next step is to look at the strategies available to pursue Chinese objectives and the responses these are likely to elicit from Taiwan and the US (Rows 3 and 4). Here three nonexclusive, "active" Chinese strategies toward Taiwan are considered: hostile rhetoric and threats, limited military action, and a full-scale invasion. Hostile rhetoric is helpful both in pursuing internal struggles for power within the CP, and in defending the legitimacy of the CP regime. It burnishes the credentials of conservative, reformist, or merely careerist factions, and it raises the regime's profile in pursuing a popular national cause. On the other hand, hostile rhetoric has predictably inflamed rather than cowed Taiwanese islanders oriented toward a distinct national path. In both the 1996 and the 2000 Taiwan elections, Chinese threats appear to have increased public support for KMT and opposition candidates more sympathetic to a distinct islander national identity.

Limited military action might take a variety of forms, from missile strikes against Taiwan's military and economic infrastructure, to blockading or mining Taiwanese ports, to shelling or invading Taiwan's offshore island groups. These are all risky strategies. All would be likely to dramatically inflame and intensify islander identity, without delivering a knockout blow. Such indecisive bloodletting would close off any prospects for voluntary unification for one or (probably) more full generations. Similarly, internal factions vying for power would be taking a big risk by pursuing such limited strategies. They would make the "loss" of Taiwan more likely in the long run and have a significant negative short-term effect on international trade and investment, in exchange for a brief public euphoria of hollow assertiveness. Limited military action only makes sense if there is a rather desperate fear that the Taiwanese model will destabilize the CP regime in the near future, and if there is a consequent willingness to try to force concessions even in the presence of a considerable risk that the bluff will be called. And called it is likely to be at present, given that military analysts do not believe PLA forces are capable of mounting a successful amphibious invasion.

Finally, if the pure national goal of unification is the primary objective, it makes the most sense to keep quiet and minimize provocations while the fruits of economic growth fuel an overwhelming military buildup. Once the buildup has proceeded far enough, a credible threat of invasion could be delivered, and unification achieved by force if necessary. Again, it is difficult to be certain of the priorities attached to the three CP objectives. But the choice of hostile rhetoric, over either preparing for invasion quietly or taking limited military action, implies a greater concern for internal power struggles and CP regime legitimacy than for Chinese national interests per se.

It is important to discuss in more detail the responses these strategies are likely to produce. As discussed, limited military action is likely to intensify islander identity and defensive military preparations, and it could lead to an immediate declaration of independence. The continued Chinese military buildup will make the informal US commitment to defend Taiwan less and less credible over time. Once China becomes capable of inflicting proportionate damage in response to any US intervention, Taiwan will probably not be important enough for the US to risk a direct military conflict. This situation will sooner or later confront Taiwan with the need to defend itself. Against a modernized Chinese military, weapons of mass destruction will be the only effective means of deterring an invasion. Again, Chinese use of hostile rhetoric, or even more so any limited military action, only pushes Taiwan to embrace this "long-term solution" more quickly.

Last, it is worth mentioning a less-anticipated consequence of China's use of hostile rhetoric. The response of the more islander-oriented leadership in Taiwan is predictably to emphasize democratic over nationalist rhetoric. Leaders can emphasize that unification must take place democratically, secure in the knowledge that democratically sanctioned unification will never occur as long as the CP regime persists. This makes sense in terms of domestic politics. The new Democratic Progressive Party President Chen Shui-bian is particularly anxious to show the Taiwanese public that he is not pursuing the islander cause in an unnecessarily risky, precipitous fashion. It appeals to Chinese nationalist public opinion by holding out the prospect of peaceful unification in a future democratic China, and it tries to turn this nationalism inward by arguing that the CP regime itself is primarily responsible for "losing" Taiwan. Judging by the recent priority given to "loud talk, no stick" strategies over "no talk, big stick" and "loud talk, little stick" strategies—indicating the priority of internal struggles for power and CP legitimacy over strategies likely to successfully reabsorb Taiwan—Taiwan's democratic rhetoric is likely to call forth continued hostile rhetoric. This in turn is likely to feed through to continued development of islander national identity and more rapid acquisition of a self-sufficient defense capability.

THE KOREAN CONFLICT

The two recent events most momentously affecting the Korean conflict have been South Korea's democratization and, above all, the Soviet Union's collapse (see Figure 1.2, Row 1). Combined with continued high economic growth, democracy in South Korea further burnishes its legitimacy relative to the North as the regime of choice to preside over a future unified Korean Peninsula. The Soviet collapse had much more fundamental effects. As communist regimes fell across Eastern Europe and, closer to home, in Mongolia and the USSR itself, the ideological legitimacy of the North Korean regime was shaken to the core. Added to this was a withdrawal of Soviet subsidies. This sent the North Korean economy reeling into deep depression and famine, and over time, it seriously eroded the technological competitiveness of the North Korean armed forces. Combined, the two events made the North Korean regime much more vulnerable to a blend of internal unrest and division and external invasion (Row 2). Although the democratic character of the regime in the South makes an invasion of the North highly unlikely except in response to serious internal unrest in the North, this consideration cannot be expected to give the North Korean regime much confidence.

Facing this economic, military, and legitimacy crisis, there were two basic paths the North Korean regime could take (Row 3). One was to follow China in moving toward market reform. Another was to intensify vigilance and try to squeeze as much as possible out of the old system. With the death of founding leader Kim Il Sung, the North Korean regime went through an uncertain succession process. This made it very difficult for his son and designated successor, Kim Jong Il, to deviate significantly from the old system—at least until he had consolidated power. However, using the conventional means of repression and centralization, there was little more that could be done to intensify vigilance and squeeze more out of the old system.

Hence North Korea seized upon a more radical alternative, the development of nuclear weapons and of long-range missiles capable of striking the US mainland. This not only solved the defensive problem created by increasing South Korean and US conventional superiority. It also opened up the possibility of a new offensive option. Maybe the US is willing to lose another 40,000 or so soldiers defending South Korea, but is the US willing to sacrifice millions or tens of millions of civilians? If this possibility were to be truly unthinkable for the US, then a withdrawal of US troops from South Korea becomes possible. This, in turn, would make a successful North Korean conventional invasion of the South conceivable. For this reason, a US withdrawal is unlikely. The US presumably believes that any first use of North Korean nuclear weapons to back an attack on South Korea can be deterred by a threat of massive retaliation, including the destruction of the North Korean ruling elite. Even if the US did prefer withdrawal, South Korea would almost certainly feel compelled to develop its own nuclear capability. For now, the US commitment to help defend the South stands, making a North Korean invasion almost certain to fail.

However, the threat of a North Korean conventional invasion backed by a nuclear threat cannot be totally dismissed. If North Korean nuclear weapons were not used, then the US and South Korean response to a North Korean invasion

Figure 1.2
Korean Conflict: Collapse of Soviet Power and Changes in South Korean Regime Type, the Structure of Preferences and Threats, and Strategic Interaction

Solid arrows denote increased probability, *dashed* arrows reduced probability.

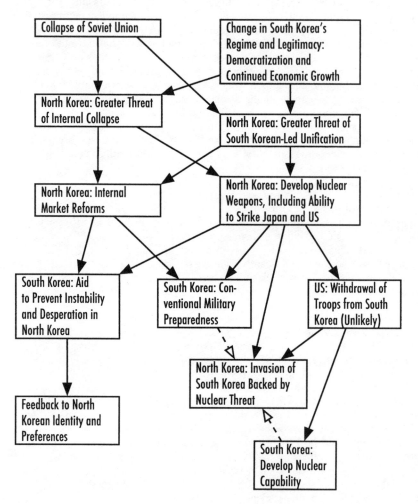

would probably be limited to repelling it and making conventional air strikes against North Korea. A US nuclear response, or even a US-South Korean retaliatory invasion of the North, would be too risky as long as there remained a possibility of some North Korean nuclear weapons surviving—not to mention the possibility of another Chinese conventional intervention into the North. Hence, a North Korean nuclear capability creates the option of an invasion which, although almost certain to fail, is also almost certain not to end in the destruction of the North Korean regime. Such an option would only be undertaken in desperation, for example amid significant civilian or military unrest, or factional infighting within the CP. But given the great uncertainty about what is happening or likely to happen in North Korea, the threat of a desperate nuclear-backed conventional invasion of the South must be taken seriously. Above all it must be taken seriously by South Korea, which would face tremendous bloodletting and destruction in the opening phases.

Consider now the options available to South Korea. The carrot would be to provide North Korea with aid to buffer the immediate emergency, and to promote trade and investment to help stabilize and rejuvenate the North Korean economy in the long run. The stick would be to intensify conventional preparations—to make a North Korean invasion as unappealing an option as possible—and maybe even to acquire its own nuclear weapons. The conventional preparations have indeed proceeded. On the other hand, the nuclear development is unnecessary and even undesirable as long as US troops remain and the US stands willing to retaliate massively against any North Korean first use of nuclear weapons.

At the same time, there are a number of mutually reinforcing reasons for South Korea to provide aid and promote trade and investment with the North. The most important is to minimize the risk of suffering and instability in the North that would be severe enough to catalyze a desperate invasion of the South. Given the qualitative conventional edge enjoyed by the South and the US, significant aid can be delivered without greatly increasing the North's chances of a conventional victory. Moreover, there appears to be little chance that withholding aid and allowing further economic hardship and famine are going to undermine the North Korean regime, whatever that regime's own fears. There are other important reasons for the South to use the carrot. As long as there are real famine conditions, there is an obvious desire to prevent further deaths of fellow Koreans, especially since this does not significantly increase the security risk. Finally, now that Kim Jong-il has consolidated power, there is still a genuine possibility of internal regime change on the Chinese model. As George Kennan pointed out in the original "X" article advancing the containment doctrine,[27] regime change in communist systems becomes more likely during generational leadership transfers. It is not at all inconceivable that South Korean trade and investment and the Chinese example might make this an attractive option to Kim—who might see it as an opportunity to preserve his rule for his lifetime without going down in history as nothing more than a crafty, self-serving playboy. This development would not be without long-term risks for South Korea. If successful on a significant scale, a Northern market reform policy might significantly increase Northern military power before producing any regime change—what might be referred to as the "China scenario." However, hypothetical future risks are liable to seem much less pressing than real, present dangers.

Finally, it is worth discussing why the collapse of the USSR and democratization of South Korea did *not* stimulate any transformation of South Korean and North Korean national and state identities. To take the South first, these events increased the legitimacy and security of the South Korean regime vis-à-vis that of the North as the most likely successor regime in a future unified Korea. With unification more likely to take place on South Korean terms, the only pressure against retaining a common Korean national and state identity in the South would arise from the estimated economic costs of unification. Moreover, even if the costs and risks associated with unification were expected to be much higher than they are, they would not easily have an impact on the common Korean national identity in the South. The division of the country is comparatively recent and is not based on any significant historical precedents. To turn to the North Korean regime, there is not much prospect of a mass response to an effort by the CP regime to create a distinct Northern identity, given the political and economic attractions of the South, and, again, the artificiality of the postwar division. In these respects, the post-Cold War identities of the two Koreas are much more similar to those of the two Germanys than to those of China and Taiwan. Unlike South Korea, Taiwan has strong economic and political reasons for staying apart, on top of a long history of separate economic, political, and cultural development.

THE INDIA-PAKISTAN CONFLICT

Two important recent changes have influenced the India-Pakistan conflict (see Figure 1.3, Row 1). In China, the post-1978 economic reforms have put Chinese economic and military power on an explosive growth path. This has intensified the Chinese military threat to India (Row 2). This threat has loomed large since China humiliated India in a brief 1962 war. There is a danger both of a second Indo-Chinese war and of Chinese intervention in a future Indo-Pakistani conflict.

The Soviet Union's collapse has had even more momentous effects, both directly and indirectly (Row 1). Eliminating the Soviet threat to China allows China to mobilize far greater military resources in the Himalayan theater along the border with India and Pakistan. Eliminating the Soviet threat to the US also reduced and altered US engagement in the region. The US was weakly allied to Pakistan during the Cold War and is likely to seek to contain China in its aftermath, a situation that represents a favorable change for India. However, it hardly compensates for the increased Chinese threat.

The Soviet Union's collapse also had significant ideological effects, particularly in delegitimizing socialism as a component of national identities and as a strategy of economic development. At the same time, two competing ideologies possessed rising appeal as alternatives. East Asian developmental nationalism, using authoritarian institutions to promote export-oriented economic development and the associated rise in national military strength, stands as by far the most successful developmental ideology of the post-World War II period. Within the Muslim world, the decline of socialism has increased the prestige of Islamist ideologies. Instead of looking to the market democracies of the developed West, or to the East Asian authoritarian followers of the Western economic development path, these ideologies hold up the great Islamic empires of centuries past as models. Islamist ideologies largely reject or ignore the modern era's traditional ideological imperative of economic development. Instead, they view state-enforced religious purity as a means of reviving the Islamic empires cherished in historical memory and religious ideology. Religious purity and fervor are understood not in terms of effects on internal economic development, but as

Figure 1.3
India-Pakistan Conflict: Collapse of Soviet Power, Increasing Chinese Power, Decline of Socialist Ideology, the Structure of Preferences and Threats, and Strategic Interaction

*Solid arrows indicate increased probability, dashed arrow reduced probability.

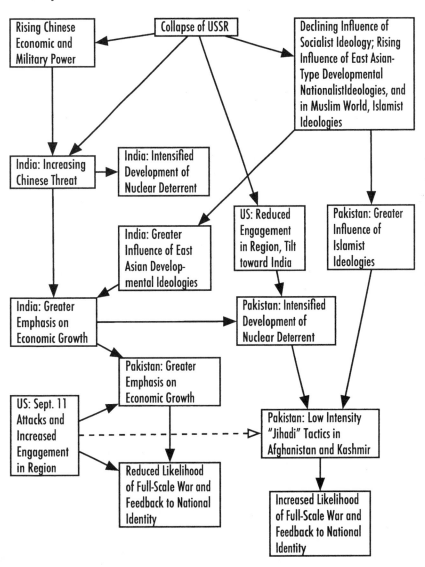

facilitating a reversal of Islamic geopolitical and cultural decline. This reversal begins with an internal purge of corrupt, largely Western influences. In the short run, this purge will facilitate overthrow of corrupt secular regimes in Islamic countries, political unification of Islamic peoples, and military victory against immediate enemies such as Israel and India. In the long run, it will take the ideological and military campaign into religiously mixed societies and even into the heart of the West in Europe and the United States.

These ideological changes have had important effects in both India and Pakistan (Row 2). Since its founding in 1947, India has long oscillated between socialist and Hindu nationalist identities. The socialist component, initially quite prominent, has long been in decline. The successes of East Asian developmental nationalism, particularly after even China began moving in that direction, gradually discredited the socialist policies of the traditionally dominant Congress Party. The Soviet collapse accelerated the process, leading to the transforming market-based economic reforms of Prime Minister P.V. Narasimha Rao in the early 1990s. Under subsequent governments led by the Hindu nationalist Bharatiya Janata Party (BJP), the new economic development strategy acquired the customary East Asian-style nationalist trappings. In India's case, greater internal stability and growing military strength promise to unleash the long-dormant geopolitical and cultural potential emphasized in Indian historical memory.

Pakistan traditionally had a more strongly secular nationalist Muslim identity, as opposed to an Islamist identity. Islamism acquired increasing influence after the disastrous 1971 war. Exploiting the discontents of Pakistan's largest ethnic group, the Bengalis of East Pakistan, India midwifed the birth of the new state of Bangladesh. This reduced Pakistan to its present Western rump. It also pointed to the danger of further dismemberment along remaining internal ethnic fault lines within West Pakistan, which divided Urdu speakers, Punjabis, Pashtuns, and Baluchis. Increased emphasis on a common Islamic identity was the obvious antidote. This policy was intensified by the 1979 Soviet invasion of Afghanistan. Pakistan mobilized Islamic identity to dislodge the Soviet-backed regime and to counter the secessionist threat posed by Afghanistan's dominant Pashtun group. The Soviet withdrawal from Afghanistan, followed by the Soviet Union's collapse, appeared to vindicate the Islamist strategy. For Pakistan's civilian and military elites as well as for the masses, Islamism emerged with increased prestige and influence.

As discussed, the increased Chinese threat and the increased influence of the East Asian development model both contributed to India's adoption of market reforms (Row 3). Growing Chinese power also increased the importance of India's nuclear capability, first demonstrated in 1974. Pakistan's nuclear program acquired urgency after the 1971 defeat, which showed that predictably permanent Indian conventional superiority carried the risk of dismemberment. The Bangladesh precedent also demonstrated that India possessed a potentially devastating response—possibly something approaching a military solution—to Pakistani support for Kashmiri separatism. In the post-Cold War period, Pakistan's incentive to retain and develop the nuclear capability demonstrated in 1988 was enhanced. The period saw both an increasing Indian economic and military power and an apparent US tilt toward India as a counterweight to China.

These events brought Pakistani identity, objectives, and strategy to a cross-roads. On the one side, China and India showed how internal economic development could be the means to greater internal political stability, military power, and regional influence (Row 4). The East Asian model also justified use of authoritarian methods, particularly against internal ethnic secessionist movements. However, an emphasis on economic growth required a conservative foreign policy, given the ways in which war and violence can disrupt trade and discourage investment. Above all, this policy implies that support for Kashmiri separatism must remain passive in order to avoid an economically devastating conflict with India.

On the other side, the victory over the Soviets in Afghanistan appeared to vindicate a more aggressive Islamist ideology. This option initially had greater influence. After the Soviet withdrawal led to civil war in Afghanistan, "jihadi" ideology, organization, and tactics were used to put a Pakistani-supported proxy in power in Kabul. Pakistani rear bases for ideological and military training, combined with military and financial support, catapulted the Taliban movement to power. As long as Pakistan had no response to India's decisive conventional superiority, such an aggressive strategy could not easily be applied to Kashmir. However, Pakistan's 1988 nuclear test provided a credible deterrent against a massive Indian conventional attack.

With one victory chalked up in Afghanistan and India restrained by a Pakistani nuclear capability, the "jihadi" strategy was applied increasingly to Kashmir. An indigenous insurgency had grown in Kashmir since 1989. In the early and mid-1990s, however, hitherto dominant local militant groups were increasingly supplanted by Islamist groups dominated by Pakistanis and other non-Kashmiri volunteers. These groups have been largely financed and armed by Pakistani military intelligence, and trained in Pakistan and in Taliban-ruled Afghanistan. The tactics of the Pakistan-based militants are far more violent, indiscriminate, and ambitious than those of their Kashmir-based predecessors. These include massacres of non-Muslim civilians in Kashmir along with spectacular attacks on politically important, ideologically symbolic targets. Most recently, the latter include the October 2001 attack on the provincial parliament of Indian-controlled Kashmir and the December 2001 attack on India's national parliament in New Delhi.[28]

However, the Islamist identity and "jihadi" strategy threaten internal economic development. An increasingly Islamist state and bureaucracy have tended to produce a multitude of ad hoc interventions in economic affairs, restricting competition and concentrating opportunities in the hands of political favorites. This promises to intensify or at least perpetuate Pakistan's traditional problems of overregulation and corruption. More important, the educational, political, and military infrastructure of the "jihadi" strategy in Pakistan gradually created a state within a state. Islamists increasingly penetrated Pakistani military intelligence and even the army itself. Secular or sectarian politicians, journalists, and businessmen were increasingly targeted and intimidated. And the Islamist movements acquired a stronger capacity to use domestic unrest and violence to secure their political demands. Finally, there was the increasing threat of war—possibly even nuclear war—with India. All this was an even greater threat to the trade and investment necessary to sustained economic growth.

With the September 11, 2001, attacks on the US, the costs of the Islamist path increased sharply. Through its decisive support for the Taliban and its use of Afghanistan as a rear base for Kashmiri militants, Pakistan could be held indirectly responsible for the September 11 attacks. If Pakistan refused to support US efforts to dislodge Al Qaeda and its Taliban protectors from Afghanistan, the US threatened Pakistan with economic and military isolation and a US alliance with India. Pakistan stared into the abyss of economic collapse, political chaos, territorial dismemberment, and possibly even nuclear holocaust. At the same time, the US and its allies offered increased financial aid and improved market access if Pakistan would support the war against the Taliban and move away from the "jihadi" strategy in general. After a tense early period in which Pervez Musharraf succeeded in purging influential Islamists from military intelligence and the army, it appears that Pakistan may be moving to shut down the "jihadi" organizational infrastructure in Pakistan. It is too early to tell if Musharraf will persist, and to tell if he does, to tell if he or others like him will be able to keep power.[29] But even a turn away from militant Islamism will not mean an end to the conflict over Kashmir. It will only mean that Pakistan will adopt more indirect, less militarily confrontational means of supporting Kashmiri separatists.[30]

LESSONS FROM THEORY AND PRACTICE

The theoretical discussion and case studies above have emphasized the lessons of theory for practice. For the China-Taiwan conflict, the changing characters of China's state identity and of Taiwan's national and state identities prove crucial to an understanding of changing state preferences and strategies. In particular, China's apparent inwardly motivated use of hostile rhetoric combined with Taiwan's democratization and increasing development of islander identity are mutually reinforcing. This dynamic makes it more likely that Taiwan will develop an independent and decisive self-defense capability before China's economic growth and military buildup create a viable invasion option.

For the Korean conflict, by contrast, the sudden decline of North Korean power and legitimacy has produced mutually compatible stabilizing responses. The North Korean regime shores up its external security with a nuclear option, and thereby stimulates South Korean efforts to shore up the North's internal economy so that the nuclear option will not increase the risk of a desperate conventional invasion. With Kim Jong-il's succession secure, the North's improving external security and internal stability make a China-style reform more feasible, although not necessarily more likely. It is difficult to detect any basic changes in North or South Korea's national and state identities, though a future China-style change in North Korea's state identity is possible.

The Chinese economic reforms and particularly the collapse of the Soviet Union reinforced preexisting trends in Indian and Pakistani national identity. India moved more sharply toward developmental nationalism, and Pakistan toward Islamist ideology and methods. This appeared to put the two nuclear-armed powers on a disastrous collision course. The US reengagement following the September 11 attacks has increased and dramatized the potential costs to Pakistan of the Islamist path and its "jihadi" strategy. This makes it more likely that Pakistan's leaders will retreat from the abyss to an inward developmental focus.

The main lesson of theory is thus that national and state identities bear close analysis as possible sources of change or stability in state preferences, strategies, and future changes in national and state identities. On the other hand, the cases also provide guidelines for theory. National and state identities are formed and constrained by the interaction of historical memories and aspirations, regime types, and contemporary opportunities. Just as they can be used instrumentally by elites interesting in preserving power or competing for power, they can also animate elites to adopt objectives and strategies that may endanger their power. But without closer analysis of particular examples, it is impossible to say how rigid or flexible national and state identities are, or what the respective roles of ideology and expediency are in generating the historical events that preserve and transform them.

NOTES

1. David A. Lake and Robert Powell (eds.), *Strategic Choice and International Relations* (Princeton: Princeton University Press, 1999).

2. Kenneth N. Waltz, *Theory of International Politics* (New York: Random House, 1979).

3. Shale Horowitz, "The Balance of Power: Formal Perfection and Practical Flaws," *Journal of Peace Research* 38, 6 (2001), pp. 705-22; Emerson M.S. Niou, Peter C. Ordeshook, and Gregory F. Rose, *The Balance of Power: Stability in International Relations* (Cambridge: Cambridge University Press, 1989).

4. Madeleine K. Albright and Joung-binn Lee, *Press Conference of Secretary of State Madeleine K. Albright and Minister of Foreign Affairs and Trade Joung-binn Lee* (Seoul: Ministry of Foreign Affairs and Trade, 23 June 2000); *Korea Herald*, "Seoul-Washington Security Session," 22 September 2000.

5. "Taiwan's China Dare," *Economist*, 25 March 2000, p. 17; "Pakistan's Musharraf Vows Crackdown on Militants," *Reuters*, 12 January 2002.

6. Similarly, during the Cold War, often-authoritarian Pakistan had stronger ties to the democratic US, and democratic India with the authoritarian USSR. However, these cannot be viewed as close alliances of the kinds built up around the China-Taiwan and Korea conflicts.

7. Mancur Olson, Jr., *The Logic of Collective Action: Public Goods and the Theory of Groups* (New York: Schocken, 1971).

8. This kind of logic is not limited to Japan. China has in the past held sway over Korea, Vietnam, and other parts of Asia, and traditionally views itself as the region's rightful political, economic, and cultural hegemon. This has caused both North Korea and Vietnam to be more pointedly nervous about their independence, making the Soviet Union a desirable counterweight. With the Soviet Union's collapse and Russia's withdrawal from an active regional role, there is still understandable nervousness about excessive reliance on China.

9. Richard Rosecrance, *Action and Reaction in World Politics: International Systems in Perspective* (Westport: Greenwood Press, 1977); Richard Rosecrance and Arthur A. Stein (eds.), *The Domestic Bases of Grand Strategy* (Ithaca: Cornell University Press, 1993); Bruce M. Russett, *Grasping the Democratic Peace: Principles for a Post-Cold War World* (Princeton: Princeton University Press, 1993).

10. Robert O. Keohane, *After Hegemony: Cooperation and Discord in the World Political Economy* (Princeton: Princeton University Press, 1984); Stephen D. Krasner (ed.), *International Regimes* (Ithaca: Cornell University Press, 1983).

11. "Meeting of Two Koreas Signals Historic Thaw," *USA Today*, 15 June 2000, p. A14.

12. Yang Jin, "New Government, New Playing Field," *Taipei Review*, August 2000; Shui-bian Chen, *Taiwan Stands Up: Advancing to an Uplifting Era. Inauguration Speech by 10th-Term Republic of China President Chen Shui-bian* (Taipei: Government Information Office, 2000), p. 16.

13. "Indian General Talks Bluntly of War and a Nuclear Threat," *New York Times*, 12 January 2002.

14. Nicholas Eberstadt, "What's North Korea Up To?" *Wall Street Journal*, 19 June 2000, p. A19.

15. Aaron Friedberg, "Will We Abandon Taiwan?" *Commentary*, May 2000, pp. 31-5.

16. "No Need for War," *Far Eastern Economic Review*, 10 January 2002.

17. Raymond Aron, *Peace and War: A Theory of International Relations* (Garden City: Anchor, 1973); Peter J. Katzenstein (ed.), *The Culture of National Security: Norms and Identity in World Politics* (New York: Columbia University Press, 1996).

18. These issues have been treated extensively in the literature on national identity. Theoretically, national identities can be viewed as more malleable, more rigid, or in between—malleable but sticky. Classic works staking out various positions on this terrain include: Benedict Anderson, *Imagined Communities: Reflections on the Origin and Spread of Nationalism* (London: Verso, 1991); Walker Connor, *Ethnonationalism: The Quest for Understanding* (Princeton: Princeton University Press, 1994); Ernest Gellner, *Nations and Nationalism* (Oxford: Blackwell, 1983); and Anthony Smith, *The Ethnic Origins of Nations* (Oxford: Blackwell, 1986). The position taken here is that models can be constructed to fit all of these positions, and that debates about particular examples can only be resolved empirically.

19. "What Now for Beijing and Taipei?" *New York Times*, 21 March 2000, p. A5.

20. "Taiwan Stands Up," *Economist*, 25 March 2000, p. 28.

21. "North Korean Diplomacy," *Chosun Ilbo*, 10 June 2000; Peter Maass, "Open Sesame: North Korea Opens Up," *New Republic* 4, 456, 12 June 2000, pp. 14-6.

22. "Ending Terror in Kashmir," *Baltimore Sun*, 10 January 2002; "South Asia's Enduring Conflict," *San Francisco Chronicle*, 4 January 2002; "The 'K' Card," *Times of India*, 10 January 2002.

23. This remains true despite Taiwan's recent recession.

24. Alexander C. Tan, "Taiwan: Sustained State Autonomy and a Step Back from Liberalization," in Shale Horowitz and Uk Heo (eds.), *The Political Economy of International Financial Crisis: Interests, Ideologies, and Institutions* (Lanham: Rowman and Littlefield, 2000), pp. 207-21.

25. A little-known but interesting parallel is the development of a distinct national identity, vis-à-vis Ceausescu's Romania, in the ethnically Romanian Moldovan Soviet Socialist Republic. With the collapse of the Soviet Union, Moldovans advocating union with Romania were decisively outnumbered by those embracing independence.

26. As will become evident, however, this mission, like the broader mission of raising China up toward her world-historical potential, is also not one that necessarily requires a CP regime.

27. "The Sources of Soviet Conduct," *Foreign Affairs* 25 (July 1947), pp. 566-82.

28. In 1999, Pakistan even took the risk of infiltrating a large force to seize parts of the strategic Kargil area in Indian-controlled Kashmir. In heavy fighting verging

on a conventional war, Indian forces later drove the infiltrators back across the border.

29. "Pakistan Is Said to Order an End to Support for Militant Groups," *New York Times*, 2 January 2002, p. A1.

30. Chindu Sreedharan, "Blood in the Snow: Ten Years of Conflict in Kashmir," *Rediff*, 8-18 December 1999 <www.rediff.com/news/1999/dec/11blood.htm>

2

China's Taiwan Policy:
Past and Present

Jing Huang

When the Chinese Communist Party (CCP) seized power and established the People's Republic of China (PRC) in 1949, the remnants of the Nationalists (the Kuomintang, or KMT) under Chiang Kai-shek fled to Taiwan. Ever since then, relations across the Taiwan Strait have been one of the most complicated riddles in the Asia-Pacific region. With the passing of the old guards in both Taipei and Beijing, the Communist-Nationalist rivalry has faded inexorably into history. But conflicts between the PRC and Taiwan continue to cast a lingering shadow over the prospects for peace and stability in the Taiwan Strait and the entire Asia-Pacific region. Given the changes in domestic politics and the international environment, PRC policy toward Taiwan has displayed considerable flexibility over the past five decades. Yet the PRC leadership has never given up its ultimate policy goal: reunification with Taiwan. And in pursuit of this goal, the PRC may, if necessary, resort to force.

In recent years, since then-Taiwanese president Li Teng-hui's private visit to Cornell University in June 1995, cross-strait relations have become increasingly volatile. In the nine months from July 1999 to March 2000, a series of events inflamed an already heated situation. These events include:

1. Lee Teng-hui's controversial statement in July 1999 that any exchanges between the two sides of the Taiwan Strait "should be based on a special state-to-state relationship";
2. Beijing's second Taiwan White Paper in February 2000, which for the first time implied that China could resort to force should Taiwan refuse indefinitely to return to the negotiating table;
3. The PRC premier Zhu Rongji's stark warning to Taiwan on March 16, 2000, on the consequences of Taiwan's presidential election, should Chen Shui-bian, the candidate of the pro-independence Democratic Progressive Party (DPP), win; and
4. Chen's victory in the Taiwanese presidential election two days later.

Yet, amazingly, Beijing's reaction to Chen's electoral victory, and his ada-
mant insistence on "two independent political entities" instead of one China,
has so far been relatively moderate and restrained. Why?

This chapter examines China's Taiwan policy from a historical perspective.
It shows how the PRC's Taiwan policy has evolved since the early 1950s, under
the impact of often-changing domestic and international environments. These
evolving Taiwan policies have, of course, strongly shaped the cross-strait relationship. The chapter then highlights the dilemma that confronts the current
PRC leadership on the Taiwan issue, laying special emphasis on the question of
how Beijing's endeavor to resolve this dilemma will affect cross-strait relations.
Finally, the chapter assesses several of Beijing's possible policy choices in dealing with Taiwan under current circumstances, attempting to shed some light
upon the basic calculus that underlies Beijing's approach to Taiwan. It concludes with a discussion of the likelihood of a renewed *modus vivendi* across the
Taiwan Strait.

Since the early 1950s, the PRC's Taiwan policy has gone through three distinct phases, each with different policy approaches and initiatives. Although
there is obvious policy continuity through the three phases, i.e., the One-China
Principle and the unchanging goal of unification, the PRC leadership's approach
to the Taiwan issue and hence PRC policy underwent profound changes: from
"liberation of Taiwan," to "peaceful unification with the one-country-two-system
model," to the current military coercion.

PHASE I, 1950-1979: CONFLICT AND COOPERATION WITHIN THE ONE-CHINA FRAMEWORK

In this phase, there were constant armed conflicts between the two
sides—while the CCP swore to "liberate Taiwan," the KMT on Taiwan pledged
to "recover the mainland." Yet both Beijing and Taipei remained steadfast in
their conviction that there is only one China in the world, and that Taiwan is
nothing but a part of China. Consequently, both sides insisted that only one
government, and not two, could represent China as a whole. Thus, each claimed
to be the sole legitimate government of the whole of China and denigrated the
other side as an illegitimate regime. Although the consensus on one China between two foes was of little help in altering the essential reality of a de facto
split China, it did ensure the de jure oneness of China in the international arena.
Ironically, this one-China framework actually provided both Beijing and Taipei
with common ground for tacit cooperation and secret communications in the
1950s and 1960s, despite frequent conflicts and hostile rhetoric between the two
sides.[1]

In retrospect, reunification by force was indeed a top priority for Chairman
Mao Zedong and his colleagues in early 1950, when a series of logistical and
military personnel training programs were initiated in active preparation for an
upcoming conquest of the island. The ambitious plan of "liberating Taiwan,"
however, faded into wishful thinking with the outbreak of the Korean War in
June 1950, Stalin's reluctance to provide necessary military equipment and
technology, and the US' determined military intervention to prevent an invasion
across the Taiwan Strait. Given its comparative military backwardness, and a

looming Sino-Soviet split that rendered adequate Soviet assistance virtually impossible, Beijing was compelled to consider the possibility of a peaceful solution to the Taiwan problem. This new approach was heralded in 1956, when then-PRC Premier Zhou En-lai declared:

The Chinese Government has repeatedly pointed out that there are two ways for the Chinese people to liberate Taiwan, that is, by war or by peaceful means, and that the Chinese people would seek to liberate Taiwan by peaceful means so far as it is possible. There is no doubt that if Taiwan can be liberated peacefully, it would be best for our country, for all the Chinese people, and for Asian and world peace.[2]

Although the rhetoric of "liberation" still remains in Zhou's words, it is obvious that the PRC began to think and signal its preference for "peaceful unification" through negotiations rather than the use of force. The process, however, was interrupted. This was partly because the PRC leaders were preoccupied with the rapidly deteriorating Sino-Soviet relationship, and partly because of the disastrous economic experiment of the Great Leap Forward (GLF). Thus, it was not until 1963, as the situation was stabilized both externally and internally, that some meaningful exchanges and negotiations took place between the secret envoys of the two sides in Hong Kong. Zhou elaborated on a peaceful solution to the reunification issue. This is summed up in the following "four points" by Li Jiaquan, a PRC official who was involved in the policymaking process at the time:

1. After reunification, the then-ruling KMT party in Taiwan would retain exclusive control over Taiwan, including the island's armed forces, while the central government in Beijing would only be in charge of Taiwan's external relations.
2. After reunification, when Taiwan's local finance was in difficulty, the central government would subsidize it to fit the circumstances.
3. After reunification, Taiwan would retain its social and economic systems, and the central government would not interfere without consulting and obtaining the consent of the KMT beforehand.
4. After reunification, both sides of the Taiwan Strait would refrain from dispatching secret agents to areas controlled by the other side, and neither side would be involved in activities that might disrupt the internal order and unity of the other side.[3]

Such a solution was all ·but impossible at the time, given the US containment policy during the Cold War on the one hand, and the fierce competition between the two sides of the Taiwan Strait for political legitimacy on the other hand. Yet the PRC leaders' vision and policy flexibility on the Taiwan issue did leave room for a negotiated settlement in the future. In fact, this approach provided a blueprint for the "one country, two systems" policy later to be formulated by Deng Xiaoping in the mid-1980s.

In shaping a peaceful approach to Taiwan, Beijing also took into account a weighty external factor—the US involvement in the Taiwan Strait. As discussed above, the US military presence in the Taiwan Strait after the outbreak of the Korean War had dashed Beijing's hope of "liberating Taiwan" for the foreseeable future. Without military assistance from the Soviet Union, which was becoming a more serious threat to China's security in the early 1960s, the PRC had no choice but to bide its time until it achieved a sufficient buildup of military capabilities. For Beijing, the US "scheme" to detach Taiwan from China legally was another cause for concern. From the PRC's point of view—which was later to be proven correct—the US' hidden intention had been to create a disengagement in the Taiwan Strait and then to introduce the concepts of "two Chinas" or "one China, one Taiwan" as an alternative to "one China."[4] At the time, the US' strategic goals in the Asia-Pacific region were to contain communism without provoking a massive confrontation with the communist world. Separation of Taiwan from China would transform the Taiwan problem from an internal Chinese issue to an international one, and therefore provide legitimacy for US involvement. This aimed not only to defend Taiwan, but also to prevent Taiwan from attacking the PRC—which could provoke a massive confrontation involving the US.

Given US policy, "liberating Taiwan" had become the mere PRC rhetoric from the late 1950s up to the early 1970s. The strategic goal of Beijing's policy toward Taiwan was, as a Chinese scholar remarks, to "cooperate with Chiang Kai-shek against the Americans" in order to safeguard the de jure oneness of China.[5] In retrospect, this approach worked well. Throughout this period, the KMT, under the successive leadership of Chiang Kai-shek and his son Chiang Ching-kuo, had opposed the concepts of "two Chinas" or "one China, one Taiwan" as vehemently as the PRC. Hence Washington's declaration in the 1972 US-PRC Shanghai Communiqué: "The United States acknowledges that Chinese on either side of the Taiwan Strait maintain there is but one China and Taiwan is a part of China. The United States Government does not challenge that position."[6]

Indeed, although the PRC's policy toward Taiwan from 1950 to 1979 appears to be fruitless in terms of the strategic goal of reunification, it did reach achieve an objective with far-reaching implications for cross-strait relations. This was the international community's recognition and acceptance of the One-China Principle—that there is but one China and that Taiwan is a part of China. However, this approach depended partly on the similar stance taken by the KMT government on the other side of the Taiwan Strait.

PHASE II, 1979-1995: THE INEFFECTUAL "SUNSHINE" POLICY

The international environment changed decisively in the PRC's favor after President Richard Nixon's historic visit to Beijing in 1972, which eventually led to normalization of US-China relations in 1979. The fundamental changes in US Pacific strategy—from non-recognition and containment of China to embracing China as a strategic partner in the Cold War, and from alliance with Taiwan to the de facto abandonment of Taiwan—relaunched the cross-strait relationship on an entirely new course. Nixon's visit to China in 1972 opened not only China to the world, but also the world to China. Meanwhile, the "reform and opening up" policy adopted under Deng Xiaoping's leadership had launched China in the direction of a "socialist market economy" and a more formalized political order. This also made China more acceptable, and indeed attractive, to the world community. All this enabled Beijing to isolate Taiwan in international affairs, with an overwhelming majority of states switching diplomatic recognition from Taipei to Beijing. The US and the PRC normalized relations in 1979, a crowning achievement of Beijing's endeavor to reduce Taipei to an international outcast. Policymakers in Washington and Beijing did not even bother to give serious consideration to a solution of the Taiwan issue, which would turn out to be the thorniest problem in US-China relations. They were convinced that, after the US' de facto abandonment of Taiwan and its acknowledgment that "there is but one China and Taiwan is a part of China," the Taiwan problem "would just go away,"[7] that is, Taiwan would have nowhere to go but back into the embrace of China. A key disagreement, which was deliberately overlooked at the time but which would later haunt policymakers in both Washington and Beijing, was about how the Taiwan problem would be solved. The US, as it would stress repeatedly in later years, saw a "peaceful solution" as a precondition for eventual reunification. By contrast, the PRC insisted that the US acknowledgment of the One-China Principle virtually amounted to an agreement that the Taiwan problem should be a matter of Chinese internal affairs. In other words, the solution, whether by force or not, was none of Washington's business.

Despite this hidden but potentially deadly dispute between the US and the PRC, Beijing's approach to Taiwan during this period could be labeled as a "sunshine" policy, as laid out by Marshall Ye Jianying, then the PRC president, in his well-known "nine-point Taiwan Policy" speech at the end of 1979. Based on the well-known "one country, two systems" formula proposed by Deng Xiaoping, this policy made a seemingly irresistible offer to Taiwan: "After unification, Taiwan could retain a highly autonomous government, with its existing political and economic systems, full authority in its internal affairs, including personnel arrangements in administration, its own law enforcement and legal system independent of the central government in Beijing, and its own armed forces."[8]

Meanwhile, the PRC government encouraged people in Taiwan to visit and invest in China. In order to promote cross-strait relations and attract investment from the island, Beijing not only offered substantial incentives for Taiwanese investing on the mainland, but also proposed the "three direct links"—direct trade, communication, and transport links—between the two sides of the strait. Taiwan's response, however, was less than enthusiastic. Taiwan's government resisted the "three direct links" (it would not accept the proposal until 2001). In 1996, it adopted a "no haste" policy to curb direct investment in the PRC.[9]

Taiwan's caution and reluctance to embrace Beijing's "sunshine" policy were well justified. All the seemingly generous offers from Beijing were based on the position that Taiwan is a renegade province of China. Thus, Beijing insisted that talks between the PRC and Taiwan should be held between the two ruling parties, namely the CCP and KMT, rather than the two governments in Beijing and Taipei. The obvious intention behind this arrangement was to deny Taiwan an equal footing in any official meetings between the two sides.

This "sunshine" policy, as Lowell Dittmer has remarked, sought to make "Taiwan's independent existence illegitimate, defenseless, and ultimately untenable while making its reunification with the mainland maximally attractive."[10]

In practice, this meant that Beijing, in an attempt to lure Taiwan back into China's embrace, did its utmost to block the island's access to the outside world (portraying Taiwan as a mere "renegade province" of China), while continuing to offer enticing incentives to Taiwan. Although such a two-pronged strategy did not extract any substantial concessions from Taipei, Beijing was confident that time would be on its side. As Andrew Nathan contends, Beijing expected that increasing international isolation would eventually leave the island "no other exit than accommodation with Beijing on Beijing's terms."[11]

But it was not to be. In implementing the "sunshine" policy toward Taiwan, the PRC leadership appeared too confident and optimistic: too confident to pay any substantial attention to unprecedented developments that were reshaping Taiwan's political and economic landscapes, and too optimistic to react promptly to the fundamental changes in the international environment caused by the end of the Cold War. Consequently, the PRC leaders' reluctance to make any adjustments of the "sunshine" policy, in response to these changes in both Taiwan and the international environment, deprived their Taiwan policy of its most effective element: flexibility.

First of all, after years of rapid export-led economic growth, Taiwan rose to become an integral and active player in the world economic system. By 1995, the island ranked as the world's fourteenth-largest trading nation as well as the world's sixteenth outbound investor, and it had accumulated the second-largest foreign reserves in the world.[12] This not only provided Taiwan with adequate resources in its effort to break Beijing's blockade in the international arena, but it also enabled Taiwanese leaders to offer attractive incentives to states that were willing to deal with them. Although most states still shun official or diplomatic ties with Taipei for fear of offending Beijing, Taiwan's economic significance has nevertheless compelled other nations to allow Taipei greater leeway in setting up more and more quasi-official representative offices on their soil. As a result, while Beijing's endeavor to box Taiwan into a shrinking international living space was offset or neutralized, a rich and prosperous Taiwan was increasingly confident in pursuing its policy of "pragmatic diplomacy (*wushi waijiao*)."

Second, full-scale democratization was gaining momentum in Taiwan, especially after the death of Chiang Ching-kuo in 1988. Over the course of a decade starting in 1986, Taiwan threw off the yoke of authoritarianism. Taiwan abolished the Martial Law that had been in place since 1946; released political prisoners who were mostly activists for Taiwan's independence; terminated curbs on speech and the press; legalized the formation of political opposition movements and parties; and conducted free elections for all the legislative bodies, local mayoralties; and, eventually, the presidency. With the CCP still holding to its coercive and exclusive one-party rule, democratization has provided Taiwanese leaders with a legitimate and convenient pretext for rejecting reunification with the PRC, in the name of "human rights and democracy." It has also stirred ever-growing US—principally congressional—sympathy toward Taiwan, which is a pivotal stimulus to Taipei's effort to raise its international profile as a political entity separate from the PRC. This effort culminated in Lee Teng-hui's private visit to Cornell University in June 1995. Beijing saw this not only as a gross violation of the One-China Principle acknowledged by the US government in the three US-China communiqués in 1972, 1979, and 1984, but also as a "dangerous step towards separation from the motherland."[13] The 1996 missile exercise conducted by the PRC's People's Liberation Army (PLA) in the Taiwan Strait demonstrated Beijing's outrage and resolve to "safeguard the sovereignty of the motherland"—by force if necessary. The threat, however, seemed to backfire. Not only did Lee Teng-hui win the very first presidential election in Taiwan, but the momentum of democratization was further reinforced. This resulted in the victory of Chen Shui-bian, the candidate of the pro-independence DPP, in the 2000 presidential election.

Chen's victory marked the end of KMT rule in Taiwan, which had lasted for over five decades since 1945. More significant, it accomplished the process of "localization" (or "Taiwanization") of Taiwanese politics, which had been a predominant theme in the island's political life since Lee Teng-hui came to power in 1988. The implications are profound and far-reaching. First, since the late years of President Chiang Ching-kuo, Taipei has lost interest in representing China as a whole and is merely interested in representing Taiwan. Second, the new-generation leaders see themselves as Taiwanese rather than Chinese.[14] Indeed, in newly democratized Taiwan, where Taiwanese leaders have become predominant in political affairs, advocating Taiwanese independence is no longer illegal but to a great extent politically correct. The momentum has been further fueled by the Taiwanese electorate's anti-China sentiments, cultivated skillfully by politicians like Lee Teng-hui and the pro-independence DPP leaders. The end result is Taiwan's inexorable movement away from its traditional commitment to one China.

While all these developments contrasted sharply with the stagnant CCP's one-party rule on the mainland, changes in the international environment also worked in Taiwan's favor. The collapse of the former Soviet Union not only blew away the "Strategic Triangle," in which China had been the US' de facto partner since Nixon's visit to Beijing in 1972, but it also restored Taiwan's strategic significance in US Pacific policy. The US' concern for Taiwan was such that, when in 1996 the PLA was conducting its missile exercise to influence the presidential election in Taiwan, the Pentagon dispatched two carrier battle groups to the waters near the Taiwan Strait. This was the largest deployment of US forces in the area since the Vietnam War. A more profound reason for the US' increasing sympathy toward Taiwan, however, was Taiwan's political democratization and economic integration in the world economy. These enabled Taiwan not only to hold the moral high ground in the international arena, but also to join in the mainstream of democracy and market economy in the post-Cold War world. Thus, behind the explicit US commitment to the "preservation and enhancement of the human rights of the people on Taiwan"[15] lies the relentless effort of the United States, now the sole superpower, to promote democracy and its intertwined value system.

Amazingly, the PRC leadership not only failed to appreciate the wide implications of these changes in Taiwan and the international environment. It also appeared extremely reluctant to revamp its "sunshine" policy, which was rendered increasingly ineffectual and stagnant by these changes. As Taiwanese politics became increasingly pluralistic, and the economy more prosperous in the late 1980s and early 1990s, the issue of reunification was no longer merely a matter that could be solved by the two "ruling parties" (namely, the CCP and the then-KMT), or even by the two governments. This lack of political vision and perspicacity on the part of Beijing not only enabled Taipei to win more initiatives in the interactions between the two sides of the Taiwan Strait, but it also handicapped Beijing's effort to box in Taiwan with the one-China policy. It is true that Beijing was still able to maintain its "blockade" against Taiwan in world affairs in the mid-1990s. But increasing support both at home and abroad emboldened Taiwan to be more aggressive in opening up "international space." This included probing the possibility of independence in defiance of Beijing.

PHASE III, 1995-PRESENT: MILITARY COERCION WITH MORE FLEXIBILITY AND INCENTIVES

The PRC leadership eventually recognized the inadequacies and ineffectiveness of the "sunshine" policy. Three days after then-US Secretary of State Warren Christopher told then-PRC Foreign Minister Qian Qichen that Washington would not grant a visa to Taiwan President Lee Teng-hui or any high-ranking Taiwan officials, the US government granted Lee an entry visa for his private visit to Cornell University in the summer of 1995.[16] Outraged and feeling betrayed, the PRC's leadership responded promptly and seemingly recklessly. Massive military maneuvers and missile firings in the Taiwan Strait in 1995-96 marked the beginning of a more realistic "carrots-and-sticks" approach to Taiwan. In other words, by increasing military pressure to deter separatist tendencies on the island, Beijing began to inject more flexibility and incentives into its Taiwan policy.

During this period, Beijing's tactics of military coercion have been evident in frequent military exercises and maneuvers. The missile exercise in the Taiwan Strait in 1996, and the massive May 2001 maneuvers and exercises along China's east coast involving the PLA army, navy and air force, have been only the most significant ones. Through these military exercises and maneuvers, Beijing has demonstrated not only its resolve to go as far as necessary to rein in Taipei's drive for independent statehood, but also its increasing military capability and readiness. Moreover, Beijing's ever-mounting military pressure on Taiwan and the PLA's frequent military exercises have formalized "military coercion" as an essential part of China's current policy concerning Taiwan.

Although it remains doubtful that the PLA's shows of force produced any substantial change of course by Taipei on the reunification issue, China's use of military measures does appear to have deterred Taiwan from openly championing either a "two Chinas" or "one China, one Taiwan" formula as alternatives to one China. There is little doubt that Lee Teng-hui was keenly aware of this. Thus, while Beijing fiercely condemned his "special state-to-state relationship" statement as yet another attempt to assert Taiwan's independence, Lee explained that the statement simply reflected Taiwan's resentment at being treated by Beijing as a local government on the one hand, and its determination to seek "equality" in dealing with the PRC on the other hand. President Chen Shui-bian has insisted adamantly on "two independent political entities" instead of one China. But he also promised in his May 20, 2000, inauguration speech that, as long as the PRC did not use force against Taiwan, his government would not seek independence or separation from the mainland.

While counting upon military "sticks" to dampen Taiwan's aspirations for independence, the PRC leadership continued to offer the island political and economic "carrots," or policy incentives, in the hope of bringing Taipei to discuss some sort of reunification. In his eight-point statement of January 1995, CCP General Secretary and President Jiang Zemin reaffirmed the PRC's staunch opposition to the notions of "two Chinas" or "one China, one Taiwan." Meanwhile, he sent a conciliatory message to Taiwan, proposing that:

1. The PRC will not oppose Taiwan establishing nongovernmental economic and cultural ties with foreign countries.
2. Different political parties, groups, and representatives [of Taiwan] will be allowed to take part in any talks concerning peaceful reunification. As a first step toward cross-strait reconciliation, both sides of the Taiwan Strait should reach an agreement on the termination of the state of hostilities under the One-China Principle.
3. Chinese should not fight fellow Chinese. The PRC's refusal to forgo the use of force against Taiwan is not directed at Taiwanese compatriots but at foreign countries that seek to interfere with China's reunification and at the separatist forces within Taiwan.
4. The two sides should develop strong economic ties and adopt pragmatic steps toward the establishment of direct mail, transportation, and commercial exchanges.
5. The rights, autonomy, lifestyle, and interests of the 23 million Taiwanese compatriots will be protected by the PRC.
6. Taiwanese officials are welcome to visit the PRC and the PRC leaders are ready to visit Taiwan at the invitation of the Taiwanese side. Cross-strait discussions of national policies, exchanges of different opinions and even casual visits will all be welcomed.[17]

One has to notice a subtle but significant change in Beijing's position in Jiang's words above. Jiang not only encourages nongovernmental exchanges between the two sides, but he also calls all "political parties, groups, and representatives" of Taiwan, not just the ruling party, to "take part in any talks concerning peaceful reunification."

Moreover, Beijing has actually reinterpreted the one-China policy to make it more flexible and acceptable. Ever since its founding, the PRC has remained steadfast in claiming that it is the sole legal government of China as a whole, while regarding the governing authorities on Taiwan as no more than a local government that exists on Chinese territory. Before the mid-1990s, this intransigence led to Beijing's apparent unwillingness to treat the KMT government on Taiwan as a political equal. Granting Taipei such political parity would be a tacit acknowledgment of Taiwan as a political entity on a par with the PRC. Consequently, as mentioned above, prior to the mid-1990s, Beijing's proposals for cross-strait negotiation had always insisted that any such negotiations be held on a "ruling party-to-ruling party" (i.e., CCP-KMT) basis. The PRC's February 2000 Taiwan White Paper, however, made a few subtle but powerful adjustments to Beijing's traditional position on one China. The adjustments are evident in the following areas.

First of all, while stressing its firm opposition to Taipei's effort to expand its diplomatic representation abroad, Beijing has actually recognized Taipei as an intra-national equal under the One-China Principle. For the first time, Beijing made it clear that cross-strait negotiations would not be regarded as one between "central and local authorities," but would be held on an equal footing under the One-China Principle.[18]

Second, the White Paper hinted broadly that: "[a]s for Taiwan, upholding the principle of one China indicates that it acknowledges that China's sovereignty and territory are inalienable. Provided that it is within the framework of one China, any question can be discussed, including various issues that are of concern to the Taiwan side."[19] This statement actually de-linked "the one China" from the PRC. This was a substantial concession to Taipei, for these "various issues that are of concern to the Taiwan side" have always included Beijing's formal renunciation of the use of force against Taiwan, the island's political autonomy, and the national name and flag for a reunified China. Thus, the White Paper was in actuality indicating that, if Taiwan agrees to joining a negotiating framework designed to achieve ultimate reunification, all these issues are negotiable. Still more recently, PRC Premier Zhu Rongji, while warning Taiwan not to seek independence, went a step further in declaring that: "We can talk with [anyone who stands for one China] and our talk can cover everything. There can also be a concession made on our part, as this concession would be one made to our fellow Chinese."[20] According to a high-ranking official in the PRC's Taiwan Affair Office under the State Council, all this has met with a deaf ear in Taipei—although Beijing passed all the messages explicitly to the Taiwanese leaders through "reliable channels."[21] What has really frustrated Beijing, according to the same sources, is not necessarily Taiwan's refusal to accept the One-China Policy. Rather, they believe that, rather than adopting a reasonable approach toward negotiation for reunification, Taiwanese politicians deliberately provoke controversies on the cross-strait relationship for political gain at home.

Third, Beijing has cultivated a people-to-people approach to Taiwan. Despite prolonged cross-strait tension, Beijing has promoted extensive economic, trade, and cultural interactions between the two sides of the Taiwan Strait. By 2000, the PRC had become Taiwan's second-largest export market, its single most important source of trade surplus, and the top recipient of the island's outbound capital flow. In 1996, for example, despite the PLA's war games in the Taiwan Strait, Taiwanese residents paid 1.57 million visits to the mainland via Hong Kong and Macao.[22] The momentum of economic and cultural exchanges has increased in recent years as Taiwan has seen some of its hardest economic times since the Vietnam War. In implementing such a people-to-people approach to Taiwan, Beijing has displayed a high degree of pragmatism, choosing to focus on substantive affairs like *san tong* (i.e., the establishment of direct trade, transportation, and telecommunications exchanges between the two sides of the Taiwan Strait), while avoiding sensitive political issues. This approach has also brought Beijing into closer contact with political parties and groups of all shades in Taiwan, not merely with important parties like the KMT and DPP.

In offering these policy "carrots," especially the economic ones, to Taiwan, the PRC also made it clear that its patience on the reunification issue is not without limits. The February 2000 Taiwan White Paper expressed this point in no uncertain terms: "If the Taiwan authorities refuse, *sine die*, the peaceful settlement of cross-strait reunification through negotiation, then the Chinese government will only be forced to adopt all drastic measures, including the use of force, to safeguard China's sovereignty and territorial integrity, and fulfill the great cause of reunification."[23] Although Beijing has yet to unveil an explicit timetable for settling the Taiwan problem, the not infrequent hinting at the existence of such a timetable, plus frequent military maneuvers and exercises, might well serve as a useful psychological weapon against Taiwan. They are a reminder that, without a strategic understanding with the PRC on the reunification issue, Taiwan's de facto independence is precarious.

CONCLUDING REMARKS: CHINA'S DILEMMA AND CHOICES ON THE TAIWAN ISSUE

The mounting military pressure from the PLA on the one hand, and the PRC leadership's obvious military restraint on the other, reveal more than a military capability insufficient to overwhelm Taiwan, as the conventional wisdom suggests. Rather, it also reflects a fundamental dilemma the PRC leadership has faced on the Taiwan issue.

For over two decades since 1978, when China began to open up to the outside world, the PRC leadership has stressed the modernization of the Chinese economy as the key element in China's long-term developmental strategy. Continuous economic growth has become an essential source of legitimacy for CCP rule, and hence vital for political stability in China. To create an auspicious context for sustained economic growth, however, China needs not only to maintain a credible climate of political stability, but to strive for a peaceful international environment as well. To advance both ends, Beijing will need to develop a stable and constructive relationship with the US, the world's sole superpower, China's largest export market, and China's most important source of investment and know-how. The use of force against Taiwan and its international implications, however, would force the PRC leadership to abandon its long-term developmental strategy centered on economic growth, which in turn would undermine the legitimacy of the CCP rule. Moreover, it would set China on a collision course with the US and its allies, for the Taiwan problem, unfortunately, happens to be the most sensitive—and potentially explosive—issue in US-China relations.

At the heart of the PRC's staunch insistence on the notion of Taiwan as Chinese territory lies Beijing's deep-seated concern for China's national sovereignty and security—matters which, indeed, leave little room for vacillation. Should Beijing decide that Taiwan's continued status as part of China can only be guaranteed by military conquest of the island, the consequences will be profound. In the first place, war with Taiwan will in all probability exact an enormous price on China's modernizing economy, depriving it of a key source of external investment and frightening off other foreign investors as well. Such a war would also be likely to incur a wide range of international economic sanctions against Beijing. Should such be the case, the PRC leadership would simply have to reconsider, if not relinquish, China's long-term developmental strategy, which has placed paramount importance upon economic growth for over two decades. The modernization of the Chinese economy, in other words, would have to be brushed aside as an objective of secondary importance compared to matters of national sovereignty and security.

Moreover, war with Taiwan is also likely to have an adverse effect upon the political life of the PRC. If the PLA proves to be incapable of prevailing over Taiwan's armed forces or pacifying the 21 million discontented inhabitants of the island in a relatively rapid fashion, it is highly dubious that public opinion on the mainland would favor a protracted conflict as the sole solution to the Taiwan problem. Should things turn more sour, strong opposition inside the CCP on the one hand and dramatic changes in the national mood within the PRC on the other hand could develop, initiating a train of events whose outcomes would be hard for the PRC leadership to predict or control. If so, the climate of political stability, which Beijing has taken great pains to promote and maintain over the past two decades, will simply vanish into thin air, along with the prospects for stable, sustained growth of the Chinese economy.

Furthermore, should Beijing set its sights upon the subjugation of Taiwan by force, it will definitely put the PRC on a collision course with the US and its ally Japan. Given Washington's ominous admonition that (to quote the Taiwan Relations Act) "any effort to determine the future of Taiwan by other than peaceful means is a threat to the peace and stability of the Western Pacific area and is of grave concern to the United States," it is extremely unlikely that the US would dismiss a full-scale PRC military attack on Taiwan as irrelevant to its strategic interests in the Asia-Pacific region—although the scope and means of US intervention in case of such an attack might vary depending on situational factors. Nevertheless, if US-China relations were once again to be characterized by mutual enmity because of Taiwan, the peaceful international environment that is essential to China's future development would be no more as well.

More significant, however, would be Japan's reaction should Beijing resort to force against Taiwan. The Japanese government has already come under increasing pressure at home to expand its "self-defense" forces into a full-scale military. Should a war break out between the two sides of the Taiwan Strait, Japan would prefer to dodge the bullet. But Japan's obligations to the US and its vital interest in the area would almost surely intervene and force a response—the question is not whether, but how and to what extent. Should this be the case, the ultimate danger to China, and indeed the entire Asia-Pacific region, is the remilitarization of Japan.

Beijing's general policy approach toward Taiwan in the foreseeable future will not depart from the policy of military coercion, with more flexibility and incentives, in the one-China framework. However, a close examination reveals that Beijing has virtually exhausted the incentives that can be offered to Taiwan, given the one-China framework. Unless the PRC leaders work out a new formula to replace this framework, there is little room for them to maneuver on the Taiwan issue. This is Beijing now stands at its bottom line. The ultimate danger of the policy of military coercion is that it could eventually corner the PRC leadership itself, rather than Taiwan, and force Beijing to go to war with Taipei, should the latter insist on its covert effort for independence. From this perspective, we can see that—unless both sides could work out a new framework for the solution of the Taiwan issue, or one side becomes willing to make substantial concessions—the policy of military coercion, with more incentives and flexibility, has in fact set the Taiwan issue in the direction of a catastrophe. For a cross-strait war would be suicidal for both sides, with disastrous implications for the entire Asia-Pacific region.

It would be surprising if the PRC leadership did not see the problem with the policy of military coercion. Ultimately, a peaceful settlement of the problem of Taiwan's future is in the best interests of the PRC, Taiwan, and the United States. In view of the dilemma that confronts the PRC leadership currently on the Taiwan issue, it is even more so to Beijing. As a result, the PRC's policy choices on the Taiwan issue will predictably follow the longstanding PRC emphasis on peaceful reunification, with mounting military pressure and the threat to use force as the very last resorts. In practice, this means that Beijing will continue the military buildup of the PLA. Although Beijing will try by every means to solve the Taiwan problem peacefully in the one-China framework, it is obvious that such an effort could not be effective without creditable military support. Such support is all the more necessary should Beijing eventually turn to military means to resolve the Taiwan problem. In fact, the PLA has already embarked upon an ambitious program to modernize its navy and air force and enhance its missile and amphibious assault capabilities. Such a military buildup will serve not only as a powerful deterrent to separatism on Taiwan, but also as a necessary condition for PLA victory in any military conflicts in the Taiwan Strait, whether with the island's military forces or with the US intervention forces.

The real focus of the PRC's Taiwan policy, however, will be in the three policy areas under the One-China Principle. First of all, the PRC leadership will continue to promote economic exchanges and cooperation between the two sides of the Taiwan Strait. The aim is to develop a cross-strait economic bond that is vital for Taiwan's economic prosperity and hence political stability. The recent economic hardship in Taiwan has indeed provided Beijing with an unprecedented opportunity as well as great hopes. The economic recession in Taiwan on the one hand and the continuous economic "boom" in China on the other has forced President Chen Shi-bian to endorse "a simple fact that many island's businessmen have recognized for years: China is where the future [of Taiwan's economy] lies."[24] Thus, not only did the Chen Shui-bian government discard the five-year-old "no-haste" policy on cross-strait investment on November 7, 2001,[25] but it also intends to lift the bans on the "three direct links" between the two sides of the Taiwan Strait. Ironically but significantly, it is the PRC that holds out this time, refusing "to open negotiations on direct links with Taipei until it accepts the One-China Principle."[26] The reversal should be encouraging to the PRC leaders. This is not because they now see an effective alternative Taiwan policy, one of increasing Taiwan's economic dependence on the PRC instead of using military coercion. This enables them to envision that reunification can indeed be achieved through economic integration, rather than military conquest.

Second, despite strong opposition from the hard-liners, the PRC leaders will continue their effort to develop a stable and constructive relationship with the United States. For they keenly realized that stable US-China relations and the US commitment to the One-China Principle are indispensable to a peaceful solution to the Taiwan problem. Thus, it is not surprising that Beijing has been seeking common ground with the United States not just on the Taiwan issue, but in all international affairs involving the two countries. The renewed US commitment to a "one-China" policy in July 1998, when President Clinton explicitly expressed Washington's opposition to the notions of "Taiwan independence," "two Chinas," and "one China, one Taiwan," as well as to the island's entry into any international organizations that require statehood, was a hopeful sign for the PRC of the deepening mutual understanding with the United States on the Taiwan issue.

US-China relations became tense after George W. Bush came to the White House because of a series of events—George W. Bush's controversial statement that the US would do "all it takes" to defend Taiwan in case of China's invasion, the collision of military airplanes, the unilateralism in George W. Bush's foreign policy, and the missile defense plan. But the US drive for an international antiterrorism coalition after the September 11 attack was a godsend to the PRC leadership. China has clearly seized the opportunity and improved its relations with the United States dramatically. As a result, in the words of a Bush administration official, "a new partnership [between the United States and China] is going to evolve over time—and as we got over the bumps of the last year."[27] Indeed, when President Bush reconfirmed to his Chinese host, President Jiang Zemin, the US commitment to the One-China Principle at the Asia-Pacific Economic Cooperation (APEC) forum, held in Shanghai in October 2001, he also failed to react to China's "undiplomatic" blocking of Taiwan's choice of its representative, forcing the island's delegates to walk out of the forum.[28] Indeed, for the PRC, a constructive working relationship with Washington would not only be instrumental in the modernization of the Chinese economy, but also serve to undermine the endeavor of the separatist forces on Taiwan to obtain their most dearly needed international recognition.

Third, Beijing has obviously learned a lesson from its inept attempt to manipulate the outcome of the 1996 presidential election. Evidently, it has adopted a new approach toward Taiwan's domestic politics. The PRC leadership realized that democratization has forever changed the political landscape on the island. It would be unrealistic to expect a rise of a dominant pro-Beijing political leader (or forces) in Taiwan. A more rational approach, as a PRC official who plays a role in policymaking suggests, is to "prevent any [such] leaders or forces from becoming dominant in Taiwan politics."[29] In other words, Beijing appears to have adopted a centuries-old approach of "divide and manipulate" (if not rule) toward Taiwan's domestic politics. By using political and economic pressures to marginalize die-hard pro-independence activists, Beijing can promote divisions within the Taiwanese independence movement.

It seems that the situation is once more developing in the PRC's favor, given the unprecedented economic recession in Taiwan and the US drive for an international antiterrorism coalition. Also evident is the confidence and "activism evident in recent Chinese foreign policy," with a focus on US-China relations and China's prominent status in the Asia-Pacific region.[30] Focusing on military preparation, seeking a stable relationship with the United States, isolating die-hard pro-independence forces in Taiwan, promoting internal divisions on the island, and most important, fostering Taiwan's economic dependence on the mainland, it seems that the PRC has finally seen some light at the end of the long tunnel toward reunification with Taiwan.

NOTES

1. See Jiaquan Li (2000), "*Zhonggong sandai Lingdao ren duiyu tongyi zhonggou wenti de zhanlue sikao* [The Strategic Thinking of the Three Generations of Chinese Communist Leadership on the Reunification Issue]." *Zhonggong dangshi yanjiu (Research on the History of the Communist Party of China)*, 2, pp. 16-7.

2. "PRC Premier Chou En-lai's Speech to the Third Session of the National People's Congress, June 28, 1954." Hungdah Chiu, ed., *China and the Question of Taiwan: Documents and Analysis* (New York: Praeger Publishers, 1973), p. 270.

3. Li, "*Zhonggong sandai lingdao ren duiyu tongyi zhonggou wenti de zhanlue sikao*," p. 17.

4. "A Brief Account of the US Two Chinas Plot," *Renmin Ribao* [People's Daily], August 7, 1961. Chiu, ed., *China and the Question of Taiwan*, p. 312.

5. Li, "*Zhonggong sandai lingdao ren duiyu tongyi zhonggou wenti de zhanlue sikao*," p. 17.

6. "Nixon-Chou Communiqué, February 28, 1973," Chiu, ed., *China and the Question of Taiwan*, p. 346.

7. Quoted from Arthur Waldron, "Chen Shui-bian's Victory and Democratization in Taiwan." Paper presented at the International Conference on the 2000 Presidential Election in Taiwan and Its Implications for Cross-Strait Relations, Taiwan, April 30-31, 2000.

8. See "President Ye Jiangying's New Year Address," *People's Daily*, January 1, 1979.

9. This "no haste" policy set a $50 million ceiling on single investment projects in China. It also requires all investment in China over $1 million to go through a strict review process.

10. Lowell Dittmer (1996), "China's Taiwan Policy," *American Asian Review*, 14, 4, p. 73.

11. Andrew Nathan (1996), "China's Goals in the Taiwan Strait," *China Journal*, 36, July, p. 91.

12. Michael Yahuda (1996), "The International Standing of the Republic of China on Taiwan," *China Quarterly*, 14, p. 1323.

13. See *People's Daily* editorial, July 28, 1995.

14. Lee Teng-hui, for example, stated defiantly in April 1994: "Now that Taiwan and the Chinese Communist regime are two political entities, one China is as yet nonexistent. How could it be otherwise? At present, there is a People's Republic of China on the mainland, and a Republic of China on Taiwan." See Lee Teng-hui, *Jingying Da Taiwan* [*Striving for a Better Taiwan*] (Taipei: Yuanliu Publishers, 1995), pp. 448-9.

15. See the US Congress: The Taiwan Relations Act of 1979.

16. This was confirmed by several reliable sources in China in interviews on June 6 and July 23, 1999, and on April 24, 2000, in Beijing.

17. For a full text of Jiang's statement, see *People's Daily*, January 31, 1995.

18. *The One-China Principle and the Taiwan Issue* (Beijing: Taiwan Affairs Office and Information Office, State Council, PRC, February 2000). *Beijing Review*, 43, 10 (March 6, 2000), p. 19.

19. Ibid, pp. 19, 27.

20. "Premier Zhu Rongji Meets the Press," *Beijing Review*, 43, 13 (March 27, 2000), p. 8.

21. Author's interviews with two PRC officials, on April 24 in Beijing and on April 26 in Shanghai.

22. Yun-han Chu (1997), "The ABCs of Cross-Strait Policy," *Free China Review*, 47, 5, p. 42.

23. "The One-China Principle and the Taiwan Issue," *Beijing Review*, 43, 10 (March 6, 2000), p. 21.

24. Maureen Pao, "Tied to China's Dragon," *Far Eastern Economic Review*, September 6, 2001, p. 28.

25. See *Far Eastern Economic Review*, November 15, 2001, p. 30.

26. Maureen Pao, "Tied to China's Dragon," p. 29.

27. Quoted from Michael Vatikiotis, Ben Doven and David Murphy, "Terror Throws Us Together, for Now," *Far Eastern Economic Review*, November 1, 2001, p. 36.

28. See ibid, pp. 36-40.

29. Author's interview with a PRC official in Beijing on September 15, 2001.

30. See David Shambaugh, "China's Ambivalent Diplomacy," *Far Eastern Economic Review*, November 15, 2001, p. 29.

3

Taiwan's Evolving National
Security Policy

Alexander C. Tan, Scott Walker, and Tsung-chi Yu

Since the Nationalists (KMT) lost China's civil war to the Communists, Taiwan has been thrust onto the world stage in a very awkward way. From 1949 to 1971, the smaller Taiwan represented all of China in the United Nations Security Council. According to the KMT's version of the one-China policy, Taiwan alone is the sole and legal representative of the Chinese people and nation. After China was admitted to the United Nations, and more important, after the de-recognition of Taiwan by the US, Taiwan was thrust to the margins of the world community. Today, less than 30 countries have official diplomatic relations with Taiwan. None of Taiwan's immediate neighbors have any diplomatic relations with Taiwan. More significant, even Taiwan's most important allies and security guarantors do not provide diplomatic recognition.

Interestingly, Taiwan has managed to survive despite all these political and diplomatic problems. How has Taiwan been able to manage to survive in this self-help world? How has Taiwan adapted itself to the changing international political and economic environment? How did Taiwan's national security policy evolve? One way to understand Taiwan's national security policy is by examining the evolution from the so-called high politics of international relations to low politics.[1]

The saying that "politics stop at the water's edge" may be precise in describing Taiwan's national security policy during the Cold War. This, however, is not appropriate to describe Taiwan's national security policy after 1979 and after the Cold War. The changing security environment in the Asia-Pacific region, coupled with the historic transformation in Taiwan's domestic political environment, i.e., political liberalization and democratization, require us to carefully examine the role of democratization and the search for national identity in Taiwan's security policy (the so-called low politics).

In the next section, I briefly trace the high politics of Taiwan's security policy, with particular emphasis on the use of development and trade as a security mechanism. In the second section, I discuss the peaceful transformation of Taiwan from an authoritarian developmental state into a democratic polity. In this discussion, I examine the implications of Taiwan's democratization and pluralization of politics and policymaking for Taiwan's national security. In the third section, I discuss the evolution of Taiwan's policy toward the PRC. Following this discussion, I briefly examine the role of the US in cross-strait relations and the changes in cross-strait interactions. I conclude by briefly discussing the implications of two contradictory trends, the converging goals of politicians on the two sides of the Taiwan Strait, and the diverging conduct of domestic politics in the two polities.

ECONOMIC STATECRAFT AND TAIWAN'S SECURITY

Since 1949, Taiwan has been under some kind of threat of an invasion from the People's Republic of China (PRC). For Taiwan, the outbreak of the Korean War in 1950 and the onset of the Cold War were fortuitous events. These events pushed Taiwan into an anticommunist alliance led by the US. The US became Taiwan's security guarantor from 1949 to 1979, and as a consequence provided Taiwan some breathing space in the international arena. However, following President Richard Nixon's visit to Beijing and the eventual de-recognition of Taiwan by the US in 1979 by President Jimmy Carter, Taiwan's security situation changed dramatically. Being diplomatically isolated, Taiwan needed to carve out an independent national security policy. The focus on national security has traditionally been on military issues, and less emphasis has been placed on the use of trade as part of statecraft. Indeed, while Taiwan's rapid economic growth and industrialization are an oft-studied topic in economic development, we understand much less about how Taiwan has used it to gain security. As Karl Deutsch (1957) suggests, international trade can stimulate acceptance and mutual responsiveness among trading nations.[2] As Steve Chan writes, "increasing commercial and noncommercial contact has the effect of deepening and widening networks of cross-national interests and institutions. These networks and shared norms underpin the rise of a security community."[3]

Taiwan's participation in the world's trading regime can be seen in terms of its need to pursue security by firmly attaching itself to the global economy and production process. As Robert Keohane defines it, regimes are "sets of implicit of explicit principles, norms, rules, and decision-making procedures around which actor expectations converge."[4] Keohane suggests that

within the context of a regime, help can be extended by those in a position to do so, on the assumption that such regime-supporting behavior will be reciprocated in the future. States may demand that others follow the norm of generalized commitment even if they are thereby required to supply it themselves, because the result will facilitate agreements that in the long run can be expected to be beneficial for all concerned.[5]

Indeed, one way to understand the evolution of Taiwan's national security is through the use of economic statecraft. By firmly integrating Taiwan's economy with the international economy, Taiwan makes itself an important player in the world manufacturing economy. As a result, the transformation to a capital-

and knowledge-intensive industrial structure in some ways decreases the substitutability of Taiwan in the world economy and increases the vulnerability of Taiwan's important trading partners. By binding Taiwan's economic "fate" to the world, Taiwan can avail itself of some security as the world becomes vulnerable to instability in Taiwan.

The diplomatic isolation of Taiwan notwithstanding, Taiwan's total trade volume has grown steadily over the years, making it one of the world's top trading nations. Table 3.1 shows Taiwan's trade with its neighboring countries and the US. Trade with the US has always been an important component of the Taiwan economy. In fact, Table 3.1 shows that the severing of official diplomatic relations in 1979 between the US and Taiwan has not affected the growth of two-way trade. Trade with Japan has also grown in total volume from $6.81 billion in 1979 to $41.2 billion in 1996.

Table 3.1
Taiwan's Trade Volume with the US and Regional Neighbors (in millions of US$)

Country	1979	1985	1990	1996
USA	9.03	19.5	34.4	46.8
Japan	6.81	9.01	24.3	41.2
Singapore	0.54	1.16	3.61	7.36
Thailand	0.25	0.38	1.87	4.46
Malaysia	0.46	0.67	2.11	6.52
Philippines	0.27	0.34	1.05	2.77
Hong Kong	1.34	2.86	10.0	28.5

Source: Taiwan Statistical Data Book, 1997.

The maintenance of strong trade relations between Taiwan, Japan, and the US has contributed to expanded commercial and noncommercial contacts between Taiwan and its two largest trading partners. Taiwan's contact with Japan and the US goes beyond the traditional government-to-government format, extending to business and civic contacts as well. Through the benefits of trade expansion and the extension of Taiwan's business contacts in Japan and the US, Taiwan has created an informal security community that may work to its benefit. As a case in point, in the renegotiation of the US-Japan security framework, Japan did not reject the idea that its naval vessels would provide necessary support for US naval operations in case of conflict in the area.[6] Based on the PRC's reaction, this is an implicit agreement that should the US get involved in a cross-Taiwan Strait conflict, Japan can probably play an important support role.

Though the revised US-Japan security guidelines do not explicitly encompass Taiwan, American and Japanese officials have not explicitly ruled it out either. American officials emphasize that the new defense agreement is not aimed at any individual nation (a vague reference to China), but it would not completely rule out that Taiwan is covered by the revised US-Japan security guidelines.[7] Interestingly, despite strategically ambiguous language by both

Japanese and American officials, one ranking Japanese official was quoted as stating that the revised security guidelines between Japan and the US do cover a military conflict in the Taiwan Strait, because of concerns about possible Chinese military action against Taiwan.[8]

Thus, trade plays an important role in Taiwan's strategy to ensure its own security and survival as a sovereign nation-state. Since the 1990s, however, Taiwan has also been able to play an important role as a financier in the region. Taiwan's large capital surplus and its huge foreign exchange reserves are seen within Taiwan's government not only in commercial terms, but also as an important tool in the fight against diplomatic isolation.

In November 1993, Taiwan launched the "Go South" policy, a program of investment and trade designed to increase Taiwan's economic integration with Southeast Asia, a region with a high level of strategic and economic importance to Taiwan. The basic objective of the policy is to make Taiwan a major supplier of capital and technology in the region. The strategy of the "Go South" policy was to provide the industrial and agricultural know-how, as well as the capital, to make Taiwan an important economic partner in the economies of the region. Of course, an important benefit of successful implementation of this policy was that these countries would be more likely to value Taiwanese friendship. Clearly, then, underlying the economic purposes of "Go South" was an attempt by Taiwan to bolster political support among its Southeast Asian neighbors.

The "Go South" campaign was an outgrowth of a well-publicized visit made by President Lee to Southeast Asia in 1994, which opened the region to Taiwanese investors. The campaign encouraged Taiwanese companies to find cheap labor and manufacturing costs in the region, a move that effectively warmed political relations between the island and Southeast Asian nations. On that trip, bitterly opposed by China, Lee met with top officials from the Philippines, Indonesia, and Thailand, promising to help the region develop agricultural and oil resources.

There were four stated goals of the "Go South" policy:

1. Expand two-way economic, trade, and investment relations with Southeast Asia.
2. Assist Taiwan's enterprises in finding beneficial production and distribution bases in Southeast Asia, expanding their size, and reducing the degree of trade dependence on mainland China.
3. Based on the principle of mutual benefit, help Southeast Asian nations create job opportunities, raise people's annual, incomes, and encourage economic prosperity, thus strengthening Taiwan's substantive relations with the nations of Southeast Asia.
4. Participate in the activities of international economic organizations in Southeast Asia.

Under the "Go South" policy, Taiwan has encouraged investment in Southeast Asia by Taiwanese businesses. According to statistics provided by Southeast Asian countries, the cumulative total of investment by Taiwanese businesses in Southeast Asia reached $40 billion in 1999. In that year, the amount of bilateral trade between Taiwan and Southeast Asia was $26.59 billion.

Table 3.2 shows Taiwan's outward direct investments since the 1990s. The US is traditionally a large recipient of Taiwanese investments. In the 1990s, however, Southeast Asia has absorbed a large proportion of all Taiwanese out-ward investments. Part of the stimulus for the increase in Southeast Asian in-vestments is the industrial restructuring occurring within Taiwan itself. As labor costs have risen and the Taiwanese dollar has appreciated in the 1990s, Taiwan-ese labor-intensive industries have moved to Southeast Asia to remain competi-tive.

Table 3.2
Taiwan's Outward Direct Investments (% share of total outward direct investments)

	90	91	92	93	94	95	96	97
USA	28	16	17	11	6	10	8	12
SE Asia	37	39	27	9	15	13	17	14
China	n/a	10	22	66	37	45	36	36

Source: Investment Evaluation Commission, Ministry of Economic Affairs.

This has made Taiwan one of the top three largest investors in Southeast Asia, making Taiwan an invaluable partner in regional economic development. Consequently, though Southeast Asian countries have not given formal diplo-matic recognition to Taiwan, the political relationship between the region's countries and Taiwan is considered to be very close. For example, compared to their experiences in other parts of the world, Taiwanese diplomats and govern-ment officials have been able to consult and visit their counterparts in Southeast Asia with relative ease. Government officials from Southeast Asian countries have also been known to pay courtesy calls to officials in Taipei.[9]

DEMOCRATIZATION AND THE SEARCH FOR NATIONAL IDENTITY

In the last fourteen years, Taiwan has been transformed from a developmen-tal authoritarian state to a democracy. For Taiwan's political elites, the end of the Cold War required a revamping of Taiwan's national security strategy. Join-ing the "third wave" of democratization became a promising strategy.

The realization that democratization can be a strategy for national security did not come directly out of careful planning and design by the ruling KMT elites. Rather, it was a consequence of conflicts within the domestic political arena between the majority islanders and the minority mainlanders. These con-flicts have underscored Taiwanese politics since the forced exile of the KMT to the island of Taiwan. With rapid economic growth and the eventual creation of a large middle class, the KMT was forced to open the political system through a process of "indigenization" of the party and the state.[10] Because of indigeniza-tion, the mainlanders' grip on power slowly eroded and political democratiza-tion settled in.[11]

For the KMT, the introduction of democracy on the island increased its po-litical legitimacy in the international arena. Efforts at political liberalization began under the late President Chiang Ching-Kuo. In 1986, the government allowed the formation of the first opposition party in Taiwan, the Democratic Progressive Party (DPP). Though opposition in Taiwan always existed under Kuomintang (KMT) rule under the umbrella name of "*Tangwai*," which means literally "outside of the KMT," the formation of the DPP is significant because it marks the true beginning of organized competitive politics in Taiwan. The formation of the DPP also signaled that the KMT was willing to allowing political liberalization to occur.

Political liberalization and eventually democracy was not fully initiated until the death of President Chiang Ching-Kuo and the succession of President Lee Teng-hui. president Lee, being the first islander to hold this top office, pushed for greater indigenization of the ruling party, the military, and the government. Democratization in Taiwan became an extension and probably an unintended consequence of Taiwanization. As Cal Clark aptly states,

Democratization in Taiwan appears to have been delayed considerably in terms of its relatively advanced level of social and economic modernization in the mid-1980s, but it certainly conformed to two central postulates of the modernization model 1) that an educated middle-class will exert considerable pressure for reform on an authoritarian regime and 2) that political liberalization will result in the party system's providing better interest representation on the major issues facing a society.[12]

This has resulted in a political system characterized by the emergence of cleavages suppressed during the authoritarian period, and by increased complexity in domestic politics.

In spite of its origins in Taiwan, democracy is a way of clearly distinguishing Taiwan from the authoritarianism of the PRC.[13] For Taiwan, the strategic goal of democratization is that by taking the moral high ground, Taiwan can secure for it a place within the "democratic alliance." Democratization can be a double-edged sword, though. The introduction of competitive elections has led to a party system largely reflecting the ethnic cleavage that is most salient in Taiwan's domestic politics. This ethnic cleavage is evident in the debate about national identity. The democratic and plural political environment allows for an internal debate on the prickly issue of reunification or independence. As a result, "the developmental states (as in Taiwan) have become less dominant in their relations with social groups, an outcome caused by the success of their economic strategy."[14]

That accountability to the whims and desires of the electorate becomes inevitable in democratic politics. This in turn leads to a tendency toward the maintenance of the status quo, since the status quo—that is, neither formal independence nor reunification—avoids open conflict with the PRC. As Cal Clark states,

Clearly, the ROC's citizens (particularly the middle class who has the most to lose) fear that a premature commitment to either Independence or Reunification could destroy the social, economic, and political progress that Taiwan has already made. In addition, except for relatively small minorities who are strongly committed to one alternative or the other, the island's citizens do not evidently see the future as a stark choice between these two alternatives . . . a public opinion poll . . . reported . . . that both Reunification or Independence were acceptable by approximately two-to-one margins if the change in status could be achieved without the dangers now associated with it (subordination to a communist dictatorship for Reunification and Chinese retaliation for Independence). [15]

Furthermore, Clark argues that

On both the key issues concerning national identity and cross-strait relations, most of the public evinced beliefs in the "moderate middle" rather than at the ideological extremes. Furthermore, the major issues in Taiwan were cross-cutting, not cumulative, in the sense that different parties represented majority opinion on different issues...[which] suggests that...democracy in the ROC attenuated, not exacerbated, cross-strait relations.[16]

As a result, the adoption of the status quo as an equilibrium strategy by Taiwan's political elites allows Taiwan to buy time to allow peaceful democratic transformation in the PRC to produce the so-called "democratic peace." Having said this, the maintenance of the status quo also means active engagement with the PRC on the economic front. Let us now turn to a discussion of the evolution of Taiwan's policy toward the PRC.

EVOLUTION OF TAIWAN'S CROSS-STRAIT POLICY

In the preceding section, I have highlighted one way of understanding Taiwan's evolving national security policy. Taiwan's national security and foreign policies are designed to break its diplomatic isolation, which has resulted from China's aggressive pursuit of its own version of the "one-China" policy. The PRC's ability to impose its version of the "one-China" policy is strengthened by China's economic growth. As China continues to open up its fast-growing economy, other countries cozy up in search of business and economic benefits. Interestingly, as the world has warmed to China, Taiwan's attitude can be characterized as ambivalent at best. The relationship between Taiwan and China can be described as frozen in the Cold War era. With the consolidation of democracy in Taiwan, the change in the international division of labor, and the changes in Taiwan's own comparative economic advantage, we are now observing a thaw in the Cold War relationship between the two entities. Let me turn now to discussing the changes in Taiwan-China relations.

Since the establishment of the People's Republic of China (PRC) as an alternative government to the Kuomintang-controlled Republic of China (ROC) in 1949, the two political entities have been competing for international diplomatic recognition. As Yu San Wang suggests, Taiwan's foreign policy can be divided into four distinct periods. The first period is what he calls Taiwan's struggle for existence in 1949-60. According to Wang, the key objective of this period was to form an anti-communist alliance, strengthen ties with the US, and prevent the PRC's inclusion in the international community. The second period of expanding international involvement, in 1960-70, continued to pursue the goals of the earlier period. The third period, from 1970 to 1979, was a period in which Taiwan's foreign and security policy was at a crossroads. This period is highlighted by Taiwan's numerous diplomatic setbacks, beginning with Canada's switch of diplomatic ties from the ROC to the PRC in 1970. Canada's switch was the first in a series, leading to a hemorrhaging of countries recognizing the PRC's claim to represent China. This period culminated in the eventual de-recognition of Taiwan by the US in 1979, which ushered in the period of unorthodox diplomacy that continues to this day.[17]

Interestingly, throughout these different periods in the evolution of Taiwan's foreign and security policy, one common strand is Taiwan's struggle to be recognized and heard in the international community. From the early stage of preventing switches of diplomatic ties by third world countries, to more recent struggles to rejoin the United Nations and other international intergovernmental forums, Taiwan continues to show a strong desire for international recognition and friendship.

From the perspective of this study, Wang's fourth period is most relevant to identifying the changes in Taiwan's policy toward PRC. The shock of losing its United Nations seat, the massive losses on the diplomatic front, and the breaking of official relations with the US, however, did not substantially change the foreign and security policies of Taiwan. This was due to a glaring lack of a stimulus in the domestic political arena. From 1970 to 1988, Taiwan continued to carry on decades-old policy of refusing to negotiate and stand side-by-side with the PRC in the international arena. As a result of this policy, Taiwan's ability to participate in the international arena substantially declined, as countries switched from recognizing the Republic of China to the PRC.

It was not until the domestic political and economic situations were dramatically transformed that we began to see changes in Taiwan's mainland China policy. As mentioned earlier, two critical factors in particular have contributed to new thinking and approaches in Taiwan's mainland China policy: 1) changes in the international division of labor and in Taiwan's own comparative economic advantage; 2) political liberalization and consolidation of democracy. Let us turn to discuss how each of these factors has contributed to changes in Taiwan's mainland China policy.

Changes in the International Division of Labor and in Taiwan's Comparative Economic Advantage

Taiwan's phenomenal economic growth after the KMT moved its government to the island had by 1986 produced tremendous pressure for industrial restructuring to sustain economic growth. From 1949 to 1986, Taiwan's export-oriented economy, aided by an open international trading regime and an undervalued currency, continued to market labor-intensive products in the world market. By 1986, with the perennial trade surpluses with the US and the world becoming sore spots for Taiwan's international economic relations, Taiwan was forced to float the New Taiwan dollar (NTD). It appreciated from NTD 40 to USD 1 in 1985, to about NTD 27 to USD 1 by 1988. With the appreciation of the NTD, Taiwan's industries were forced to confront changes in comparative advantage within the international division of labor. From 1986 onwards, as domestic wage pressures and competition from neighboring countries began to cut into its international competitiveness, Taiwan could no longer rely on labor-intensive industries and cheap manufactured products.

The opening of the PRC in the early 1980s provided an outlet for Taiwan's products, and more important, a production base for labor-intensive industries. As shown in Tables 3.1 and 3.2, Taiwan's trade and investment to Hong Kong and China account for a large percentage of Taiwan's total trade and outward investment. By 1996, Hong Kong had become the thirdlargest trading partner of Taiwan, and the PRC received more than one-third of all Taiwanese outward investments.

As larger and larger numbers of Taiwanese businesses relocated their production bases to China, domestic pressure to address the "hollowing out" of Taiwan's economy and national security began to mount. With the phenomenal growth in cross-strait economic activities, Taiwan began to espouse a policy of "no haste, be patient" in regard to its relations with China. With much fanfare, it launched the "Go South" policy, urging business to invest in Southeast Asia rather than mainland China.[18]

Yet by the end of President Lee Teng-hui's administration, the "Go South" policy can be judged a total failure. Not only are labor-intensive businesses from Taiwan continuing to relocate to China. Increasingly, Taiwan's brand-name companies and high-tech industries are to shifting production to China. In the first year of Chen Shui-bian's administration, Taiwan's domestic politicians have been pressured by local business to change economic policy toward the PRC. President Chen Shui-bian has responded. His promise to open direct links between the three islets of Kinmen (Quemoy), Matsu, and Penghu (the Pescadores) and the PRC represents a fundamental policy shift in cross-strait relations, in favor of regional economic integration based on mutual interests. With Taiwan experiencing a recession—due in part to global market weakening and in part to the domestic political situation—economic policymakers have suggested that Taiwan may consider some form of closer economic relations with China, similar to the European Union. For example, discussions are under way at the highest levels of Taiwan's government that Taiwan seriously consider opening up its economy to allow capital inflows and direct investments from the PRC. Though these policies are still in the discussion stage, they signal a drastic departure in Taiwan's economic policy toward the PRC in the near and long-term future.

Political Liberalization and Consolidation of Democracy

Consolidation of democracy has also changed Taiwan's policy toward the mainland. This can be observed from the plurality of viewpoints now discussed in Taiwan. Under the leadership of Lee Teng-hui, the KMT and Taiwan saw a continued indigenization of its bureaucracy and its key decision makers. In the thirteen years of Lee Teng-hui's presidency, Taiwan's key politicians have been islanders who do not trace any political roots to the mainland. Interestingly, to signal the islanders' commitment to the "one-China" concept, it was under President Lee that we saw the formation of the cabinet-level Mainland Affairs Council and, within the president's office, the National Unification Council, as well as the adoption of the National Unification Guidelines. From avoiding all contacts prior to 1988, it was during Taiwan's democratization that Taiwan opened up contacts with the PRC. These contacts included the high-profile meeting between the heads of Taiwan's Straits Exchange Foundation and the mainland's Association for Relations across the Taiwan Straits.

Despite these efforts, current negotiations between Taiwan and China have reached an impasse, as PRC authorities insist that any resumption of talks be predicated on Taiwan's acknowledgment of the "one China" principle. Taiwan's reluctance to acknowledge the PRC's version of the "one China" principle is a direct result of the impact of pluralist politics and the increasing influence of public opinion. This has resulted in an interesting situation. The politicians are reluctant to move any closer to China because of the electorate's general reluctance. The very influential business community, seeking to gain economic benefits and maintain international competitiveness, is pressing the government to negotiate with China (at least on economic issues). These contradictory pressures have placed Taiwan's politicianss between a rock and a hard place. As a consequence, Taiwan's mainland policy, while maintaining the spirit of the National Unification Guidelines and the policies during the Lee administration, can be more aptly described as "under construction."

THE ROLE OF THE US IN CROSS-STRAIT RELATIONS

Examining the role of the US is important in discussions of Taiwan-China relations. Before the US severed diplomatic relations with Taiwan, the US played the key role in explicitly securing Taiwan's security. After 1979, the US' commitment to Taiwan is largely spelled out in the Taiwan Relations Act of 1979. However, the commitment to a one-China policy on the one hand, and to the spirit of the Taiwan Relations Act on the other, has made it difficult for the US to define its position on cross-strait relations. This so-called "strategic ambiguity" in American policy toward Taiwan and the PRC has been deemed important in maintaining peace and the status quo. But it has also contributed to substantial change in the American approach toward Taiwan and the PRC.

The emphasis on peaceful negotiations rather than the use of force to settle the Taiwan issue is the most preferred option for any US administration. While opposing any use of force by Beijing, the US also opposes any new initiatives by Taiwan. This is evident in the Clinton administration's "Three-No's" policy: (1) no independent Taiwan; (2) no two Chinas or one Taiwan, One China; and (3) no Taiwan membership in intergovernmental organizations.[19] Clinton's "Three-No's" policy acts as a catalyst for Taiwan and the PRC to recalibrate their approach to bilateral relations, by emphasizing the maintenance of the status quo.[20]

From the perspective of Taiwan, the US' "Three-No's" policy constrains the possible options for its own dealings with the PRC. Moving away from the traditional focus on sovereignty issues, the "Three-No's" policy prods the two sides to move toward areas of mutual agreement, such as economic cooperation and establishment of direct links on shipping, communication, and transportation.[21] Furthermore, the relative clarity of the US position against a unilateral declaration of Taiwan independence has forced Taiwan's leadership (both in government and opposition) to tone down its rhetoric and actions in support of an independent Taiwan, so as not to anger the PRC and the US.[22] More recently, President Chen's toning down of Taiwan's summer 2001 war games and military exercises signals the island's commitment to smoothing relations with the PRC. This move to placate Beijing is coupled with statements that Taiwan is ready to defend itself if attacked. This signals the new administration's commitment to maintaining the status quo.[23]

As for the interactions between the US and the PRC, the opening of US markets to PRC exports and the increased investments by US businesses in the PRC have expanded the basis of common interests between the US and China. These common interests resulting from functional economic relations (e.g., trade and investments) can spill over to other areas, such as common security.

China's 2001 entry into the World Trade Organization, with strong US and European support, enhances economic incentives to maintain the cross-strait status quo. US policymakers hope that, by bringing China into the international trading regime, China's cost calculation will shift away from resolving the cross-strait conflict by force. According to neo-realist thinking, as functional and economic interactions increase in frequency and iteration, a state's incentive to be nonconfrontational and cooperative in its international dealings increases. In other words, as the PRC economy continues to benefit from participation in the international trading regime, the benefits of trade and maintaining the regime are more likely to outweigh any benefit associated with destroying the established equilibrium. As Gill and Reilly point out,

Since the People's Republic initially opened up in the 1970s, China's strict sovereign prerogatives have been gradually eroded. Today the nexus where defense of Chinese sovereignty meets the imperative of engaging the outside world defines both the limits and the possibilities of enmeshing China within international society. The challenge for the international community is to understand the dynamics of China's sovereignty-integration nexus and to identify policies that will strengthen Beijing's commitment to international peace and stability.[24]

This is the challenge that exists for the US and Taiwan in its dealings with the People's Republic of China.

CONCLUSION

Finding the optimum balance between the goals of growth, order, and security may lead East Asian political leaders to diverging conduct and paths. Chan suggests that "economic prosperity may increase the danger of war because it makes armament expenditures more affordable and influences leaders to be more aggressive and self-confident in their foreign policies."[25] If this is correct, then, "the recent economic dynamism and expansion of capitalist East Asian countries may suggest a greater danger of warfare and military competition in the years ahead."[26] This would suggest that while the goals of leaders on both sides of the Taiwan Strait may be converging, the paths to achieving those goals are diverging. However, this will depend on the relative importance attributed to economic growth relative to national identity and sovereignty goals. As discussed, Taiwan under democracy is not likely to be the source of destabilizing emphasis on national identity and sovereignty goals.

We would also be remiss not to consider the US role in cross-strait relations. As the hegemon, it is in the interest of the US to maintain the status quo and prevent an open conflict between the PRC and Taiwan.[27] To maintain relative peace in the area, then, American policymakers want to actively engage the PRC, using diplomatic and economic incentives to draw the PRC into the existing international regime. This will not only require the PRC to comply with economic norms such as the protection of intellectual property rights, but also with political norms such as respecting human rights and the principle of "negotiation instead of confrontation." The US policy thinking is based on the premise that the higher the trade interdependence between the PRC and the USA, and the PRC and Taiwan, the less likely it is that the PRC will use force to try to absorb Taiwan. If this premise proves false, the outcome will depend on US calculations of the costs and benefits of aiding in the military defense of Taiwan.

NOTES

1. Some arguments in this chapter were originally suggested in Alexander C. Tan, Scott Walker, and Tsung-chi Yu, "Risk Diversification: Ensuring Taiwan's National Security," in Alexander C. Tan, Steve Chan, and Calvin Jillson (eds.), *Taiwan's National Security: Dilemmas and Opportunities* (Aldershot, UK: Ashgate, 2001), pp. 119-33.

2. Karl Deutsch, *Political Community and the North Atlantic Area* (New York: Greenwood).

3. Steve Chan, "Taiwan in APEC's Trade Structure," in Alexander C. Tan, Steve Chan, and Calvin Jillson (eds.), *Taiwan's National Security: Dilemmas and Opportunities* (Aldershot, UK: Ashgate, 2001), p. 104.

4. Robert Keohane, "The Demand for International Regimes," *International Organization*, 36, 2, p. 141.

5. Ibid. p. 159.

6. Dennis Hickey, "The Revised US-Japan Security Guidelines: Implications for Beijing and Taipei," paper presented at the Conference on Dilemmas and Opportunities: Taiwan's National Security, Dallas, Texas, April 1998.

7. Ibid. p. 9.

8. Ibid. p.10; Nicholas Kristof, "For Japan, A Quandary on Pleasing Two Giants," *New York Times*, August 24, 1997, p. 9, in *Lexis/Nexis*.

9. Several countries in Southeast Asia have maintained a close military relationship with Taiwan. It is an open secret that Singapore, for example, conducts many of its training exercises in Taiwan. The Philippines is known to have received preferential prices on Taiwanese surplus military equipment.

10. Cal Clark, "Changing Middle Class Constituencies and Party Competition on Taiwan: Implications for the Security Challenge," paper presented in the Conference on Dilemmas and Opportunity: Taiwan's National Security, Dallas, Texas, April 1998.

11. Taiwanization was a process begun under President Chiang Ching-Kuo. This process involves bringing islanders into important positions in government and the KMT party.

12. Cal Clark, "Changing Middle Class Constituencies," p. 35.

13. This is a view strongly held by the DPP leadership and later the KMT itself.

14. Steve Chan, *East Asian Dynamism: Growth, Order, and Security in the Pacific Region* (Boulder: Westview, 1990), p. 63.

15. Cal Clark, "Successful Democratization in the ROC: Creating a Security Challenge," in Alexander C. Tan, Steve Chan, and Calvin Jillson (eds.), *Taiwan's National Security: Dilemmas and Opportunities* (Aldershot, UK: Ashgate, 2001), p. 45; see also Myra Lu, "Taiwan People Prefer Cross-strait Status Quo," *Taipei Journal*, September 16, 2000, p. 1.

16. Cal Clark, "Successful Democratization in the ROC," p. 46.

17. Yu San Wang, "Foundation of the Republic of China's Foreign Policy," in Yu San Wang (ed.), *Foreign Policy of the Republic of China on Taiwan: An Unorthodox Approach* (New York: Praeger, 1990), pp. 1-12.

18. Robert Scalapino, "Taiwan—Opportunities and Challenges," in Alexander C. Tan, Steve Chan, and Calvin Jillson (eds.), *Taiwan's National Security: Dilemmas and Opportunties* (Aldershot, UK: Ashgate, 2001), pp. 1-17.

19. Elizabeth Freund, "President Clinton's Three-No's and the Taiwan Question," *Working Paper in Taiwan Studies* No. 32.

20. This status quo is a position that can be equated to a Nash equilibrium outcome. Though not exactly Pareto optimal from the perspective of PRC and Taiwan domestic politics, it is an equilibrium position that is nonprovocative to all parties involved.

21. To gradually reduce the tension across the Taiwan Straits, current president Chen Shui-bian proposed a minidirect link between Taiwan's outer islands of Kinmen, Matsu, and Penghu with the mainland province of Fujian.

22. For example, former President Lee Teng-hui in 1999 was quoted in an interview with *Deustche Welle* as stating that negotiations between the PRC and Taiwan should be based on a "special state to state" status. The US and the PRC were swift to criticize this particular statement. The US sent top emissaries to express Washington's displeasure with the statement's apparent attempt to change or move away from the status quo. As a result of this interview, Washington and Beijing viewed President Lee Teng-hui as a troublemaker.

23. "Taiwan Tones Down Its War Games," *Reuters*, September 22, 2000.

24. Bates Gill and James Reilly, "Sovereignty, Intervention, and Peacekeeping: The View from Beijing," *Survival*, 42, 3 (Autumn 2000), p. 41.

25. Chan, *East Asian Dynamism*, p.112.

26. Ibid, p. 112.

27. American action in the area has shown that the status quo is the preferred American position. For example, Washington sent warships during the PRC's 1995 missile exercises off the coast of Taiwan. This was meant to deter any outbreak of open conflict between the two sides, which would have disrupted the status quo. Similarly, Washington's decision to include Taiwan in the Theater Missile Defense is a clear signal that it prefers maintenance of the status quo in cross-strait relations.

4

Ambiguity and US Foreign Policy on China-Taiwan Relations

A. Cooper Drury

Although the Taiwan Strait has seen multiple violent crises between the People's Republic of China and Taiwan, not one of these crises escalated into a full-scale war. Without trivializing either the loss of life or the continued tensions that have plagued the Strait, a de facto negative peace or tense stability has been the norm for more than 50 years.[1] The United States' policies toward China and Taiwan have played a large role in maintaining this tense stability. Via weapons sales, military shows of force, and diplomacy, the US has stopped the dispute from escalating into a full-scale war.

In plain terms, the current US policy on China-Taiwan relations is to (1) maintain the status quo of official recognition of the PRC as the one China (2) while preserving Taiwan's autonomy, and (3) wait until China liberalizes enough to make some form of reunification acceptable on both sides of the Strait. This current, largely unofficial, and unexplicated policy seems to have evolved over the past 50 years. Originally, in the 1950s, the goal was to maintain Taiwan's sovereignty and contain China, ultimately leading to a settlement. *Settlement* was defined as the collapse of the communist regime and the return of the nationalists to power, although the vehicle for this transition was not part of the US policy and was hotly debated in Washington. This goal shifted to maintaining Taiwan's autonomy and engaging China while still seeking settlement.[2] The definition of settlement was in flux, because engaging the communists seemed to contradict the desire for their collapse, and still there were many who hoped for this collapse.

The more recent Taiwan Relations Act and its amendments solidified the US policy toward maintaining the status quo of stability and at least a negative peace. Providing military support to Taiwan and a declaration that any transition must be peaceful balanced recognition of Beijing as China's true government. In 1996, two US aircraft carrier battle groups moved close to Taiwan, balancing China's effort to intimidate Taiwan with large-scale military exercises in the straits. This reinforced the idea that US involvement is aimed simply at stemming hostilities, without aspiring to greater goals.

The US policy toward the China-Taiwan relationship is not perfectly consistent. However, the policy can be portrayed as a steady, harmonious evolution of decisions from Harry Truman to Bill Clinton.[3] Observing the over 50 years of relative peace in the Taiwan Strait suggests that US foreign policy toward China-Taiwan relations follows, at a minimum, a long-term plan similar to Cold War containment. The US commitment to peace and stability in the region coupled with the containment of communism appears to follow a rather logical, planned course.

Such may seem the American master plan, but there is no master plan. The US policy toward the Strait is more like the proverbial duck paddling in the water: serene on the surface but chaotic beneath. From the first decisions to defend Formosa and the offshore islands to the Shanghai communiqué and subsequent de-recognition of Taiwan, the policy toward China and Taiwan has been anything but consistent. Truman wanted to let Formosa go to the communists, Dwight Eisenhower waffled back and forth on whether or not and how to defend the offshore islands, and Richard Nixon's trip to China and Jimmy's Carter's recognition of Beijing were complete surprises. Ronald Reagan consistently commented during his campaign and administration that Taiwan was independent and represented China, leaving his staff the headache of reassuring Beijing that this was not exactly what he meant. Clinton first publicly rejected Taiwanese President Lee's request for a visa to visit his alma mater, Cornell University, but later reversed that decision without any communication with Beijing (which strenuously objected to the visit).

It is outcome-oriented hindsight that suggests US policy has been well formulated and consistent. Closer inspection of the process shows that since 1949, US policy is ambiguous and has been made on an ad hoc basis. Instead of coherent planning, the policy has emerged from a combination of international pressures and lobbies, domestic politics, and ideologies of presidents and their advisors. Further, the process has been jarred by each new president's interest and efficacy in foreign affairs, goals for American security, and approach to the Asia-Pacific region.

To predict possible policy decisions by the White House, one must understand the history and pattern of American foreign policy toward the Strait. Simply viewing the current president's stated preferences toward a China policy will not provide much, if any, guidance in understanding possible decisions in a crisis situation. The statements made by presidents are often merely statements aimed toward satisfying particular groups. To actually forecast what the US president will do given a crisis in the Strait, one must also look at prior policy decisions. A host of studies show that the US military has the capacity to defend Taiwan, so that is not the question. The question is, what will the White House do when faced with such a choice?

Thus, the lack of planning and consistency in the decision process may have grave repercussions. While the duck's paddling may be chaotic, it does have direction and purpose. The US policy does not benefit from such direction. True, achieving peace and stability is the overall goal, but that is like saying the duck wishes to survive—it provides little information. To date, the US has seemed to have direction, but only because the decisions made in the past 50 years have effectively diffused the crises of the day. There is no contingency plan for responding to future crises. True, the military has options it can offer to the White House, but the president himself is not afforded a contingency plan. Had the Soviets rolled their tanks into Western Europe, NATO would have acted, or at a minimum, the president had such a strategy before him. If China launched an invasion of Taiwan, it is uncertain what the White House might do; the president must make each decision on an ad hoc basis.[4]

While there are many scenarios involving the possibility of US military intervention, the China-Taiwan situation poses one of the most dangerous. China's economic and military power's are growing; China is a nuclear-armed nation with limited but viable intercontinental delivery systems; and, most important, the Taiwan dispute is one that could easily lead to hostilities. Further, while US policy toward the region may seem well planned and stable, it is in fact no better planned than US policy toward other hot spots in the world. Worse, the policy has become more ambiguous with time. The lack of a consistently planned foreign policy risks a massive loss of life in the region, as well as a wider conflict.

Below, I spell out the ad hoc nature of the policy by turning to five watersheds in the formation of America's China-Taiwan policy. In the first two cases, the 1954-55 Taiwan Strait Crisis and the 1958 Quemoy Crisis, two factors played a role in influencing Eisenhower's decision to protect the offshore islands: domestic politics and international pressures from Taipei. The third case, Carter's recognition of Beijing and the subsequent Taiwan Relations Act, was almost completely driven by a domestic political battle between the president and Congress. Fourth, Reagan's constant referral to Taiwan as the official government of China was driven by his anti-communist ideology and administrative style. Finally, Clinton's bow to congressional pressure led directly to the 1996 Taiwan Strait crisis. Each of these cases demonstrates how US policy toward the region is not only formed by nonrational factors, but is also quite fluid. At no point has a plan been developed. In fact, policy has changed from president to president. I conclude with a discussion of how US policy has become more ambiguous and the consequences for US foreign policy.

WATERSHED DECISIONS

Prior to the first crisis in the Taiwan Strait and Eisenhower's election, President Truman had no intention of protecting Taiwan. After the People's Liberation Army crossed the Yangtze River in force, Truman wrote that the US "had picked a bad horse" in the Nationalists. While disliking Mao Zedong, Truman also had no respect for Chiang and his corrupt regime.[5] While Truman saw no feasible way to support the KMT, a growing China Lobby in the US forced his administration to develop such a policy. The State Department struggled to devise a policy that would limit US involvement and still keep Mao from taking all of China, but it became painfully obvious that no such policy existed. The struggle in Truman's administration exemplified what was to come: a fight between those seeing little value in Taiwan and those who saw it as key to the containment of communism and American security in the Pacific.

"On the eve of the Korean War, therefore, the direction that US policy toward Taiwan would take lacked clear definition."[6]

The battle to form a policy toward China came to an abrupt end with the start of the Korean War.[7] Truman used the Seventh Fleet to separate Formosa and the Pescadores from the mainland, preventing both an attack from the mainland and an attack on the mainland. Initially, this decision was meant to be temporary, but Beijing's entrance into the war began to solidify the security relationship between the US and the Nationalists. In 1951, the Mutual Defense Assistance Agreement paved the way for a US guarantee of Taiwan's safety. However, this did not include the offshore islands.

The Taiwan Strait Crisis

"[O]ne of the most serious problems of the first eighteen months of my administration."[8] Eisenhower's presidential campaign stressed that his administration would not only contain communism but roll it back. At this point, the issue of the offshore islands became a part of US policy. Eisenhower suggested that he would "unleash" the Nationalists on the mainland—a comment made more for psychological effect than as a statement of military policy.[9] While aiming for a psychological effect on Beijing, the US did encourage Chiang to better arm the islands. The Joint Chiefs of Staff (JCS) advocated that "a few of their regular American-equipped units" be rotated to the islands, once the islands were fully equipped.[10] The idea was to bolster the Nationalists to help themselves, frighten Beijing, and keep the American commitment to a minimum.

Despite these symbolic moves, Eisenhower had ambivalent feelings toward protecting the offshore islands. For the most part it appears that he concurred with the majority of the JCS, who believed the offshore islands were not critical to the defense of Formosa and the Pescadores, and were instead a serious strategic liability.[11] However, the JCS and the president were concerned that the islands had great psychological significance for the Nationalists, and that losing them would have a demoralizing effect.[12] Left alone with his advisors, Eisenhower probably would have chosen to evacuate Quemoy and Matsu, instead of providing a US security guarantee. However, there was a strong outside force at work.

First and foremost was Chiang's constant push for more aid and stronger US security commitments. While his requests were never granted openly and without great conditions, his constant pressure was an effective strategy. It never allowed the US to get further than suggesting that certain islands should be evacuated after the PRC began shelling. Much like a salesman who never gives the buyer a chance to form a solid counteroffer, Chiang kept pressure on the Americans to work out a way to defend the offshore islands without unacceptable American involvement. He also tried to influence what was considered *unacceptable*. The effect of this pressure was to make US commitment to the offshore islands more likely once the shelling began.

Chiang also effectively convinced the US that the loss of Quemoy and Matsu would destroy the Nationalists' will to fight and defend the main island itself. The combination of tying Formosa's security to the offshore islands and maintaining constant pressure for more aid kept the White House from imposing a deal on Chiang. Had Eisenhower's administration been able to make the Mutual Defense Assistance Agreement conditional on the evacuation of the offshore islands, the shelling would more likely have led to a withdrawal from those strongholds. Instead, Chiang's efforts limited the options the White House considered.

Chiang's efforts placed him in a good position to gain American support on September 3, 1954, when the People's Liberation Army (PLA) began shelling Quemoy and Matsu. While a decision had not been made, Eisenhower listed his reasons for holding the offshore islands: not appeasing the communists, maintaining morale on Formosa, and most of all, not losing Chiang as an ally.[13] The last two reasons were result's of Chiang's diplomacy.

I do not mean to overstate Chiang's influence. When the PLA landed troops in the Tachen Islands after shelling the Nationalist emplacements, the White House convinced Chiang to evacuate the islands, but only after private assurances of protection for the larger offshore islands of Quemoy and Matsu.[14]

Eisenhower asked Congress to authorize presidential action in the Taiwan Strait. Eighteen days later, the Formosa Resolution was signed into law. The resolution explicitly approved the protection of Formosa and the Pescadores, but only suggested that the offshore islands could be included.[15] This rather vague language was used to placate Congress, where a strong and vocal opposition to abandoning the offshore islands existed. Clearly, Eisenhower was trying to get as much authority as possible to keep his own options open, but doing so required threading a domestic political needle.

In this rather delicate political environment, Chiang made public statements that he had strong US support, including American ground forces to aid in providing security for Nationalist holdings. Eisenhower, angry with Chiang's lack of discretion, reacted strongly and rejected his aid request. The ambivalent signals coming out of the White House—the resolution and the denial of aid—certainly gave Beijing no reason to halt the shelling. As a result, Eisenhower stepped up the pressure on Beijing by saying that atomic weapons might be used if a conflict broke out in the Strait. This comment sparked a war scare in the US. The president had to backpedal and say that war was not very likely, sending the PRC yet another ambivalent message. The continued domestic fight over the policy further muddied the waters.[16]

In a last-ditch effort to avoid direct American involvement on the offshore islands, Eisenhower sent Admiral Radford and Assistant Secretary of State Robertson to convince Chiang that the offshore islands were not important. The mission was confused from the start, as it was Eisenhower's intent to try one last time to convince Chiang to leave the offshore islands. Failing that, the US would have to become directly involved. However, both Radford and Robertson believed in an American security guarantee for the islands, and as such, they did not make the most effective emissaries.[17] As always, Chiang rejected the idea of leaving the islands. However, before the mission was over, the PRC ceased its shelling.

Originally, I attributed the cessation of hostilities to luck on the part of the US. Certainly, none of the messages sent were clear enough for Beijing to realize that war might be likely. However, recent documents suggest that Chiang signaled Beijing that America was backed up against the wall and would quite possibly enter the dispute, escalating it to a dangerous level for all involved. The US policy toward the Strait stayed in an uneasy flux throughout that crisis and into the next. Instead of fixing the leaky policy, the US seemed only able to put buckets around to catch the falling water.

The Taiwan Strait Crisis II: The Quemoy Artillery Blockade

A short three years after the initial shelling of the offshore islands, Beijing targeted Quemoy with another sustained attack. The island was effectively blockaded by artillery fire. In every way, this second crisis was a continuation of the first. Over the three years only one factor had changed, but it was a critical one that pushed Eisenhower into a firmer commitment to defending the offshore islands: Chiang had enhanced the importance of Quemoy and Matsu by dramatically increasing the number of troops on them.

Eisenhower still believed that the offshore islands should be downgraded to a military outpost with a minimal troop detail. However, Chiang realized that if he increased his forces there, he could make losing the islands militarily unacceptable. This is exactly what he did, and it worked.[18] While the blockade looked as though it would hold, ingenuity and resourcefulness (and a certain amount of luck) allowed the Nationalists, with American help, to break through and resupply the island. Shortly after, the shelling ceased.

It is unclear if, prior to the blockade, Eisenhower planned to defend the offshore islands. He never signaled Beijing that the US would defend the offshore islands, so it is not surprising that the second crisis erupted. The PRC leaders had no reason to believe they would not succeed. Had the blockade held and the conflict escalated, however, the US would have been drawn into a war alongside Taiwan against the PRC. The US would have entered the conflict very grudgingly, since it was never interested in holding the offshore islands. Thus, the *only* reasons for a US security commitment were (1) the China lobby's earlier pressure for greater assurances that effectively set the stage for US involvement, and (2) Chiang's heavy troop deployment on the islands.

As these conditions changed through time, so did the US commitment toward defending the offshore islands. While the crises took place over 40 years ago, they show that the US security commitment was not a product of careful strategic decisionmaking. Instead, the White House found itself in a situation it perceived as strategically moribund and inane.

Carter and the Taiwan Relations Act

Following Nixon's visit to China earlier in the decade, President Carter, on December 15, 1978, issued a communiqué that established relations with Beijing, de-recognized Taiwan, and terminated the Mutual Defense Treaty of 1954. Following Nixon's historic trip, policy focused more on China and less on Taiwan. Thus, Taiwan's security became less critical to the US and subsequently became less stable. This instability is exemplified by the constant quarreling between Carter's advisors over what to do about China.[19] After a series of less-than-friendly interactions with the Soviets, both Beijing and Washington realized that normalization was in their mutual best interests.

Seven days after the communiqué, however, Senator Barry Goldwater mounted a legal suit claiming that the president alone did not have the power to terminate a treaty. While the lawsuit failed, it was the beginning of strong congressional activism that led to the Taiwan Relations Act of April 10, 1979. The TRA included provisions for continued arms sales to Taiwan and a call for the peaceful resolution of the China-Taiwan conflict, but it did not mention the defense of the offshore islands. Once again, US policy toward the Strait was being made on an ad hoc basis. Beijing was furious with the TRA, and President Carter had to assuage the anger with assurances that he would interpret the act in a manner favorable to the PRC.[20]

While the Sino-American relationship blossomed through cultural and economic exchanges, Carter still faced serious domestic pressures. As part of the normalization agreement, the president promised not to sell arms to Taiwan during the year in which the Mutual Defense Treaty was terminated.[21] However, toward the end of his term, he was forced by Congress to accept a large arms sale to Taiwan.[22] Clearly, the White House was not dictating policy toward the region, and as such, the policy was quite unstable going into the 1980 presidential election.

A Change in Administrations and Reagan's Waffling

During Ronald Reagan's campaign for president, George Bush (then the Republican vice presidential nominee) was sent to China to highlight Republican abilities in foreign affairs. During the send-off, then candidate Reagan spoke of "government-to-government" and "official relations" when referring to Taiwan.[23] After Bush arrived in China and began reassuring the Chinese government that Reagan had simply misspoken, Reagan (back on the campaign trail in America) suggested that he would reopen official relations with Taiwan. Not surprisingly, Bush's entire trip was consumed with trying to calm Chinese fears of Reagan's future policies.

Reagan's passionate anticommunist beliefs, coupled with his inexperience and low level of interest in foreign affairs, made policy toward China and Taiwan rather unsteady. While it was the Soviet Union that the president considered evil, he did not perceive much of a difference between communists—they were all evil in his eyes. Due to his focus on domestic affairs, Reagan turned over foreign policy to Secretary of State Alexander Haig. Haig was particularly interested in creating better relations with Beijing. But because of personality problems and political tactics, Haig's tenure was very short. Relations with China were particularly affected by the turmoil during and immediately following Haig's time in the State Department. This was almost entirely because of the fighting and inconsistent behavior regarding arms sales to Taiwan—the administration regularly flopped back and forth on how many and what types of weapons to sell to Taipei. A great deal of time was spent drafting and issuing a joint communiqué, which in part stated that the US had no intention of selling arms to Taiwan indefinitely. Reagan told reporters a week later that the US would continue to sell arms until such a time as it saw fit—that there was no termination date in the foreseeable future.[24]

This type of wavering cooled Sino-American relations considerably, and it highlights the dramatic effect a switch in administrations can have on foreign policy. During the Carter presidency, relations were rapidly becoming more than cordial—they were actually becoming friendly. Once Reagan stepped into the White House, all bets seemed to be off. From Secretaries of State Haig to Shultz, the Reagan administration's policy toward the Strait was nothing like that of the Carter administration. There was no clear guiding principle for the administration to follow or even feel obliged to consider. Without such a schema, American policy toward China has shifted in response to international conditions, domestic political considerations, and changes in ideology.

Clinton and the 1996 Taiwan Strait Crisis

In June, 1995, Taiwanese President Lee Teng-hui visited the US as a private citizen to attend his alumni reunion. While such a visit may seem innocent, it sparked the most militarized crisis in the Strait since the 1950s. Prior to Lee's visit, US policy did not allow top Taiwanese government officials to enter the US. In 1994, Lee had stopped for refueling in Hawaii, but he was not permitted to exit the aircraft. The policy sought to respond to China's insistence that the US not give any form of official recognition to Taiwanese officials. Clinton upheld this policy and rejected Lee's request for entry. To put pressure on the president, Congress almost unanimously passed non-binding resolutions calling for Clinton to allow Lee to visit. Congress argued in the resolutions that Taiwan's status as America's fifth-largest trading partner required better treatment for her officials. While Clinton originally resisted, he gave in to congressional pressure and allowed Lee to visit as a private citizen. The reversal was made without warning or consultation with Beijing.

The PRC responded with diplomatic outrage, and initiated a series of missile tests shortly after Lee's visit in June 1995. While the White House downplayed the missile tests, it sent the aircraft carrier *Nimitz* and its battle group through the Taiwan Strait in December 1995.[25] As the Taiwan national elections approached, Beijing escalated its reaction into large-scale live-fire war games in the first quarter of 1996. In response, the US sent two aircraft carrier battle groups to the area. Immediately following the elections, the Chinese military exercises ended without incident.

As with many previous incidents, the president set out with one policy in mind and was redirected by strong congressional pressure. The Chinese reaction (missile tests and war games) was well scripted and under control, but it was largely a result of American policy instability.[26] In other words, had Clinton held his ground and not allowed Lee to visit the US, Beijing probably would not have felt compelled to react so strongly. True, some action would have been likely with the coming elections in Taiwan, but the magnitude of the exercises was immense.

The crisis illustrates the danger involved in China-Taiwan relations. Beijing was surprised at America's response to the war games; the leaders felt that sending two aircraft carrier groups was an overreaction.[27] Had Beijing felt threatened and reacted to the US response, the two naval groups could conceivably come into contact with each other. Although unlikely, the contact might have become lethal. This danger was the direct result of the US' ambiguous policy toward the region and its ad hoc decision-making process. Had US policy been transparent, the 1996 crisis might not have occurred and would at least have been less dangerous.

CONSEQUENCES

The above decisions suggest two very important factors in American foreign policy: (1) the process, not simply its outcome, is key to understanding the changing nature of a foreign policy, and (2) domestic political influences must be taken into account. US policy toward the Strait over time appears stable, as though it evolved through a series of crises and decisions into Washington's coherent policy program. Nothing could be further from the truth. While Washington would like Beijing to democratize enough to allow for a peaceful settlement of the Taiwan issue, it has no plan other than to wait. The term *evolve* is too consistent or logical for America's China policy. Evolution implies a series of coherent, traceable adaptations to changing environments. The only regular aspect of US policy has been the almost random changes occurring over the past 50 years. Instead of evolution or even the duck paddling in the water, US policy toward China and Taiwan has taken a path more like a rabbit escaping a predator—a series of quick shifts, sharp turns, and backtracking.

Because of the ad hoc nature of US policy, it is impossible to predict future policy decisions from past ones. Recall that Truman was not interested in protecting Formosa, nor was Eisenhower interested in protecting the offshore islands, but they both did so. Had Carter and the Democrats held the White House and the Senate, Sino-American relations would not have declined for a period. They lost both.[28] Had Clinton resisted congressional pressure, the 1996 crisis would not have occurred, or at least it would have been less severe.

A PRC attack on Taiwan would almost certainly incur the wrath of the US. But what form that wrath would take depends on a variety of factors. As the Chinese PLA's deputy chief of staff put it: "You [America] will not sacrifice Los Angeles to protect Taiwan."[29] If the American people, the answer would almost certainly be a resounding, "No, we would not!" As many reports attest, a full-scale attack on Taiwan is unlikely to succeed or even occur.[30] The danger is not as much from such a large-scale offensive, however, as it is from a smaller attack on the offshore islands, for example. Even the most skilled and popular president would have difficulty engaging the American public in a costly battle over some small islands with two of its biggest trading partners.[31] Particularly with the recent obsession with military casualties, the US would have a difficult time persuading the public that any loss of life would be justified.[32] If one looks to history for a solution, it provides little guidance. US policy toward China has worked in the past because its resolve was never truly tested.

History also suggests that US policy is becoming more ambiguous with time. The higher levels of trade and concern with human rights create conflicting interest groups within the US. These, added to those concerned with Chinese ascent to superpower status, create political pressures within the US that make it difficult for the White House to make policy. Even within either major political party there are pressures from at least two of these three groups. The result is greater ambiguity and, ultimately, instability in US policy.

What is so interesting about the ambiguity of American policy toward China-Taiwan is that it is the only realistic choice. If the US were to side with Taiwan, it would engender severe animosity in a rising power and strong trading partner. The economic costs of such a policy would be dramatic for both sides. Containing China is not an option, as the US would stand alone with such a strategy. Similarly, siding with Beijing would abandon Taiwan and its new democracy, as well as end the possibility that the PRC would eventually de-mocratize.[33] Thus, the American policy toward China and Taiwan is ambiguous and unstable, but it is the best option available.

This argument appears rather pessimistic about Sino-American relations, especially during a period when trade is flourishing. Diplomatic controver-sies—particularly due to the US bombing of the Chinese embassy in Belgrade, and the offshore collision between a Chinese fighter and a US intelligence-gathering aircraft—have challenged relations. But Beijing does not seem inter-ested in losing US trade and support for WTO entry. I do not dispute that a conflict in the Strait is unlikely, and that such a conflict is deterred even more effectively now because of all the economic carrots each nation is enjoying. If American resolve is tested, however, it is not clear what the outcome will be.[34] US foreign policy is stable because the situation in the Strait is stable. Simi-larly, if the Strait becomes unstable, so may US policy.

NOTES

1. This characterization is similar to similar to Gaddis' description of the Cold War as the Long Peace. See John Lewis Gaddis (1986), "The Long Peace: Elements of Stability in the Postwar International System," *International Security* 10, 4, pp. 92-142).

2. The debate over whether or not the US should contain or engage the People's Republic of China continued at the time. The point here is that Nixon moved the US policy of strict hostile containment toward diplomatic engagement. This shift repre-sented a massive change from antagonistic relations to an initial, uneasy anti-Soviet partnership. Following Nixon's visit, there were of course many ups and downs in this relationship.

3. It is too early to tell with the administration of President George W. Bush.

4. It is possible that ad hoc decision making may be reasonable under the circum-stances. The consequence is still uncertainty.

5. David McCullough, *Truman* (New York: Simon & Schuster, 1992), pp. 742-44; Robert Accinelli, *Crisis and Commitment: United States Policy Toward Taiwan, 1950-1955* (Chapel Hill: University of North Carolina Press, 1996), p. 5.

6. Accinelli, *Crisis and Commitment*, p. 27.

7. Accinelli, *Crisis and Commitment*, p. 29.

8. Dwight D. Eisenhower, *Mandate for Change 1953-1956: The White House Years* (New York: Doubleday & Company, 1963), p. 459.

9. Alexander L. George and Richard Smoke, *Deterrence in American Foreign Pol-icy: Theory and Practice* (New York: Columbia University Press, 1974), p. 270.

10. Karl Lott Rankin, *China Assignment* (Seattle: University of Washington Press, 1964), p. 168.

11. Dwight D. Eisenhower, *Waging Peace 1956-1961: The White House Years* (New York: Doubleday & Company, 1965), p. 293.

12. Eisenhower, *Mandate for Change 1953-1956*, p. 463; see also Rankin, *China Assignment*; George and Smoke, *Deterrence in American Foreign Policy.*

13. Eisenhower, *Mandate for Change 1953-1956*, pp. 470-74.

14. Eisenhower, *Mandate for Change 1953-1956*, p. 466; George and Smoke, *Deterrence in American Foreign Policy.*

15. Eisenhower, *Mandate for Change 1953-1956*, p. 459.

16. Eisenhower, *Mandate for Change 1953-1956*; George and Smoke, *Deterrence in American Foreign Policy.*

17. Eisenhower, *Mandate for Change 1953-1956*; George and Smoke, *Deterrence in American Foreign Policy.*

18. Eisenhower, *Waging Peace 1956-1961*, pp. 292-94.

19. Robert S. Hirschfield, "The Reagan Administration and US Relations with Taiwan and China," in Louis W. Koenig, James C. Hsiung, and King-yuh Chang, eds., *Congress, The Presidency, and the Taiwan Relations Act* (New York: Praeger, 1985), pp. 111-40; Cecil V. Crabb, "An Assertive Congress and the TRA: Policy Influences and Implications," in Louis W. Koenig, James C. Hsiung, and King-yuh Chang, eds., *Congress, The Presidency, and the Taiwan Relations Act* (New York: Praeger, 1985), pp. 85-110; Harry Harding, *A Fragile Relationship: The United States and China since 1972* (Washington, DC: The Brookings Institution, 1992).

20. Harding, *A Fragile Relationship.*

21. Harding, *A Fragile Relationship.*

22. Hirschfield, "The Reagan Administration and US Relations with Taiwan and China."

23. Hirschfield, "The Reagan Administration and US Relations with Taiwan and China."

24. Hirschfield, "The Reagan Administration and US Relations with Taiwan and China."

25. Dennis V. Hickey (1998), "The Taiwan Strait Crisis of 1996: Implications for US Security Policy," *Journal of Contemporary China* 7, 19, pp. 405-19.

26. Andrew Scobell (2000), "Show of Force: Chinese Soldiers, Statesmen, and the 1995-1996 Taiwan Strait Crisis," *Political Science Quarterly* 115, 2, pp. 227-46.

27. Scobell, "Show of Force."

28. It is possible that Carter's focus on human rights would have become a problem, but that is only speculation.

29. James Mann, "Between China and the US," *Washington Post*, 10 January 1999.

30. See Bates Gill, "Chinese Military Modernization and Arms Proliferation in the Asia-Pacific," in Jonathan D. Pollack and Richard H. Yang, eds., *In China's Shadow: Regional Perspectives on Chinese Foreign Policy and Military Development* (Rand Corporation, 1998); and Bates Gill and Michael O'Hanlon, "China's Hollow Military," *The National Interest*, Summer 1999.

31. Note how the question of defending the offshore islands remain unresolved, even after more than 45 years.

32. It is possible that the concern to avoid casualties is a fallacy created by the media and White House, and reinforced by the successes in Kosovo. However, US

involvement would still be very difficult to sell if it involved a protracted conflict on the mainland.

33. This is not to mention the technology and resources the PRC would gain from reunification. These would significantly enhance China's military capabilities.

34. Such a test may be more likely as Taiwan democratizes. This strengthens Taiwan's distinct national identity and decreases its willingness to reunify.

5

Assessing North Korean Behavior: The June 2000 Summit, the Bush Administration, and Beyond

Terence Roehrig

On June 13, 2000, North Korean leader Kim Jong Il strode out onto the tarmac at the airport in Pyongyang, North Korea's capital, to greet arriving South Korean President Kim Dae Jung. Many had to rub their eyes in disbelief, unsure that what they saw was really happening. Never before had these two Korean heads of state met. Soon after the leaders arrived at the state gues thouse, Kim Jong Il remarked, "June 13 will be a day recorded in history." Kim Dae Jung replied, "Let's go on and make that history."[1] Few expected a meeting of this type so soon into the new millennium, and even the usually restrained North Korean media reported the event as "a landmark turning point on the road toward national reconciliation, cooperation, peace and unification."[2] The personal greeting from Kim Jong Il at the airport, a gesture few anticipated, ushered in three days of talks. These culminated in a historic agreement moving both Koreas further along the path of reconciliation and eventual reunification.

These were amazing developments in inter-Korean relations, rekindling hope that the two Koreas might reconcile soon. Yet, many argued that the hopes engendered by these events and others that followed in 2000 should be tempered with caution. North Korea remains a heavily armed state, with intentions and policy preferences that are not always clear. Though the historic summit agreement was a tremendously positive step in improving relations on the peninsula, one scholar quipped, "Let's not get summit slap-happy."[3] In September 2000, a US Defense Department report concluded that: "While the historic summit between the North and the South holds the promise of reconciliation and change, no evidence exists of the fundamental precursors for change. There is little or no evidence of economic reform or reform-minded leaders, reduction in military spending or a lessening of anti-US rhetoric."[4] Early in its term, the new George W. Bush administration announced its "skepticism" toward Kim Jong Il and the North Korean regime.

How to assess North Korea and its policy preferences in the wake of these events? Does North Korea remain a serious threat in the region? Or have Pyongyang's policy goals turned away from confrontation? Assessing North Korean behavior has long been a difficult endeavor. Though South Korea and the US have viewed the North as a serious threat for many years, North Korea's intentions have never been easy to measure precisely. This chapter will assess North Korea's security posture, applying the theoretical frameworks of neo-realism, neo-liberalism and constructivism outlined by Shale Horowitz in Chapter 1. First, it will be necessary to provide some historical background on North-South relations, along with a review of the June 2000 agreement and subsequent events.

HISTORY OF NORTH KOREAN POLICY TOWARD THE SOUTH

The end of World War II in 1945 was an important turning point for Korea. Since 1910, Korea had been a possession of the Japanese Empire, enduring a long and painful occupation. With the end of the war, Koreans assumed that liberation and independence were finally at hand. After all, they were on the side of the victors. However, it was not to be.[5] Following the Japanese surrender, the US and the Soviet Union divided the peninsula at the 38th parallel, with the US to accept the surrender in the south while the Soviets did so in the north. Though the intention was to reunite Korea soon after the war, it was not long before Cold War hostility overtook these plans and talks on reunification stalled. In 1948, separate regimes were established in the two Koreas. Syngman Rhee was elected president of the Republic of Korea (ROK) in the South, and soon after, Kim Il Sung assumed the leadership of the Democratic People's Republic of Korea (DPRK) in the North. Both North and South claimed to be the legitimate rulers of the entire peninsula, and both pledged that they would eventually reunify Korea under their leadership.

On June 25, 1950, North Korea made a bid to reunify through force. Encouraged by US actions that seemed to indicate reduced support for the South and, in any case, hoping to win the war before the US could respond, Kim Il Sung launched a massive assault across the 38th parallel. The North almost succeeded in its goal, driving ROK and US forces into a small region on the southeastern tip of the peninsula. In September 1950, US forces under General Douglas MacArthur launched a counteroffensive behind DPRK lines at the western port city of Inchon, and eventually drove North Korean forces back across the 38th parallel.

Now, the scope of the war changed. As US and ROK forces continued their push north, it appeared that instead of merely defending South Korea, the US and its allies had the opportunity to "roll back" communism in Korea. However, as US and South Korean units approached ever closer to the Yalu River that separates North Korea from China, Beijing began to send warning signals that it would not tolerate these adversaries so close to its border. When US commanders would not heed the warning, the Chinese launched an assault in late November 1950 that succeeded in driving US and ROK forces back south of the 38th parallel. By early January 1951, the battle lines were approximately where they had been in June 1950. The remainder of the war was a stalemate fought roughly along the 38th parallel, with little ground changing hands. Finally, in July 1953, the US and North Korea signed an armistice ending the conflict. South Korean President Syngman Rhee refused to sign the armistice, believing that it short-circuited his goal of reunifying the peninsula under his leadership.[6]

After the war, North-South relations remained tense. For Kim Il Sung, the war was a disaster. The conflict produced great loss of life and tremendous destruction to the economy, results that caused many to question his hold on power. The early years following the war were spent purging political opponents, solidifying his power, and rebuilding the North. By the 1960s, Kim Il Sung was ready to pursue again his goal of reunifying the peninsula. However, the Korean War had taught him that so long as the US remained a staunch ally of the South, a direct attack was destined to fail.[7] Instead, Kim embarked on a different approach.

Realizing that he could not succeed in the face of US-ROK military power, he opted instead for a campaign to destabilize the South Korean regime through infiltration and subversion. In a 1964 speech to the Korean Worker's Party, he noted three steps necessary to achieve reunification. First, North Korea had to strengthen its own revolutionary base by educating and training its own people in the proper doctrine. Second, the revolutionary forces in South Korea needed strengthening. Utilizing Marxist doctrine, Kim believed that the South Korean masses suffered from false consciousness, not realizing the extent of their oppression under US imperialism and ROK rulers subservient to the Americans. To address this situation, Kim Il Sung called for greater organization of the masses through a vanguard party in the South, which would lead the effort to overthrow the corrupt southern regime and reunify with the North. Finally, Kim also called for improved relations with other third world states exploited by US imperialism.[8]

As a result, North Korea greatly escalated its efforts to infiltrate agents and operatives into the South. These efforts reached their peak in 1967 and 1968, with ever more numerous and bold acts of violence. During 1967, 224 North Korean infiltrators were killed while on missions in the South.[9] In November 1968, 120 North Korean commandos infiltrated along the east coast of South Korea but most were either captured or killed, causing little damage to the South.[10] The most serious action came on January 21, 1968, when a team of 31 commandos attempted to assassinate South Korean President Park Chung Hee at his residence, the Blue House in Seoul. The effort failed to kill the president, but it demonstrated the lengths to which North Korea was willing to go to destabilize the South.[11]

While Kim undertook these measures to weaken the South, he also made contradictory efforts at reconciliation. In 1960, North Korean Foreign Minister Chung Il Hyung stated that his country renounced the policy of using force to liberate the South.[12] Later in 1962, Kim Il Sung declared that "unification must be attained gradually through a series of intermediate steps."[13] Whether these statements were a bluff or a sincere effort was not clear.

The strategy of subversion and infiltration may have been a prelude to invasion. Given the results of North Korea's previous attempt to invade the South, this also seems unlikely. Instead, efforts to destabilize South Korea indirectly avoided a direct military confrontation and allowed the North to control the risks of its policy. Pyongyang could "ratchet up" its efforts, yet allow room to back off should the ROK-US response be too threatening. Thus, North Korea could control its policy so as to keep the costs within a tolerable range.

After several years of efforts to destabilize the South, the cost in soldiers and resources was becoming excessive, and Kim had little to show for it. In fact, many of his infiltration attempts did more to galvanize ROK opinion against the North, so the efforts were scaled back significantly. Thus, by the 1970s, North Korean behavior began to moderate somewhat, though not without continued contradictions.[14] The two Koreas began a dialogue that produced an agreement in July 1972 stating their shared principles for reunification. The joint communiqué stated:

First, unification shall be attained independently, without reliance upon or interference from an external power. Second, unification shall be realized through peaceful means rather than the use ff force. Third, both sides shall promote a great national unity as a homogenous people, transcending differences in ideas, ideologies, and systems.[15]

Despite the improvement in North-South relations indicated here, little in the agreement was ever implemented. Also, other ominous signals continued, including a massive buildup of DPRK conventional forces and construction of tunnels crossing under the Demilitarized Zone (DMZ). Three tunnels were found during the 1970s, with a fourth discovered in 1990. In August 1974, another attempt was made to assassinate President Park, presumably by a North Korean agent. The effort failed, but Park's wife was hit by a bullet and later died from the wound. Finally, in August 1976, North Korean soldiers killed two US officers at Panmunjom in the DMZ.

In the 1980s, two terrorist incidents further soured North-South relations. North Korean agents planted a bomb in Rangoon, Burma, in 1983, which was intended to kill South Korean President Chun Doo Hwan during a visit to Southeast Asia. The bomb went off prematurely, missing Chun. However, 17 other members of the President's party were killed, including four cabinet ministers. Four years later, North Korean agents planted a bomb aboard Korean Airlines flight 858, which exploded over the Gulf of Thailand. ROK leaders believed the North was attempting to disrupt presidential elections scheduled for December 1987 and to discourage international attendance at the 1988 Summer Olympics to be held in Seoul. The 1987 bombing still haunts North Korea, as it prompted the US State Department to place the DPRK on its list of states that support terrorism. The designation, still held by Pyongyang, prevents access to numerous sources of international economic assistance and loans. To no avail, North Korea has sought desperately to be removed from the list.

Yet relations showed some signs of improving when negotiations between the North and South began again in the early 1990s. These culminated in two major agreements. On December 13, 1991, North and South Korea signed a treaty of reconciliation and nonaggression, pledging to recognize each other's political system, refrain from the use of force against each other, and work toward a more permanent peace. On the last day of that month, the two Koreas inked another deal banning nuclear weapons from the peninsula. However, the two sides could not agree on measures to verify the nuclear ban and both agreements saw little progress in actual implementation. The nuclear weapons issue was particularly important, because the ROK and the US were becoming increasingly worried that North Korea was developing a nuclear capability. This issue will be addressed later in the chapter.

Why the sudden change again in North Korean behavior? As the Cold War context of global politics was rapidly changing in the late 1980s and early 1990s, Pyongyang was becoming less important to its major patrons, the Soviet Union and China. Both Moscow and Beijing began to make overtures to South Korea. China was urging Kim Il Sung to undertake some economic reform, as the PRC had done. Increasingly, the North was feeling more isolated. Also, South Korean President Roh Tae Woo had taken a more conciliatory position toward the North, asking Kim Il Sung to join him for a summit meeting. While Kim refused, other high-level Korean officials did meet.[16]

It has been difficult to gauge North Korean intentions over the years. North Korean behavior has often been erratic and difficult to explain. As a result, the DPRK and its longtime leader, Kim Il Sung, have often been labeled crazy and irrational. When Kim Il Sung died in 1994, the new leader of North Korea, his son Kim Jong Il, was viewed in a similar manner. Despite the end of the Cold War, North and South Korea appeared to be locked in a continuing cycle of tension and suspicion. Though the level of tension had decreased significantly over the years, there seemed little hope for any permanent improvement in relations.

In 1997, South Korea elected a new president, Kim Dae Jung. Kim was a longtime opposition leader against the old military governments in South Korea, and he was determined to improve relations with the North. Implementing what became known as the "sunshine policy," Kim Dae Jung attempted to reach out to the North and break the deadlock in North-South relations. In June 2000, Kim Dae Jung received his wish, making the historic trip to North Korea for a summit meeting and raising hopes that perhaps a more permanent peace could be achieved on the Korean Peninsula.

THE JUNE 2000 SUMMIT

After several days of talks in Pyongyang, the two leaders concluded an agreement. Many hoped that it would be the basis for improved relations and the eventual reunification of the two Koreas. In the opening paragraphs, both sides recognized "the lofty wishes of the Korean people yearning for peaceful reunification of the fatherland" and called for "promoting mutual understanding," "achieving peaceful, national reunification." The agreement contained five specific provisions:

1. Both North and South "will join hands" to "resolve the issue of national unification independently."
2. Acknowledge that each has "different formulas" but also "common factors" to reach the goal of unification.
3. North and South Korea will facilitate visits between relatives and families separated by the division of the two
4. Koreas, and the South will repatriate Communist prisoners held in South Korean jails who have finished serving their sentences;

5. Both Koreas will "pursue a balanced development of their national economies" and seek to "build mutual trust"
6. with further exchanges in cultural, sports, health and environmental areas; and
7. Agree to continue meetings, including a visit to Seoul by Kim Jong Il "at an appropriate time."[17]

In September, the progress of the summit was followed up with meetings between the two respective defense ministers, the first time these occurred since before the Korean War.[18] The meeting produced an agreement to reopen a railroad connection that had been cut off since the war. South Korea hoped for discussion on a much broader range of issues, including increased confidence-building measures between the two militaries. In the end, both sides decided to establish a hot line between the two military commands and begin regular "working level" meetings.[19] Further meetings between defense officials followed to address other security issues, but little concrete progress was made. However, that the meetings occurred at all was a significant shift in North-South relations.

In October, other important visits occurred. North Korean General Jo Myong Rok, first vice chairman of the National Defense Commission, made a historic visit to Washington. He met President Bill Clinton for discussions on North Korea's ballistic missile program, nuclear weapons, and the search for the remains of Korean War veterans.[20] In particular, General Jo brought an invitation for President Clinton to visit Pyongyang, and reiterated that the North was willing to scrap its missile program in return for help in launching civilian satellites.[21]

Soon after, Secretary of State Madeleine Albright made a trip to the North in hopes of further narrowing differences for a final agreement on ballistic missiles. At the conclusion of her trip, Secretary Albright announced that "important progress" had occurred during the talks, especially to "restrain missile development and testing, as well as missile exports."[22] Though there was speculation President Clinton would accept an invitation to Pyongyang to conclude a missile deal, he decided that time had run out for him to finish the deal. The incoming Bush administration had already indicated it was lukewarm to such a deal and so the issue was put on hold.[23]

The North has also kept up an ambitious pace to establish diplomatic contacts in various corners of the world. The DPRK has established formal relations with over 140 countries, including the Netherlands, Belgium, Italy, Australia, the United Kingdom, Canada, Spain, the Philippines, Kuwait, and Germany. In July 2000, North Korea began participation in the ASEAN Regional Forum (ARF) with all of ASEAN's members—excluding Myanmar—agreeing to open diplomatic relations with Pyongyang.[24] In May 2001, a delegation from the European Union visited Pyongyang, and later announced the EU's intention to open diplomatic relations with the DPRK.[25] A few months earlier, Pyongyang had also agreed to give German diplomats, journalists and aid workers unobstructed access to travel throughout North Korea—which allowed aid workers to monitor the use of German economic assistance more effectively. This was the first time the North had granted such privileges.[26]

North-South relations also saw improvement at other levels. As part of the June 2000 Summit Agreement, on August 15, 2000, one hundred families each from North and South journeyed across the border to visit family members whom they had not seen, in many cases, since the Korean War. The four-day visit coincided with the anniversary of Korea's liberation from Japanese colonial rule and marked only the second time the two sides had allowed exchanges of this sort.[27] Two more visits followed in November 2000 and February 2001. After a six-month lull, a fourth visit was scheduled for October 2001, but it was cancelled at the last minute by the North.[28] In September 2000, observers marveled at another amazing sight. For the opening ceremonies of the 2000 Olympic Games in Sydney, Australia, athletes from both the DPRK and the Republic of Korea (ROK) entered together under one banner.[29]

THE BUSH ADMINISTRATION

The optimism of the June Summit soon faded. The new George W. Bush administration declared its skepticism toward Kim Jong Il and the North Korean regime. In February 2001, President George W. Bush announced that his administration was conducting a review of North Korea policy, and that any further talks with the DPRK would be suspended pending the results of that review. President Bush followed with questions about Kim Jong Il and his trustworthiness, stating that "we're not certain as to whether or not they're keeping all terms of all agreements."[30] This statement was in reference to the 1994 Agreed Framework that halted any North Korean nuclear weapons program. Later, even administration officials admitted that North Korea had not reneged on any of its obligations pertaining to this agreement.[31] Secretary of State Colin Powell added further to this in remarks following the March 2001 meeting between President Bush and President Kim Dae Jung. Secretary Powell stated:

It [North Korea] is a threat; it has got a huge army poised on the border within artillery and rocket distance of South Korea. . . . and they still have weapons of mass destruction and missiles that can deliver those weapons of mass destruction. So we have to see them as a threat. We have to not be naïve about the nature of this threat, but at the same time, realize that changes are taking place."[32]

Moreover, the Bush administration has often cited the threat from "rogue states," such as North Korea and Iraq, to justify its proposed deployment of the national missile defense system (NMD).[33]

The North Korean response might have been expected. An editorial broadcast on North Korean radio labeled the US "a cannibals' nation," accused the Bush administration of "escalating its provocative and reckless diatribe" against the DPRK, and declared that revenge would be "thousand-fold" if "the US imperialists turn to confrontation."[34] In other actions, North Korea told EU delegates that it would not halt the sale of ballistic missiles or missile technology, claiming, according to EU delegate Javier Solana, that "technology was part of trade."[35] However, the North did reaffirm its intent to continue the moratorium on missile tests until 2003. Finally, North Korea threatened to restart its nuclear program that has been shut down since 1994, in response to perceived intentional delays to build the new reactors that are part of the Agreed Framework.

The US finished its policy review in May 2001 and declared its willingness to reopen talks with the North. However, this time talks would have a comprehensive agenda, including restricting the development, testing, and export of ballistic missiles; making early inspections of the North's nuclear facilities; and reducing the North's conventional military threat—all with expectations of rigorous verification regimes. The Bush administration is likely to be a tougher negotiating partner than the Clinton team and far less willing to compromise or provide incentives for North Korean behavior. Despite US willingness to restart talks, North Korea has so far refused to return to the negotiating table, being particularly unhappy with an agenda it sees as imposing preconditions on it. As the DPRK Foreign Ministry stated, "we cannot construe this otherwise than an attempt of the US to disarm" the North "through negotiations."[36] As of November 2001, the talks between the US and North Korea remained on hold.[37]

However, North-South talks, also on hold since the start of the Bush administration policy review, began again in September 2001. They yielded several important developments, including arranging another round of family reunions, restarting construction on a cross-border railway, and opening an east coast tourist route. Hopefully a US-DPRK dialogue can resume soon, but following the September 11 terrorist attack, other policy issues are likely to be more pressing.

ASSESSING NORTH KOREAN CAPABILITIES AND INTENTIONS

To examine the North's security posture, this chapter will use two dimensions: capabilities and intentions. Capabilities refer to the specific assets possessed by Pyongyang, including military and economic assets. Intentions refer to North Korea's objectives and willingness to employ certain policies to achieve those objectives.

Capabilities

Despite the improvement in North-South relations, Pyongyang still maintains a large military arsenal. According to figures contained in the *The Military Balance*, the DPRK has an armed force of over 1 million soldiers, 4,000 tanks, over 11,000 artillery pieces, 2,500 multiple rocket launchers, and 621 combat aircraft. In 1999, the North spent approximately $1.3 billion dollars on defense, a figure that represented 15 percent of its overall budget.[38] A recent US Defense Department report indicated that over 70 percent of these forces are deployed within one hundred kilometers of the demilitarized zone, reducing warning time in the event of a North Korean attack.[39] There is considerable question regarding the age and effectiveness of equipment. But in the short term, these forces remain formidable.[40] North Korea also possesses a chemical and biological weapons capability.

Of particular interest in recent years is North Korea's nuclear and ballistic missile program. In 1994, in an effort to keep North Korea from developing nuclear weapons, the US and the DPRK signed the Agreed Framework.[41] Under the agreement, North Korea suspended use of its nuclear energy facilities in the Yongbyon region, where old gas-graphite nuclear reactors produced large amounts of waste that could be diverted for weapons production. To compensate for the lost energy generation, the US, South Korea, and Japan formed the Korean Peninsula Energy Development Organization (KEDO) consortium to construct two light-water reactors to replace the old gas-graphite models.[42] By 2005, the nuclear components of the first light-water reactor are scheduled for delivery. Then, North Korea will be required to open up its nuclear facilities to inspection by the International Atomic Energy Agency (IAEA). There is considerable uncertainty over the exact nature of North Korea's nuclear status. While the North remains a signatory of the Nuclear Nonproliferation Treaty (NPT) and maintains it has no nuclear weapons, there is suspicion they may have diverted some spent fuel prior to the 1994 agreement. At an April 2001 conference on North Korea, CIA Deputy Director John E. McLaughlin stated that, based on estimates of unaccounted for nuclear material, "the North probably has one or two nuclear bombs."[43] The full inspections of North Korean nuclear sites required under the Agreed Framework may help to clarify this issue. The US has asked for an early start to verifying North Korea's nuclear status, a process experts predict could take at least two to three years. However, North Korea has refused the request, declaring its anger with delays in construction of the light-water reactors and demanding compensation for lost energy. Inspections, highly desired by the US and its allies, are an important trump card that Pyongyang is reluctant to give up until required to do so by the Agreed Framework. Under the terms of the agreement, the North is not obligated to conduct early inspections. So far, North Korea has been in full compliance with the Agreed Framework, despite some questions from time to time.[44]

Another serious concern has been Pyongyang's burgeoning ballistic missile program. In August 1998, North Korea test-fired the three-stage *Taepodong* 1 missile, supposedly to put a satellite into orbit.[45] The missile crossed Japanese airspace and caused a firestorm in the region. Japan halted deliveries of badly needed food aid and suspended talks to reestablish relations with the DPRK. The following year, Pyongyang began preparations for testing another missile, the *Taepodong* 2. A combined US-Japanese-South Korean effort put tremendous pressure on the North not to conduct another test. Intelligence estimates indicated that the *Taepodong* 2 had a much longer range, capable of reaching Hawaii or Alaska, and that by 2005, the North would have a missile capable of reaching the continental US with a nuclear-tipped warhead. In September 1999, North Korea agreed to suspend testing. They extended the moratorium in June 2000, shortly after the summit meeting and following the lifting of some US economic sanctions.[46] In July 2000, Kim Jong Il traveled to Moscow for meetings with Russian President Vladimir Putin. Reportedly, he offered to give up the North's missile program if other countries furnished the North with rockets for launching satellites into orbit.[47] However, Kim Jong Il later denied he had made the offer, saying there must have been a misunderstanding. Ongoing talks with the US were close to achieving a final agreement. But President Clinton felt time had run out in his presidency. This left it up to the new Bush administration to continue negotiations.[48] Kim Jong Il later extended the moratorium on missile test flights until 2003; in a visit to Russia in August 2001, Kim confirmed the ban.[49] While the moratorium covers flight tests, it does not include research and development of components and engines, or the sale of missiles and missile technology.

Despite this large array of military capabilities, North Korea's overall strength is greatly compromised by a failing economy and ongoing food short-ages. The DPRK economy continues to struggle with outdated technology, a deteriorating infrastructure, and a lack of investment capital. Throughout much of the 1990s, the economic output of North Korea declined, as industrial and mining production operated at only 30 percent capacity.[50] Using Bank of Korea data, one scholar notes that from 1991 to 1996, the DPRK economy shrank approximately 30 percent, while running large trade deficits. The greatest source of hard currency for the North's economy is likely money sent by ethnic Kore-ans living in Japan.[51] North Korea's ballistic missile program also represents an important option for export income, and Pyongyang has already made sales to Iran, Syria, and Pakistan. It is estimated that North Korea earns over $500 mil-lion per year from the sale of ballistic missiles and related technology.[52] In ear-lier rounds of negotiations with the US on the missile issue, North Korean offi-cials offered to give up the missile program if compensated with $500 million annually. However, the US refused to consider the offer.

The problem of food shortages was building throughout the 1980s, due to inefficient practices and bureaucratic mismanagement of the farming sector.[53] Beginning in 1995, these problems were exacerbated dramatically by a series of droughts and floods that decimated North Korea's agricultural production. Many have died of starvation and some estimates place the death toll at over one mil-lion. The North's diplomatic blitz has been in part an effort to obtain increased food aid and attract foreign investment. A massive foreign aid effort, including an estimated $380 million in 1999, has improved the DPRK's food problem. But further food donations will be necessary to help the North make it through the years ahead. In August 2001, Catherine Bertini, executive director of the World Food Program, noted after a visit to North Korea: "There is no question that for the foreseeable future North Korea will be the recipient of international assistance. It is not possible for the country to be food self-sufficient in the next few years."[54]

Despite these economic problems and much to the consternation of many observers, North Korea continues to divert scarce resources to maintain a large armed force. It is possible that Pyongyang's development of ballistic missiles along with the suspected one or two nuclear weapons may be an effort to im-plement less expensive security measures rather than maintain a large and costly conventional force. The development and sale of ballistic missiles also provide an important source of hard currency for the North Korean economy, with much of this money going into the coffers of the military. Yet, it is disconcerting that North Korea devotes such a significant share of its limited resources to military endeavors when there is such great need in other areas.

Intentions

The more difficult aspect of assessing any country is determining inten-tions. This is no less difficult here, given North Korea's sometimes seemingly erratic behavior and the lack of available information. Many have argued that

North Korean actions are irrational and unpredictable, well deserving of the title "rogue state" often used to describe the North. Yet others have argued that North Korea is indeed quite rational, as it fights for survival with few allies, a deteriorating economy, and constraints caused by its limited power resources.[55] As one scholar notes about North Korea, its "periodic ratcheting of tensions," though dangerous, has earned it a place at the bargaining table, and "capturing international headlines has afforded a poor and strategically disadvantaged state great attention."[56] However, as time has passed, North Korea's strategy of "crisis brinkmanship" has become less effective and, according to one scholar, one of the "predictable elements of North Korea's negotiating style."[57] While the summit and other actions noted earlier are very positive signs, doubts remain in the minds of many regarding North Korea's purposes. The discussion of intentions here will focus on two dimensions, the North's willingness to use force to achieve policy goals, and its desire to institute economic reform.

Military analysts and practitioners have long debated whether or not North Korea would feel emboldened to launch another strike to reunify the peninsula as it did in 1950. Would the North really consider such an attack again? It seems very unlikely the North would conclude that an attack on the South would have much chance for success. Despite its sizeable armed forces, the North faces a South Korean military that is prepared and modernized and a US-ROK alliance that remains strong and determined to maintain peace and stability in the region. The North would likely receive strong condemnation from others in East Asia, including China and Russia, for taking such action. Initiating an armed attack on the South might have some limited success in the short run, and be tremendously destructive for the South, but the US-ROK response would be devastating and likely lead to the end of the North Korean regime. It would be difficult for North Korean leaders and military planners not to realize that the use of force to reunify the peninsula would be a desperate gambit destined to fail.

Rather than an indication of its aggressive intentions, the North's military arsenal may increasingly be a hedge against the uncertainty of what is evolving in North-South relations. Several elements of this reasoning may be present here. First, possessing weapons of mass destruction and developing a ballistic missile capability become cheaper alternatives to maintaining the North's conventional capabilities and competing with ROK and US conventional strength.

Second, in the North's view, these weapons may have value as a deterrent against having reunification rammed down Northern throats on the South's terms. The North's military assets are a source of leverage for it to maintain some degree of control over the process, while pursuing policy goals that include attracting further economic aid and investment for its desperate economy.[58] Thus, some have suggested that the nuclear weapons and ballistic missile programs are useful as "bargaining chips" for the North to parlay into increased assistance from the US, South Korea and Japan.[59]

Finally, the nuclear weapons option, if in fact North Korea has one, and ballistic missiles provide a deterrent against the US, compensating the North for the loss of its major allies, China and Russia. After returning from his trip to Pyongyang in 1999, former Defense Secretary William Perry answered a question concerning North Korean motives on this issue. "I believe their primary

reason . . . is deterrence. Whom would they be deterring? They would be deterring the United States. We do not think of ourselves as a threat to North Korea,
but I truly believe that they consider us a threat to them."[60] A nuclear and ballistic missile capability poses the prospect that a military conflict with North Korea could mean the delivery of nuclear-tipped missiles against the continental
US, causing Washington to flinch in its support for Seoul.

Even a suspected, as opposed to an actual, nuclear program has been argued
to have benefits for Pyongyang. Michael Mazarr has maintained that "Going
Just a Little Nuclear" has been an important part of North Korean strategy,
where a full-blown nuclear program would have brought down certain condemnation and sanction. Yet, having no nuclear ambitions would have meant far
less attention for North Korea and its policy concerns. By maintaining a somewhat ambiguous nuclear program, the North has reaped many economic and
political benefits, while avoiding the wrath it would incur as a declared nuclear
state.[61]

Some have feared that a collapsing North Korea—with many making dire
predictions of its imminent economic demise—might lash out against the South
to preserve the failing regime. However, the North, despite all of its problems,
has displayed a dogged determination to survive. More important, the South,
the US, and others in East Asia have realized that a North Korean collapse could
be extremely destabilizing. It could lead to use of force by the North, a serious
refugee problem, and, from South Korea's perspective, the tremendous economic
costs associated with sudden reunification with the North. As a result, the countries in the region are working to avoid just such a collapse, which could make a
desperate use of force possible.

The second important issue regarding intentions is the degree to which the
North is sincerely interested in reforming its economy, opening up its isolated
society, and pursuing normalized relations with the South and the rest of the
world. According to many scholars and analysts, the primary goal for North
Korea at this stage is regime survival. Kim Jong Il and the leadership in Pyongyang are well aware of the economic difficulties they face. However, change
most likely will come slowly. According to one scholar, "to survive, the regime
needs to be more open and to embrace reform. However, interest in this is limited to the extent that such reforms do not penetrate too deeply the political-
military or social institutions and destabilize the regime."[62] North Korea is also
keenly aware of the need to normalize relations with the US, to gain access to
American and other international aid sources that are contingent on removal
from the US State Department terrorism list.

The June Summit was an important signal that the North is moving in the
direction of change, though the process appears to be carefully measured and
slow. The summit agreement was short on substance, as many skeptics maintain. But the summit talks and the agreement were an important first step, and
an indication of Kim Jong Il's willingness to move the North in a new direction. The meeting also changed some of the perceptions of Kim Jong Il, who
emerged from the summit a personable and humorous individual—a very different image from the irrational, fanatical leader of a "rogue state." However, much
work remains between the two Koreas and, should the agreement not be implemented, it would not be the first time this has happened. One very important

part of the summit agreement that has yet to occur is Kim Jong Il's promised visit to South Korea. This is a very important reciprocal measure that would give Kim Dae Jung's sunshine policy a huge boost at home. At the moment, there are no scheduled plans for such a visit.

The move toward greater dialogue with the South and more extensive economic contacts between the two Koreas will pave the way for further improvement in North-South relations. Indeed, the North-South dialogue has resumed after a six-month hiatus with a September 2001 meeting between top-level ministers. Among the several agreements reached during the meeting was the scheduling of another round of family reunions, and resuming construction of a cross-border railway and overland road across the DMZ to facilitate trade ties. Ministers also agreed to further meetings on North-South economic cooperation to promote trade and investment. North Korea had requested increased food aid and 500,000 kilowatts of electricity to prop up its ailing economy, but these issues were placed on the agenda for later meetings.

According to Park Jong Chul, a researcher at a Seoul think tank, North Korean efforts in these talks were likely designed to provide support for Kim Dae Jung's "sunshine policy," which has increasingly come under fire in the South for producing few tangible results.[63] Before leaving Seoul, the North Korean delegation noted: "The important agreements reached in the talks will undoubtedly give hope and confidence to our people."[64] While these are positive signs that efforts to improve North-South relations may again be gathering momentum, implementation remains a question mark.

Following the June 2000 Summit, the North demonstrated other signs that its intentions were shifting. Small but important signals included turning off the 108 loudspeakers that boomed propaganda messages across the DMZ, a measure that occurred under a direct order from Kim Jong Il in the wake of the June Summit agreement.[65] Kim Jong Il also stated that he would send a 15-member fact-finding team to South Korea to study Seoul's capitalist economic system. The group is likely to have younger economists in the delegation, and it represents another sign of Kim Jong Il's interest in economic reform. Though it is unlikely that the North will completely abandon its state-planned economic system, one press report noted that the DPRK may follow the state-guided economic development model utilized by South Korean President Park Chung Hee in the 1960s and 1970s.[66] Finally, in January 2001, Kim Jong Il journeyed to Shanghai, where he visited the city's stock exchange, a Buick plant and a semiconductor factory—the latter two being joint ventures with General Motors and Japan's NEC, respectively. According to one press report, the Chinese Foreign Ministry noted that Kim congratulated China on the outstanding changes brought about by Beijing's "correct" policies.[67]

Despite the optimism generated by the summit and subsequent events, critics have suggested that North Korea has had to give little in return for all that it has gained. Before the South and others continue to provide more and more aid, this view maintains the North should provide evidence that it is truly on the path of economic reform and willing to draw down its threatening military posture. This has largely been the outlook of the Bush administration in demanding a more comprehensive approach to further talks, greater reciprocity in North Korean concessions, and a generally tougher line toward North Korea. According to a senior Bush administration official, "We need to see some progress in all areas. We are prepared to wait. We don't feel any urgency to provide goodies to them in response to their rhetoric or threats."[68] When the North becomes more forthcoming, according to this view, the shift in North Korean intentions will truly be clear. Yet, this argument may be misplaced. According to one scholar, the US

cannot expect specific and equal reciprocity for the initial rounds of interaction. Engagement is almost always implemented in relationships based on years, if not decades, of hostility and distrust. The decades of Cold War animosity between Washington and Pyongyang will only be thawed if the engager [US], in a relative position of strength and confidence, is willing to forgo reciprocity, at least in the initial stages of the policy, to overcome the cognitive biases created by past enmity.[69]

Given North Korea's position of weakness vis-à-vis the US and South Korea, it has far less to give up in a reciprocal deal and will feel a great need to hold onto whatever leverage it has until the last possible moment.

The discussion of the last several pages demonstrates that North Korean intentions are not entirely certain at this stage. Given the low level of trust, it should not be surprising that this is so. Also, it is still possible that North Korea's apparent willingness to move toward engagement could be reversed by the North Korean leadership. Yet, as the engagement process continues, it becomes increasingly more difficult for the DPRK to reverse course to the hostility and violent actions of previous years. As norms of cooperation and dialogue become further established in North-South relations, a reversal of the North's willingness to engage is likely to have steeper costs in lost economic aid, trade, and investment, items the North Korean economy desperately needs. Obtaining concessions from North Korea may have to wait until a greater degree of trust has been established among the players and the engagement and reform process has had more time to operate.

WHAT DOES THE FUTURE HOLD? A THEORETICAL EXAMINATION

Following the June Summit, there was tremendous progress in relations between North and South Korea. Yet, the situation also remains uncertain, as many difficult issues remain, especially those related to security. Dialogue with the US has not yet resumed, given the Bush administration's hesitation in dealing with the North Korean regime. Neo-realism maintains that this should be no surprise. Military security issues will continue to be paramount here, as all sides make careful calculations regarding their threat perceptions in the region. For North Korea, there are some legitimate security concerns. Pyongyang is working under severe constraints as it faces well-armed adversaries, has limited resources to ensure its own security, and no longer has its chief alliance partners—China and the Soviet Union. Given these circumstances, neo-realism would argue for continued military vigilance and skepticism regarding North Korea and its intentions. Indeed, that has been the most recent approach of the US government. A strong US-ROK defense posture that does not underestimate DPRK capabilities or intentions is necessary to contain North Korea, while forcing it to alter its system and lessen its threatening military posture.

This approach does not hold all the answers and does not seem to be empirically accurate. Kim Dae Jung's "sunshine policy" and a willingness by US officials to negotiate with the DPRK regime have been important vehicles in drawing Pyongyang out of its isolation. The policy has downplayed military confrontation, while providing economic aid and investment, and seeking confidence-building measures. Examples of these efforts include significant amounts of food aid supplied by South Korea, the US, and Japan; exchanges of family members separated during the Korean War; Hyundai's Mt. Kumgang tourism project; and the construction of two light-water reactors under the US-North Korea Agreed Framework. These are important approaches stressed by neo-liberalism, whereby a growing economic and social interdependence can enhance stability and trust while discouraging the use of force—since the cost in these areas of interdependence is now greater. Consider the program of family exchanges that began in August 2000. As the exchanges increase and the personal ties grow, it becomes more difficult for either side to demonize the other, hopefully making it less likely that either North or South will use force to settle disputes or reunify. Also, North Korea is desperately in need of aid and investment to maintain the regime. This has encouraged Pyongyang to break its isolation and establish relations with over 140 countries. Certainly, growing economic and social ties are no guarantee of a peaceful transition to a unified Korea. However, these interactions establish a base to launch further confidence-building measures, while creating the impetus within North Korean society to push for reform, and to raise the cost should North Korea reverse course.

How shall we interpret the North's reactions to the Bush administration? It should be no surprise that the Bush administration's early actions brought a critical response from Pyongyang. While a review of US policy was expected and necessary, and caution is always an important ingredient in assessing the North, the public criticism of Kim Jong Il and the North Korean regime before concluding the policy review damaged the climate for continued talks. Caution and prudence are essential when dealing with North Korea, but to proclaim this publicly, given the progress made during the summer and fall of 2000, was problematic. These actions no doubt embarrassed North Korean leaders and reinforced the views of their hawks, who oppose any negotiation with the US and South Korea. In time, the damage done to the negotiation climate will heal, and North Korea will return to the bargaining table. The US has already offered to resume talks, but so far Pyongyang has been hesitant to return. Sufficient time has elapsed for the North to express its displeasure with the early pronouncements of the Bush administration, and it is time to restart talks. However, progress will be harder to come by with a Bush administration that believes too many concessions have already been made to a North Korean regime that is unlikely to move in any meaningful way towards political and economic reform.

And here is the key question. To what degree is North Korea capable of implementing reform? Must reform come through the collapse or disintegration of the current system? The final answers to these questions are difficult to predict, making the Korean Peninsula a region of great uncertainty over the next ten to twenty years. North Korea will likely move toward some type of Chinese-style economic reform that maintains tight control over the political system. Yet, it is not certain North Korea, or China for that matter, can indefinitely stall movement toward political reform. However, it seems relatively certain that, as constructivists might maintain, North Korea is going through some sort of reshaping of its policy preferences and national political identity. It is difficult to discount its many actions—reaching out to other states for diplomatic contacts, willingness to meet with the South in many different forums, reducing its bellicose rhetoric, and studying the Chinese economic system—as simply maneuvering by the old North Korea. While South Korea, the US, and Japan are correct to maintain a vigilant watch over North Korean actions, Pyongyang needs time to "reshape" its previous policy preferences and national identity against the inevitable opposition from various groups within North Korea. Kim Jong Il, who now may feel sufficiently secure in his hold on power, and other more pragmatic members of North Korea's leadership, need time to sell the changes. This is especially so in a society whose national identity has been steeped in the ideology of *juche*, which preached the North's need for self-reliance and hostility toward the South. Slowly, Pyongyang will have to make the case to its people for increased economic integration and reconciliation with the South. This will be a gradual process; to expect sudden changes in North Korean preferences is to invite the circumstances that may produce the very instability all sides wish to avoid. As efforts to engage North Korea proceed, the forces for reform within the DPRK will grow and become more difficult for any leader in the North to reverse. This will hopefully be encouraged by the passing of a generation of leadership rooted in *juche* and maintaining the status quo. North Korea needs time to reshape policy preferences and national identity—a process already under way as tension in the region continues to recede.

CONCLUSION

While each of the theories outlined in Chapter 2 and utilized here—neo-realism, neo-liberalism and constructivism—provide some insight, none of the three provides the entire answer. As a hedge in an environment of uncertainty, South Korea must continue to maintain a robust military capability along with a strong US-ROK alliance to ensure stability as the engagement process continues to unfold. Even North Korea indicates from time to time its support for the continued presence of US forces in Korea as a stabilizing influence in the region,[70] though Kim Jong Il also calls for the removal of US troops to speed efforts toward reunification.[71]

Yet at the same time, efforts to engage North Korea must continue, not only by those in the region but also by others outside East Asia (as has occurred with ASEAN and EU member states). Hopefully the series of talks on several fronts begun after the June 2000 Summit will resume again. Yet this process has no guarantees, especially as the positions of the US and North Korea will likely harden a bit. But continued engagement will slowly bring North Korea into the larger circle of the international community and encourage further change in the North. As this process continues, and it may take some time, tension on the peninsula will subside and progress will be made toward the eventual goal of reunification. Tough issues remain to be addressed. That may be one of the few certainties here. South Korea and the US should retain a firm deterrence posture and quietly prod North Korea toward reform. However, North Korea must be allowed the time, without complete reciprocity, to reshape a domestic policy environment that has not been overly concerned with reform. Then, change in the DPRK may begin to occur at a faster pace.

APPENDIX 5.1: North-South Summit Agreement, June 15, 2000

Upholding the lofty wishes of the Korean people yearning for peaceful reunification of the fatherland, President Kim Dae Jung of the Republic of Korea and Kim Jong Il, chairman of the National Defense Commission of the Democratic People's Republic of Korea, held a historic meeting and summit talks on June 13-15, 2000.

Noting that the meeting and talks held for the first time in the divided Korean history carry grave significance in promoting mutual understanding and developing South-North relations and achieving peaceful, national reunification, the top leaders of South and North Korea declared as follows:

1. The South and North, as masters of national unification, will join hands in efforts to resolve the issue of national unification independently.
2. Acknowledging that the different formulas that the North and South favor for reunification have common factors, they will strive to work together to achieve this goal.
3. The South and North will exchange groups of dispersed family members and their relatives around Aug. 15 and resolve as soon as possible humanitarian issues, including the repatriation of Communist prisoners who have completed their terms in jail.
4. The South and North will pursue a balanced development of their national economies and build mutual trust by accelerating exchange in the social, cultural, sports, health and environmental sectors.
5. In order to put these agreements into practice, the South and North will hold a dialogue between government authorities at an early date. President Kim Dae Jung cordially invited National Defense Commission chairman Kim Jong Il to visit Seoul, and he agreed to do that at an appropriate time.

Source: *New York Times*, June 15, 2000, A 10.

NOTES

1. Howard French, "Two Korean Leaders Speak of Making 'A Day in History,'" *New York Times*, June 14, 2000, p. A1.

2. Ibid.

3. Victor Cha, "Let's Not Get Summit Slap-Happy in Korea," *Nautilus Policy Forum Online*, June 27, 2000 <http://www.nautilus.org/fora/security/0005B_Cha.html>.

4. Steven Lee Myers, "Pentagon Says North Korea Is Still a Dangerous Military Threat," *New York Times*, September 22, 2000, p. A10.

5. At the Cairo Conference in 1943, Franklin D. Roosevelt, Winston Churchill, and Chiang Kai-shek announced that following the war, Korea would receive its independence "in due course." However, Roosevelt believed that might entail a period of trusteeship to prepare Korea for independence under US, Soviet, and Chinese guidance, a period Roosevelt thought might be 20-30 years.

6. It is important to note that the armistice was not a peace treaty. Recently, North Korea has made numerous efforts to replace the armistice with a permanent peace agreement. Given the South's refusal to sign the armistice, the North has maintained a new peace treaty should be concluded only between Washington and Pyongyang, a proposal that Seoul vigorously rejects.

7. Soon after the war, the US and South Korea signed a defense pact that committed the US to "act to meet the common danger in accordance with its constitutional processes." South Korea had hoped for wording to the effect of "an attack on one was an attack on both," wording that gave greater assurance of a prompt US response. However, the "constitutional processes" wording was required by the Congress, to prevent any usurpation of congressional power to declare war. The US also stationed two combat divisions in South Korea to act as a tripwire, further ensuring a US response should North Korea attack again. Since that time, US forces have gradually been reduced, at present to approximately 37,000.

8. Byung Chul Koh, "Unification Policy and North-South Relations," in Robert A. Scalapino and Jun-Yop Kim (eds.), *North Korea Today: Strategic and Domestic Issues* (Berkeley: Institute of East Asian Studies, University of California, 1983), pp. 274-75.

9. US Department of State, *American Foreign Policy: Current Documents, 1967* (Washington, DC: Government Printing Office, 1967), pp. 788-90.

10. Koh, p. 277.

11. Shortly after, North Korea seized the *Pueblo*, a US intelligence ship, in what the US maintained to be international waters. The ship and its crew were held for over a year. North Korean motives here were unclear. One scholar maintains that the seizure was not planned, and that, while Kim Il Sung delighted at this chance to embarrass the US, he and his generals "knew the price they had paid for such military adventurism" and realized they were lucky to have avoided a shooting war with the US over the issue. See Dae-Sook Suh, *Kim Il Sung: The North Korean Leader* (New York: Columbia University Press, 1988), pp. 233-4.

12. Rhee Sang Woo, *Security and Unification of Korea* (Seoul: Sogang University Press, 1984), p. 144.

13. Koh, p. 273.

14. In testimony before the Senate, US ambassador to South Korea William Porter provided his explanation for why the infiltrations decreased after 1968. "I think initially they were losing too many trained men to go on the way they were. I think that probably somebody had to account in North Korea for the loss of the 120, and then, of course, the 31 who participated in the Blue House raid . . .. No doubt, someone had advocated that kind of program and someone had to explain the lack of success." US Senate, *United States Security Agreements and Commitments Abroad: Republic of Korea*, Hearings before the Subcommittee on US Security Agreements and Commitments Abroad of the Committee on Foreign Relations, 91st Congress, 2nd Session, Part 6, February 24, 25, and 26, 1970 (Washington, DC: Government Printing Office, 1970), p. 1611. The following year, Kim Il Sung quietly purged several of his generals for these actions, which had brought the DPRK dangerously close to war. Suh, pp. 238-42.

15. Koh, p. 281.

16. Don Oberdorfer, *The Two Koreas* (Basic Books, 1997), pp. 260-61.

17. *New York Times*, June 15, 2000, p. A10. See Appendix 5.1 for the complete text of the agreement.

18. Howard W. French, "Defense Chiefs of Two Koreas Meet on Reducing Tensions," *New York Times*, September 26, 2000, p. A10.

19. Howard W. French, "After Pact on Rebuilt Railway, Two Koreas Plan More Talks," *New York Times*, September 27, 2000, p. A5.

20. David E. Sanger, "North Korean at White House, Continuing a Warming Trend," *New York Times*, October 11, 2000, p. A3.

21. Michael R. Gordon, "How Politics Sank Accord on Missiles with North Korea," *New York Times*, March 6, 2001, p. A1.

22. Jane Perlez, "Albright Reports Progress in Talks with North Korea," *New York Times*, October 25, 2000, p. A1.

23. David E. Sanger, "Clinton Scraps North Korea Trip, Saying Time's Short for Deal," *New York Times*, December 29, 2000, p. A13.

24. The membership of ASEAN is composed of Brunei, Cambodia, Indonesia, Laos, Malaysia, Myanmar, the Philippines, Singapore, Thailand, and Vietnam. ARF members include ASEAN states plus Australia, Canada, China, the European Union, India, Japan, Mongolia, New Zealand, North Korea, Papua New Guinea, Russia, South Korea, and the US.

25. The EU hoped this would "facilitate the European Community's efforts in support of reconciliation in the Korean Peninsula and, in particular, in support of economic reform and easing of the acute food and health problems" in North Korea. Suzanne Daley, "North Korea May Get Help Under Plan By Europeans," *New York Times*, May 15, 2001, p. A3.

26. "Great Strides Toward Opening," *Korea Now*, March 10, 2001, p. 9; and Howard French, "With US Pulling Back, North Korea Opens Up to Other Nations," *New York Times*, March 29, 2001, p. A11.

27. The first exchange occurred in 1985, but further reunions were halted soon over various disagreements.

28. In explaining its decision, North Korea cited an anti-terrorism security alert in South Korea. This is unlikely to be the true reason for the postponement.

29. The joint entrance took a good deal of negotiation. The number of North Korean athletes was considerably smaller than that from the South. In order for the states to have relatively equal numbers of athletes in the entering delegation, many ROK athletes could not join the procession.

30. David E. Sanger, "Bush Tells Seoul Talks with North Won't Resume Now," *New York Times*, March 8, 2001, p. A1.

31. After Bush made the remark, a White House spokesman clarified that the President's concern was directed toward any future agreements. Ibid.

32. "*Remarks by Secretary of State Colin Powell to the Pool*," March 7, 2001 <www.whitehouse.gov/news/releases/2001/03/20010307-3.html>.

33. Soon after the June summit, US officials changed the designation of states like North Korea from "rogue states" to "states of concern." However, that language has returned as the Bush administration increasingly uses Iraq and North Korea to argue for funding of a national missile defense system.

34. Don Kirk, "North Korea Turns Up the Heat; Calls US a Nation of Cannibals," *New York Times*, March 15, 2001, p. A8.

35. Don Kirk, "North Korea Refuses to Stop Arms Exports, Delegation Says," *New York Times*, May 5, 2001, p. A4.

36. Howard W. French, "North Korea Rebuffs US on Troop Talks," *New York Times*, June 19, 2001, p. A3.

37. At the October 2001 Asia-Pacific Economic Cooperation forum meeting in China, Bush urged Kim Jong Il to restart talks, stating "I would hope that he would accept not only our invitation, but seize the opportunity to bring more peaceful relations to the Korean peninsula. This is a moment in history where he can prove his worth." After affirming Kim Dae Jung's sunshine policy, President Bush continued, saying "I must tell you that I've been disappointed in Kim Jong Il not rising to the occasion, being so suspicious, so secretive." Soon after, North Korea shot back, declaring "It is a senseless attitude from even elementary diplomatic etiquette for the head of state of the US to speak ill of the leader of another country, who is a stranger to him, for no reason. Such reckless deed [*sic*] tells that he has no image as a politician, to say nothing of that of a head of state. Then, how can we trust the United States though it makes honeyed words?" Despite Bush's assertions that restarting negotiations was now up to North Korea, the Foreign Ministry continued, saying: "It is universally known that it was none other than Bush who began casting a string of doubts, saying he feels skeptical about the North Korean leader as soon as he assumed the presidential office. And it was again his administration which put the DPRK (North Korea)-US dialogue which was under way to a stalemate." See "Bush Seeks Meeting with N. Korea Leader," *The Associated Press*, Shanghai, October 19, 2001, and "N.Korea Says US Must Ease Stance for Talks to Resume," *Reuters, Tokyo*, October 23, 2001, as quoted in NAPSNet Daily Report, Nautilus Institute, October 19, 2001 <NAPSNet@nautilus.org>.

38. *The Military Balance, 1999/2000 and 2000/2001* (London: International Institute for Strategic Studies).

39. Don Kirk, "Threat From North Korea Rising, US Army Warns," *The International Herald Tribune, Seoul*, September 9, 2000, as contained in *Northeast Asia Peace and Security Network Daily Report*, September 8, 2000 <http://www.nautilus.org>. It is also important to note that, while critics of North Korea often point to their threatening forward deployments, South Korean and US forces are also forward deployed in an effort to halt any deep advance into ROK territory should the DPRK launch an invasion.

40. According to a report issued in 1999 by a US House of Representatives Advisory Group that was very critical of US policy, "North Korea is less capable of successfully invading and occupying South Korea today than it was five years ago, due to issues of readiness, sustainability, and modernization. It has, however, built an advantage in long-range artillery, short-range ballistic missiles, and special operations forces. This development, along with its chemical and biological weapons capability and forward-deployed forces, gives North Korea the ability to inflict significant casualties on US and South Korean military personnel and civilians in the earliest stages of any conflict." North Korea Advisory Group, "Report to The Speaker, US House of Representatives—Report Summary," p. 5 <http://www.house.gov/international_relations/nkag/report.htm>.

41. For more detailed discussion, see Michael J. Mazarr, *North Korea and the Bomb* (New York: St. Martin's Press, 1995); Leon Sigal, *Disarming Strangers: Nuclear Diplomacy with North Korea* (Princeton: Princeton University Press, 1998); Don Oberdorfer, *The Two Koreas* (Basic Books, 1997); and Scott Snyder, *Negotiat-*

ing on the Edge: North Korean Negotiating Behavior (Washington, DC: United States Institute of Peace Press, 1999).

42. South Korea provides the bulk of KEDO's funding, $3.2 billion, to construct the reactors. An ROK company, Korean Electric and Power Company (KEPCO), is the prime contractor. Japan contributes another $1 billion to the effort, and the European Union has given over $140 million. The US provides $55 million annually for 500,000 tons of fuel oil, to supplement the North's energy needs until the two light-water reactors come on line.

43. Tim Connolly, "US Urged to Talk with North Korea," *Dallas Morning News*, April 20, 2001, p. A24.

44. A major disagreement surfaced in 1998 when US satellites discovered an underground complex at Kumchangri in North Korea, which was suspected of being a nuclear weapons site. However, visits to the location in 1999 and 2000 by inspectors confirmed that the site was not used for nuclear weapons. North Korea cooperated fully with the visit. "US Inspects North Korean Military Site," *New York Times*, May 31, 2000, p. A14.

45. Nicholas D. Kristof, "North Koreans Declare They Launched a Satellite, Not a Missile," *New York Times*, September 5, 1998, p. A5.

46. Jane Perlez, "North Korea Urged Again Not to Test New Missile," *New York Times*, July 28, 1999, and Jane Perlez, "North Korea's Missile Pledge Paves the Way for New Talks," *New York Times*, June 22, 2000, p. A8.

47. Michael R. Gordon, "North Korea Reported Open to Halting Missile Program," *New York Times*, July 20, 2000, p. A6.

48. Michael R. Gordon, "How Politics Sank Accord on Missiles With North Korea," *New York Times*, March 6, 2001, p. A1.

49. Michael Wines, "North Korean, With Putin, Vows to Curb Missile Program," *New York Times*, August 5, 2001, p. A4.

50. Kim Hak-joon, "Prospects for Change under Kim Jong-il Regime," *New Asia* (Autumn 1998), reprinted in *Korea Focus* 6, 5, p. 29.

51. Marcus Noland, "Why North Korea Will Muddle Through," *Foreign Affairs* 76, 4, pp. 107-8.

52. Chun Chae-sung, "Missile Technology Control Regime and North Korea," *Korea Focus* 8, 1, p. 28.

53. Noland, p. 108.

54. Elisabeth Rosenthal, "North Korea Still in Need of Food Aid," *New York Times*, August 22, 2001, p. A7.

55. See Scott Snyder, *Negotiating on the Edge: North Korean Negotiating Behavior*.

56. Stephen Noerper, "Summit Success: Toward a New Stability on the Korean Peninsula," Northeast Asia Peace and Security Network Special Report, August 21, 2000 <*http://www.nautilus.org*>.

57. Snyder, p. 9.

58. According to Mazarr, " officials in Pyongyang learned how useful an ambiguous nuclear capability could be in getting the attention of the world community, wringing security concessions out of Seoul and Washington and acquiring pledges of economic assistance and expanded diplomatic relations." Mazarr, *North Korea and the Bomb*, p. 182.

59. Selig Harrison makes an interesting point here. In addition to fears of US moves in Korea, Pyongyang is also deeply concerned about Japanese intentions to develop nuclear weapons. As a result, North Korea may be more willing to forgo re-

search and development of the long range *Taepodong* missiles that can reach the US, but less eager to halt manufacture and deployment of the medium range *Nodong* missile that can target Japan and US military bases there. Selig S. Harrison, "Time to Leave Korea?" *Foreign Affairs* 80, 2, p. 65.

60. As quoted in ibid., p. 64.

61. Michael J. Mazarr, "Going Just a Little Nuclear," *International Security* 20, 2, pp. 92-122.

62. Victor D. Cha, "Engaging North Korea Credibly," *Survival* 42, 2, p. 138.

63. "Where Roads Converge," *Korea Now*, September 22, 2001, p. 5.

64. Ibid., p. 7.

65. "Hostility Subsides at DMZ," *Korea Now*, July 1, 2000, p. 7.

66. "More Funds, Less Guns," *Korea Now*, September 9, 2000, p. 6.

67. Craig S. Smith, "Shanghai Gets Visit by Chief Of North Korea," *New York Times*, January 18, 2001, p. A9, and Kim Ji-ho, "North Korea Braces for Economic Reform," *Korea Herald*, January 22, 2001.

68. Michael R. Gordon, "US Toughens Terms for North Korea Talks," *New York Times*, July 3, 2001, p. A7.

69. Victor D. Cha, "Engaging North Korea Credibly," p. 149.

70. According to Kim Dae Jung, during one of his meetings with Kim Jong Il during the summit, the North Korean leader remarked something to the effect that, "We are surrounded by big powers—Russia, Japan and China—so the United States must continue to stay for stability and peace in East Asia." There is considerable doubt concerning North Korea's commitment to this position, since it never publicly confirmed the statement. Jane Perlez, "South Korean Says North Agrees US Troops Should Stay," *New York Times*, September 11, 2000, p. A3.

71. Michael Wines, "North Korean, With Putin, Vows to Curb Missile Program," *New York Times*, August 5, 2001, p. A4.

6

The "Sunshine" Policy Revisited: An Analysis of South Korea's Policy toward North Korea

Uk Heo and Chong-Min Hyun

Since Kim Dae Jung took office as president in 1998, South Korea's approach toward North Korea has changed dramatically, from a hard-line policy based on the Cold War mentality to an engagement policy (called the "sunshine" policy).[1] This change was expected because of Kim Dae Jung's already-introduced unification policy, which is based on the gradual increase of exchanges between the two Koreas until unification is completed.[2] The "sunshine" policy, therefore, is the initial step of President Kim Dae Jung's unification policy.

The core of the "sunshine" policy is bringing North Korea out of isolation and integrating it into world politics. For that purpose, Seoul has not only provided food and economic aid to Pyongyang, but has also eased its own regulations on South Korean business activities in North Korea. As a result, business between the two Koreas increased and overall relations between Seoul and Pyongyang improved. The most successful example of the "sunshine" policy may be the 2000 summit meeting between the two Koreas.

The "sunshine" policy was generally supported by the US Clinton administration. Washington wanted to negotiate an end to North Korea's development of nuclear weapons and long-range missiles, and easing tensions between the two Koreas seemed an advance toward that goal. Therefore, Washington and Pyongyang were engaged in a series of talks covering nuclear and missile issues and overall improvement of the US-DPRK relationship. As a result, North Korea's Vice Marshal Jo Myong-rok met with President Bill Clinton in October 2000, and US Secretary of State Madeleine Albright reciprocated by visiting Pyongyang.

Since George W. Bush took office, however, the overall picture between the three countries has changed. The reason is that the Bush administration has employed a hard-line policy toward North Korea, emphasizing reciprocity between aid and nuclear and long-range missile development. Washington has even said that it is not going to provide any more aid until Pyongyang makes significant changes—although Washington is willing to resume dialogue and continue humanitarian aid.

This approach is different from the Clinton administration's, which heavily relied on carrots (economic and food aid) to stop North Korea from developing nuclear weapons and long-range missiles. This change has led the South Korean government to be concerned about potential discord between the US and South Korea with respect to North Korea policy. In order to fine-tune, South Korean Foreign Affairs and Trade Minister Lee Joung-binn and Director of the National Intelligence Service (NIS) Lim Dong-won visited the United States in February 2001. In the US-South Korea summit meeting on March 7, 2001, George W. Bush and Kim Dae Jung also discussed how to approach North Korea, but failed to agree on a joint framework. In the meeting, the two leaders only confirmed that there is a difference in their perception of North Korea. How to coordinate South Korean and US policies was left to future discussions.

In this paper, we revisit the "sunshine" policy to analyze how effective the policy has been in dealing with North Korea. We also attempt to make policy suggestions for Seoul, in order to make the "sunshine" policy work better in a changed international environment.

The paper consists of four parts. First, we analyze the inter-Korean relationship using a simple game. Second, we describe the "sunshine" policy in the context of the evolution of South Korea's policy toward North Korea over time. Third, we discuss Washington's role in the inter-Korean relationship. Finally, we make some policy suggestions designed to make the "sunshine" policy more effective.

A GAME-THEORETIC ANALYSIS OF THE INTER-KOREAN RELATIONSHIP

In this section, we attempt to explain the inter-Korean relationship using simple game theory. The inter-Korean relationship resembles the prisoner's dilemma game. The reason is that these two countries, although they have common as well as conflicting interests, do not trust each other. They both know that an arms race is not good for them. But due to a lack of confidence in each other, neither side has been willing to make a positive gesture prior to the recent "sunshine" policy. Thus, the inter-Korean relationship can be described using a prisoner's dilemma setting (Figure 6.1).[3] Figure 6.1 describes the inter-Korean relationship as a one-shot game. However, the repeated version of this game would be a more accurate description of the relationship.

As described in Figure 6.1, South Korea has two broad options: (1) armaments (improving its military power to better defend itself and to absorb North Korea by force); and (2) peace (providing economic aid to encourage peaceful coexistence). North Korea also has two general options: (1) armaments (continuing to develop nuclear and conventional weapon systems and long-range missiles to strengthen the military, to better defend itself, and to absorb South Korea by force); and (2) peace (opening the country to the rest of the world and receiving economic aid from South Korea, the US, and others). The game depicts South Korea's options as the two rows of the figure and North Korea's as the two columns.

Figure 6.1
The Inter-Korean Relationship

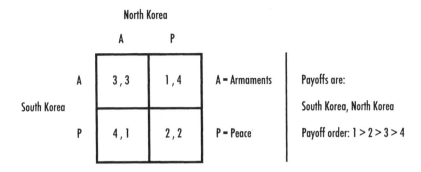

The combination of the choices made by these countries determines the outcome of the game. The game represents the outcomes of each intersection of choices as an ordered pair {x, y}, where x is the outcome for South Korea and y is the outcome for North Korea. Each outcome is a cardinal number from 1 to 4, where 1 is the most preferred outcome and 4 the least preferred.

In this game, both countries attempt to obtain the greatest payoff from the game. In their calculation of the payoffs, both countries try to maximize economic development and military strength. The reason is that these two countries do not trust each other. Therefore they want to make sure that their security is firmly guaranteed. At the same time, they want to develop their economies. Given that economic prosperity is an important element of national power, this is a reasonable assumption. The relative importance of strengthening the military as against pursuing economic development varies over time.

The optimization of the prisoner's dilemma game in a one-shot game setting produces an outcome called a Nash equilibrium. Given the choice of the other actor, neither actor can obtain a better outcome by choosing another option. In other words, each country's policy choice is the best response to the other country's strategy according to an expected payoff calculation. The ordered pairs in Figure 6.1 represent the interaction between South Korea and North Korea. In the game, both Koreas prefer to focus on strengthening their militaries (maintaining the status quo), regardless of the other's strategy. This is the reason that, since the division of the country in 1945, both Koreas have been involved in an arms race.

However, the Nash equilibrium described above is an outcome in a one-shot game. The actual inter-Korean relationship is, however, a repeated game of the prisoner's dilemma. According to Robert Axelrod, a tit-for-tat strategy, in which each player reciprocates the other's strategy, is most likely to be employed in the repeated prisoner's dilemma situation.[4] In other words, if either country starts employing a "peace" strategy—such as South Korea's "sunshine" policy of providing economic aid and using cooperative rhetoric—the other is likely to follow the same path. The question is whether North Korea is really going to follow this path. In the next section, we first discuss the evolution of South Korea's policy toward North Korea and then we apply the game discussed here to the current inter-Korean relationship. Later, we also discuss relevant factors that may affect the outcome of this repeated game, such as the role of international actors.

THE EVOLUTION OF SOUTH KOREA'S NORTH KOREA POLICY

The Rhee Syngman and Chang Myon Administrations

With the establishment of the South Korean government in 1948, South Korea considered North Korea an illegal entity occupying the northern territory of the Korean Peninsula. According to the National Assembly Resolution of September 12, 1948, the Republic of Korea (ROK) is the sole legitimate government with sovereignty over the whole Korean Peninsula. The United Nations (UN), in its third general assembly meeting on December 12, 1949, also recognized the ROK government as the sole legitimate government of the Korean Peninsula. With the UN's recognition, President Syngman Rhee stated on January, 31 1950, that the ROK has the right to use force to recover the northern part of the peninsula should the free will of the people in the North continue to be repressed.[5] In other words, the main policy position toward North Korea (unification policy) during the Rhee administration was forceful absorption. However, this changed after the Korean War.

In 1950, North Korea crossed the 38th parallel to unify the country. With the UN intervention, the war ceased. However, the damage caused by the war was huge, leading people to rethink the method of unification. On May 3, 1960, Heo Jung, the head of the interim government, announced that South Korea would pursue peaceful unification under the UN resolutions.[6] Since then, South Korea has maintained a peaceful unification policy along with strong anti-communism.

The Park Chung Hee Administration

Although Park Chung Hee announced that South Korea's security policy was based strongly on anti-communism, his policy approach was different from his predecessor's. In contrast to Rhee's policy of unification first and development next, Park Chung Hee argued that economic development should be the primary objective. Thus, Hee changed Seoul's approach to reunification by recognizing North Korea. On August 15, 1970, Hee announced that South Korea would not oppose North Korea's presence during the United Nations (UN) deliberation on the Korean question, as long as North Korea recognized the UN's efforts for the achievement of a unified, democratic, and independent Korea and accepted the UN's authority.[7] This announcement had two important implications. First, South Korea was willing to accept peaceful coexistence for now and pursue unification later. Second, President Park Chung Hee regarded economic development as the basis of national power.[8]

With this positive gesture, Seoul and Pyongyang had a number of contacts between government officials. As a result of these meetings, the two countries agreed upon the three principles of unification announced in the joint communiqué of July 4, 1972: (1) unification shall be achieved without external influence or interference; (2) unification shall be achieved through peaceful means; and (3) a great national unity shall be sought transcending differences in ideas, ideologies, and systems.[9] However, nothing was followed up because of conflicting interests between the two countries.

All of the Park administration's efforts to conduct a dialogue with the North were unsuccessful. With the lack of contacts, both countries were heavily involved in an arms race. For instance, South Korea's military spending was 5 to 6 percent of GNP, which is about 30 percent of the government budget. Despite the high levels of defense spending during the Park administration, South Korea still managed high rates of economic growth. North Korea is estimated to have spent even more of its GNP on its military, and the North Korean economy struggled.

The Chun Doo Hwan and Roh Tae Woo Administrations

On January 12, 1981, South Korean President Chun Doo Hwan proposed a summit meeting to discuss all the issues related to unification. He invited North Korean President Kim Il Sung to visit Seoul without any preconditions. On January 22, 1982, President Chun proposed to create a South-North consultative conference for the purpose of drafting a constitution of a unified Korea. However, North Korea rejected all these proposals. After the October 1983 Rangoon incident, in which North Korean agents set off a bomb that killed a number of visiting South Korean government officials, contacts between the two countries stopped.[10]

On July 7, 1988, President Roh Tae Woo resumed efforts to ease tensions between the two Koreas. In the special presidential declaration for National Self-Esteem, Unification, and Prosperity, President Roh announced that South Korea would actively promote exchanges and visits between the people of South and North Korea and would make necessary arrangements to ensure that Koreans residing overseas could freely visit both Koreas. He also proposed that both Koreas open doors for trade and cooperate to achieve balanced development of the national economy.

Although these efforts did not materialize, the two Koreas finally joined the UN in September 1991. Moreover, the two Koreas signed the Agreement on Reconciliation, Nonaggression and Exchanges and Cooperation in December 1991. With this agreement, the two Koreas agreed to recognize each other's political systems and pledged not to intervene in each other's domestic affairs. This was an important change in the inter-Korean relationship.[11] Moreover, the two Koreas also signed the "Joint Declaration on the Denuclearization of the Korean Peninsula."[12] This was designed to stop North Korean nuclear development, although it appears that North Korea has not fulfilled her obligations under the agreement.

In January 1993, the US and South Korea announced the Team Spirit military drill. North Korea threatened that there would be no dialogue between the two Koreas if the US-South Korea joint military drills did not stop. With the Team Spirit drills continuing, dialogue between the two countries stopped.

The Kim Young Sam Administration

When President Kim Young Sam came to power in 1993, there was no contact between the two Koreas. In his inauguration speech, President Kim Young Sam proposed a summit meeting between the two Koreas. However, the inter-Korean relationship did not improve for two reasons: (1) the North Korean nuclear crisis developed, which led North Korea to withdraw from the Nuclear Nonproliferation Treaty (NPT); and (2) South Korea and the US continued the Team Spirit military drill.

In order to solve the North Korean nuclear crisis, Seoul proposed high-level talks. North Korea agreed, and five high-level discussions were held. In 1994, Pyongyang proposed a summit meeting. After two preliminary meetings, the summit meeting was scheduled in Pyongyang on July 25-27. However, Kim Il Sung died on July 8 and the meeting was cancelled. All contacts between Seoul and Pyongyang also stopped.

In order to improve the inter-Korean relationship, the Kim Young Sam administration examined various alternatives. The outcome was a four-party formula also including the US and China. On April 16, 1996, the US and South Korea proposed a four-party summit. Moreover, Seoul announced that it would not oppose US-North Korea talks if North Korea participated in the four-party talks. This proposal, according to Koo, was significant in a number of ways. First, with this proposal, Seoul changed its policy on US-North Korea relations. Until then, South Korea had insisted that the relationship between Washington and Pyongyang should be contingent upon the improvement of inter-Korean relations. However, with the four-party talks proposal, Seoul no longer insisted on its erstwhile linkage policy and allowed Washington and Pyongyang to engage in political talks separate from the four-party talks. Second, the four-party talks proposal involved Washington's recognition of Pyongyang, which opened the door for US economic aid to North Korea.[13]

With the September 1996 incursion of North Korean submarines into South Korean waters, tensions mounted. Despite these tensions, four-party talks were held twice, on December 9, 1997, and on March 16, 1998. However, the talks failed to produce any meaningful results.

The Kim Dae Jung Administration and the "Sunshine" Policy

Before Kim Dae Jung came to power, he introduced a unification policy design called the "three principles and three stages unification formula." The three principles are "peaceful coexistence, peaceful exchange, and peaceful unification." The three stages consist of the first stage of union of the republic (or the state), the second stage of union by federalism, and the third stage of completed unification.[14] This policy design requires acknowledging each other's existence, building confidence for economic exchanges, and making sincere efforts to cooperate to reach unification.

In order to implement his unification policy design, Kim Dae Jung announced three principles of South Korea's security policy toward North Korea: (1) maintenance of a solid security posture, (2) no pursuit of unification through absorption, and (3) improvement of inter-Korean relations by actively promoting exchange and cooperation in various fields. Given that the two Koreas have confronted each other numerous times in the past several decades, Kim Dae Jung clarified that all efforts to assure South Korea's security would include commensurate efforts to improve the inter-Korean relationship. For example, the presence of US troops in South Korea is perceived to be positively contributing to the regional order.[15]

Since German reunification, North Korea has been concerned about being absorbed by the South. Thus, the lingering food shortages in North Korea generated much speculation about the collapse of the North Korean regime.[16] For instance, in his outgoing speech on December 29, 1996, former US Central Intelligence Agency Director John Deutsch predicted the demise of the North Korean regime.[17] On April 10, 1997, after completing a round of top-level consultations in South Korea, US Defense Secretary William Cohen also viewed the food crisis as a sign that the communist government in Pyongyang was headed for collapse.[18] Newspapers also reported that the most recent North Korean missile test may be an effort to conceal instability.[19] Thus, Seoul made it clear that South Korea pursues balanced prosperity in the whole Korean Peninsula, rather than absorption. Seoul also stated that it regards North Korea as a partner on the road to peaceful unification.

As a first step to peaceful unification, Kim Dae Jung wanted to improve exchange and cooperation between the two Koreas. This principle suggests that promotion of mutually beneficial relations through exchange and cooperation in all fields is the best way toward a common national community. Thus, economic activities have been encouraged, and the Seoul government removed the ceiling on investment by South Korean companies in North Korea. This move opened up opportunities for many private sector companies to start businesses in North Korea—most notably, the large-scale tourism business conducted by the South Korean conglomerate Hyundai.[20]

According to Kihl , there are two reasons for separating non-political activities from politics. First, Seoul wants to assure the US and Japan that they could change their policies toward North Korea, on the grounds that normalization between these countries will enhance the engagement of North Korea with the rest of the world. Second, due to limited resources, the South Korean government cannot provide "enough" economic aid to North Korea; so the government wants the private sector to contribute to the efforts.[21]

SEOUL'S "SUNSHINE" POLICY AND PYONGYANG'S RESPONSE

During the Cold War, both South and North Korea pursued an arming method, like that in the Nash equilibrium of the one-shot prisoner's dilemma game described in Figure 6.1. The reason is that they both wanted to maximize security. However, South Korea's economy developed over time while North Korea's did not. Currently South Korea's GNP per capita is eleven times higher than that of North Korea, and its GNP is twenty times higher. Thus, Seoul feels comfortable enough to pursue a peaceful strategy, such as the "sunshine" policy.

President Kim Dae Jung argues that economic exchanges between the South and the North will ease tensions on the Korean Peninsula and help prompt reform of the North Korean economy. To this end, Seoul has provided a lot of economic aid, including food and fertilizer, to Pyongyang. Moreover, business ties between the two countries rapidly increased through subcontracting arrangements. Since average wages in the South are ten times higher than those in the North, many South Korean companies—particularly small and medium-sized companies—pursued this route to make quick profits. As a result, more than 200 South Korean companies have subcontracting relationships with North Korean manufacturers, and Hyundai is going to develop one of the investment zones at Kaesong in addition to the tourism business.[22] In sum, the South-North economic cooperation has increased dramatically, although North Korea has hardly reduced its efforts to strengthen the military.

According to Horowitz, there are reasons for Seoul to provide aid and promote trade and investment with the North. The most important one is reducing the possibility that North Korea, due to its severe economic conditions, might launch a desperate invasion of the South.[23] In addition, an improved relationship is likely to reduce tensions between the two countries, which will provide a better environment for economic activities.

Despite Seoul's positive gesture, Pyongyang has not reciprocated. The lack of reciprocity led the opposition Grand National Party to criticize the "sunshine" policy and question its effectiveness. Moreover, Hyundai's tourist business in North Korea has been a failure, creating another obstacle to the continuation of the Kim Dae Jung administration's "sunshine" policy.[24] The South Korean economy has been struggling since the 1997 financial crisis; but despite economic difficulties and the lack of reciprocity, the Kim Dae Jung government has continued to provide aid to the North.

BUSH'S NORTH KOREA POLICY AND ITS IMPACT ON THE "SUNSHINE" POLICY

Since George W. Bush took office, there has been a lot of concern in South Korea about how the Bush administration's policy toward North Korea may affect the improved inter-Korean relationship. With the recent revelation of Bush's hard-line North Korea policy, the concern has increased. However, Washington's current approach to Pyongyang—dialogue with transparency and reciprocity—is likely to continue for a number of reasons. First, Seoul's "sunshine" policy has backfired, due to the lack of reciprocity from Pyongyang. For instance, despite Seoul's economic and food aid, Pyongyang has made no contribution to easing tensions on the Korean Peninsula. As a result, the South Korean public is becoming skeptical about the effectiveness of the "sunshine" policy.

In addition, according to General Thomas A. Schwartz, Commander in Chief of the US-Korea combined forces, North Korea continues to invest 25 to 33 percent of its GNP annually in the military despite its great economic difficulties. As a result, the 1.2 million-strong North Korean forces are "bigger, better, closer, and deadlier than before the summit meeting."[25] Schwartz describes the recent North Korean military improvement as follows:

Recent force improvements include forward repositioning key offensive units, emplacing anti-tank barriers in the forward areas, establishing combat positions along major routes between Pyongyang and the Demilitarized Zone, improving coastal defense forces in the forward area, constructing missile support facilities, and procuring air defense weapons and fighter aircraft. Applying lessons from US operations in Europe and Southwest Asia, the North Koreas also modified key facility defenses, dispersed forces, and improved camouflage, concealment, and deception measures. Training levels over the past two years have been record-breaking, with the focus on improving the readiness of major offensive forces. Immediately following the June 2000 summit, the North Korea People's Army training cycle in the summer of 2000 was the most extensive ever recorded. It was preceded by the most ambitious winter training cycle for the past ten years. High levels of training continue as we speak to you today.[26]

Because of North Korea's continuing efforts to improve its military, US Department of Defense (DOD) and Central Intelligence Agency (CIA) officials raised the possibility that North Korea is diverting South Korea's cash aid through Hyundai's tourism business to military preparations. Moreover, the US considers North Korea a "rogue state," due to its efforts to develop nuclear weapons and long-range missiles. Controlling nuclear and missile development is deemed critical to US security. This is why, during the Clinton administration, the Geneva Agreed Framework was signed and missile talks occurred. In the Geneva Agreed Framework, the US promised to provide North Korea with crude oil in exchange for giving up nuclear development. The oil aid is to be provided until South Korea and Japan finish building two light-water nuclear reactors in the North. However, the Bush administration is not sure that North Korea has fully complied with the agreement. Therefore, Washington wants Pyongyang to make significant policy changes before discussing improvement of relations between the two countries. These changes may include opening up the economy, reducing conventional weapons, and giving up nuclear and missile development and exports.

However, these expectations are difficult for North Korea to meet in the near future, because North Korea has remained a closed Stalinist country for several decades. Opening up the country immediately may change the perception and attitude of the North Korean people toward the government, which may create a problem for the leadership. Reducing conventional weapons systems may leave the North Korean leaders with a feeling of insecurity. Therefore, North Korea needs time to make changes. In spite of that, North Korea has signaled the possibility for change. For instance, Kim Jong Il indicated that North Korea might attempt to follow the Chinese economic development model by partially opening up the economy. Recent North Korean economic officials' visits to US industrial sites and to Wall Street are another possible sign of change.

North Korea is signaling the possibility of change to the US because Pyongyang needs Washington's help. North Korea has been undergoing severe food shortages and economic difficulties for over a decade. Regardless of the type of government, long-lasting economic difficulties can be a threat to regime survival. That is why Pyongyang is considering opening up its economy. Due to its poor economic infrastructure, however, North Korea needs extra help for its effort to have a serious chance of success. In addition to foreign direct investment, the North also needs financial assistance from international organizations, such as the IMF and World Bank. In order to get all these, it is necessary for Pyongyang to obtain Washington's support, including complete removal of US economic sanctions.

In the recent foreign ministerial talks, US Secretary of State Colin Powell asked the South Korean government to play the role of mediator between Washington and Pyongyang. This request implies that the US government does not want to use force and is willing to talk with North Korea. North Korea has also expressed an interest in negotiating with the Bush administration under the Geneva Agreed Framework. In other words, both Washington and Pyongyang have interests in improving the relationship and have something to offer each other. This provides South Korea with an opportunity to implement the engagement policy more successfully than before.

FACTORS AFFECTING THE SUCCESS OF THE "SUNSHINE" POLICY AND POLICY SUGGESTIONS FOR THE SOUTH KOREAN GOVERNMENT

With President Bush's hard-line policy toward North Korea, the international environment has changed. Moreover, North Korea has not employed a tit-for-tat strategy, as Axelrod predicts for a repeated game of the prisoner's dilemma. In this situation, how can the "sunshine" policy succeed? That will depend on three things: 1) How long can the South continue to employ this policy without a positive response from the North? 2) Will North Korea reciprocate, and if so, when? (3) What kind of role will the US play in the inter-Korean relationship? The first two factors are related to each other, since Seoul can continue to provide economic aid to Pyongyang if Pyongyang cooperates to reduce tensions.

Until recently, it has been believed that Pyongyang perceives that being engaged with Seoul would increase the risk of weakening its regime security. That is why Pyongyang has allowed only limited material and human exchanges. On the other hand, Seoul needs some confidence that Pyongyang will not take any military measures to reunify the country. Therefore, confidence-building between the two countries is necessary for the success of the "sunshine" policy.

For confidence-building measures, Seoul made several proposals to Pyongyang in 1990, which are as follows:

1.   Prior notification of military movements and exercises above the brigade level, and mutual invitations to observe the military exercises.
2.   Withdrawal of forward-deployed offensive arms and troops to rear areas and reduction of offensive arms and troops to prevent surprise attack and recurrence of war.
3.   Maintenance of military balance based upon parity in the arms and troops of both sides, namely, the superior side's reduction of its arms and troops to the level of the inferior side.

4. Reduction of troops corresponding to that of arms, and reduction of reserve and paramilitary personnel corresponding to that of armed forces.
5. On-the-spot verification and monitoring to guarantee the implementation of the agreements in the process of arms reduction, and the establishment and operation of both a joint verification team and a standing monitoring team for the purpose.
6. Decision about a final military strength level should be made by mutual consultation based upon the expected level of military strength appropriate to the unified nation.

However, North Korea did not respond to the proposals, and there has been no discussion of confidence-building measures or arms reduction since 1991. According to Goodby, Seoul and Pyongyang cannot agree on confidence-building measures due to their different purposes and perspectives. Seoul wants to test the possibilities for cooperation and convey security benefits by reducing the risks of miscalculation or surprise attack. On the other hand, Pyongyang wants to use confidence-building measures to achieve progress in the political and economic areas.[27] Since both parties know what the other wants, the only question left would be how they can compromise to achieve the goals. Thus, Goodby recommends the European confidence-building measures employed in 1994. The measures are as follows:

1. Information on organization, manpower, and weapons/equipment, including plans for deployments of weapons/equipment.
2. Information on defense planning, including defense policy and doctrine and force plans.
3. Consultation and cooperation as regards unusual military activities and hazardous incidents.
4. Voluntary hosting of visits.
5. Military-to-military contacts.
6. Joint military exercises and training to work on tasks of mutual interest.
7. Prior notification and observation of certain military activities, including an annual calendar of such activities.
8. Constraints on size and frequency of exercises and prohibition of any large unannounced exercises.
9. Inspections and evaluations.
10. An improved communications network.
11. An annual implementation assessment meeting.[28]

Although not all of these can be adopted on the Korean Peninsula, some could certainly be employed. This is why South Korea wants to discuss military issues, such as installing a hot line between the two leaderships, sharing information on the size and deployment of military forces, and allowing mutual observation of military exercises.[29] President Kim Dae Jung said that "the talks will help the Koreas ease tension and build up confidence in each other by establishing a hot line between the two military authorities and exchanging information about the movements of military units and the sizes of drills."[30]

Getting North Korea to agree to some of these measures will depend on how Seoul approaches Pyongyang. The "sunshine" policy has three guidelines: separation of politics and economics, the reciprocity rule, and the linkage of issues for negotiation. However, with the separation of politics and economics, these guidelines have not been implemented. For instance, no agreement in response to providing fertilizer to the North in 1998 was reached. This failure of the reciprocity rule and linkage of issues for negotiation can undermine South Korean public support for the government's "sunshine" policy. This is the reason that Seoul changed its reciprocity policy to the principle of "provide first and expect later."

Then, how do we get Pyongyang to reciprocate Seoul's peace-oriented policy? In addition to economic aid, some type of pressure (or motivation) must be brought to bear. In order to do this, as Kihl pointed out, cooperation between the US, Japan, and South Korea is critical.[31] Thus far, Seoul has tried to take the initiative in approaching North Korea. The US has been interested in preventing North Korea from developing nuclear weapons and long-range missiles. Japan has been interested in normalizing relations with North Korea. North Korea has taken advantage of this ineffective coordination of North Korea policy by Seoul, Tokyo, and Washington. Therefore, synchronized action from the US, Japan, and South Korea will affect the success of the "sunshine" policy. The synchronized action should start by discussing the approach to North Korea before taking any policy actions, and by employing agreed-upon tactics (aid or pressure) jointly. For instance, when economic aid is provided, Seoul as well as Washington needs to demand a return for the favor, such as sharing military information. If Pyongyang refuses to do so, aid must be stopped. Since North Korea is in desperate need of economic aid and thus needs help from Seoul and Washington, North Korea will come to dialogue.[32] Effective negotiations may be possible if this approach is performed with a yeoman-like tenacity and consistency.[33] Thus, Seoul should try to play the mediator role between Washington and Pyongyang. In the process, Seoul should also require Pyongyang to reciprocate the "sunshine" policy.

Another type of potential pressure measure is severing all the food aid. Forty percent of North Korea's population relies on foreign food aid. Without the foreign food aid, North Korea's food crisis would be much more severe, which would affect the public view of the leadership in Pyongyang. By synchronizing the measure with the US with respect to aid (continuing and/or severing) depending on North Korea's reaction, the "Sunshine" policy could be much more effective than it has been.

CONCLUSION AND DISCUSSION

During the Cold War, according to Koo, there were structural constraints on inter-Korean relations, such as the rivalry between the US and the Soviet Union.[34] However, the end of the Cold War removed the constraints, and nowadays South and North Korea can be the primary actors in pursuing reunification. However, that is only possible if North Korea is interested in peaceful unification, beginning with cultural and economic exchanges. However, because of North Korea's nuclear program and long-range missiles, the US does not want to be left out. Moreover, Pyongyang seems to be more interested in dealing with Washington than with Seoul. Because of that, Pyongyang has not employed a tit-for-tat strategy in dealing with Seoul. Thus, some kind of change is necessary for the "sunshine" policy to work better.

The change should be based on the current situation. North Korea has experienced food shortages, and this problem cannot be resolved without Seoul's help.[35] In other words, Seoul has some bargaining leverage that can be used to pressure the North. The key here is Seoul's willingness to wait with patience. Pyongyang is unlikely to respond to the pressure immediately. Therefore, patience and tenacity are critical.

Another important factor is that there are other international actors, such as the US, Japan, and other international organizations and programs, which can also help North Korea. Seoul needs to take advantage of these international actors to make the "sunshine" policy work better. As reported in news media, Washington is not very happy with Pyongyang. Thus, Seoul must take advantage of Washington's concern to apply pressure to the North.

When Seoul first introduced the engagement (sunshine) policy, it started as an effort to bring Pyongyang out of isolation and thus ease tension on the Korean Peninsula. In the beginning, reciprocity was one of the policy principles. After vice-ministerial talks were cancelled in 1998 and 1999, however, the principle changed to "provide first and expect later." Since then, Seoul has had a tendency to rush in its approach to Pyongyang, which resulted in Pyongyang's insincere negotiation attitude. Using the opportunity to play the mediator role between Washington and Pyongyang, Seoul can try to change Pyongyang's attitude. The reason is that the Bush administration's new policy may provide Seoul with a possible stick, which is a critical means of successful foreign policy. Thus, Seoul needs to take time to find a common denominator that both Washington and Pyongyang can accept. By doing so, Seoul can solidify its initiative in the North Korean negotiations and return to the original reciprocity principle of the engagement policy. As discussed in General Schwartz' statement before the US Senate Armed Services Committee, unilateral aid without reciprocity will not take Seoul where it want's to be with the "sunshine" policy.

In conclusion, it is time for Seoul's engagement policy to change. To make the "sunshine" policy more effective, Seoul needs to form a new cooperative framework with Washington in approaching North Korea.

NOTES

1. On July 25, 1998, the South Korean government announced that it would no longer use the expression "sunshine," because North Koreans might be misled to think of it as an absorption policy. However, the expression has been commonly used in academic and policy discussions. US Deputy Secretary of State Richard Armitage recently suggested that Seoul change the name to "engagement" policy. See Kihl Young Whan (1998), "Seoul's Engagement Policy and US-DPRK Relations," *Korean Journal of Defense Analysis* 10, 1, p. 21.

2. Before coming to power, Kim Dae Jung introduced a unification policy design called the "three principles and three stages unification formula." The three principles include "peaceful coexistence, peaceful exchange, and peaceful unification," and the three stages consist of "the union of the republic (state), union by federalism, and completed unification."

3. See Peter C. Ordeshook, *Game Theory and Political Theory: An Introduction* (Cambridge: Cambridge University Press, 1986); Eric Rasmussen, *Games and Information: An Introduction to Game Theory* (Cambridge, MA: Basil Blackwell, 1989); George Tsebelis, *Nested Games: Rational Choice in Comparative Politics* (Berkeley: University of California Press, 1990).

4. Robert Axelrod, *The Evolution of Cooperation* (New York: Basic Books, 1984).

5. Jung, Kyu-Seop, "Unification Diplomacy," in Kim, Dal-Choong, ed., *Korea's Foreign Policy* [in Korean] (Seoul: Orum Publishers, 1998), pp. 235-60.

6. Jung, "Unification Diplomacy," pp. 236-40.

7. Ministry of Unification, http://www.unikorea.go.kr.

8. A theoretical base of this argument can be found in international conflict literature. For instance, proponents of power transition theory such as A.F.K. Organski, Jacek Kugler, and David Lemke argue that economic power can be easily converted to military power. Thus, they use Gross National Product (GNP) as an indicator of national power in their study of international conflicts. See A.F.K. Organski and Jacek Kugler, *The War Ledger* (Chicago: University of Chicago Press, 1980).

9. Ministry of National Unification, *A White Paper on National Unification, 1997* [in Korean] (Seoul: Ministry of National Unification, 1997), p. 26.

10. Ministry of Unification, http://www.unikorea.go.kr.

11. By joining the UN, both Koreas are now formally recognized as sovereign countries by the world community.

12. Koo, Bon-Hak (1998), "Challenges and Prospects for Inter-Korean Relations Under the New Leadership," *Korean Journal of Defense Analysis* 10, 1, p. 79.

13. Kim, Dae Jung, *Three-Phased Unification by Kim Dae Jung* [in Korean] (Seoul: Asia-Pacific Peace Press, 1995), pp. 34-44.

14. Kihl, "Seoul's Engagement Policy and US-DPRK Relations," p. 22.

15. Koo, "Challenges and Prospects for Inter-Korean Relations Under the New Leadership," p. 85.

16. See Heo, Uk, Kwang H. Ro, and Chong-Min Hyun (2000), "Redirecting South Korean Security Policy," *Pacific Focus* 15, 1, p. 61.

17. *Los Angeles Times*, 30 December 1996.

18. *Voice of America*, 10 April 1997.

19. *Digital Chosun Ilbo*, 31 August 1998.

20. Mr. Chung Ju-Young, the former CEO of Hyundai, also delivered 500 head of cattle during his visit to North Korea to discuss the business projects.

21. On June 10, 1998, President Kim Dae Jung explained why the "sunshine" policy is needed in his address at the joint session of the US Congress, as follows: "To lead North Korea toward reconciliation, the Republic of Korea and the United States should promote a 'sunshine' policy—offering inducements against the backdrop of strong security measures. And we should extend to North Korea both goodwill and sincerity, so suspicion dissolves and openness emerges ... Above all, we need a flexible policy. To get a passerby to take off his coat, so the fable goes, sunshine is more effective than a strong wind ... We hope such an overall approach gives North Korea psychological room to open its mind—and its doors. To be sure, we will never relax our vigilance against North Korea. But neither will we be afraid of pursue peace" (cited in Kihl, "Seoul's Engagement Policy and US-DPRK Relations," pp. 30-31).

22. Selig S. Harrison (2000), "Time to Leave Korea?" *Foreign Affairs* 80, 2, pp. 71-72.

23. Shale Horowitz (2001), "Reconstructing Conflict in East Asia: Preserving Two Koreas, and Moving towards One China and One Taiwan," *Pacific Focus* 41, 1, p. 53.

24. In order to help Hyundai continue its North Korean business, the Kim Dae Jung government provided more than 860 billion won ($682 million) in fresh loans. This move was criticized by the opposition party, because of potential conflicts with World Trade Organization (WTO) rules. See *Korea Herald*, 3 February 2001.

25. Thomas A. Schwartz, *Statement before the Senate Armed Services Committee*, 27 March 2001, p. 4.

26. Schwartz, *Statement before the Senate Armed Services Committee*, p. 5.

27. James Goodby (1999), "Confidence-Building Ten Years On: What Has Changed," *Korean Journal of Defense Analyisis* 11, 1, p. 203.

28. Gooby, "Confidence-Building Ten Years On: What Has Changed," p. 199.

29. See the discussion of the second defense ministers' talk in *Digital Chosun Ilbo*, 9 September 2000.

30. *Korea Herald*, 9 September 2000.

31. Kihl, Young Whan, "Seoul's Engagement Policy and US-DPRK Relations," p. 48.

32. Forty percent of North Korea's population depends on food provided through foreign aid.

33. Kihl, "Seoul's Engagement Policy and US-DPRK Relations," p. 48.

34. Koo, "Challenges and Prospects for Inter-Korean Relations Under the New Leadership,"p. 88.

35. Koo, "Challenges and Prospects for Inter-Korean Relations Under the New Leadership," p. 87.

7

Recent US Foreign Policy Regarding the Korean Peninsula

Karl DeRouen Jr. and David J. Jackson

The border between North and South Korea, defended in part on the southern side by 37,000 US troops, is one of the last vestiges of the Cold War. Whether or not this border continues to remain a point of contention into the twenty-first century will be determined in large part by American politics. President George W. Bush has an important choice to make. He can proceed cautiously by honoring the 1994 Agreed Framework, supplying North Korea with food aid,[1] and conducting four-way talks with China, South Korea, and North Korea. The Bush administration appears more inclined to be more risk-acceptant. Domestic politics, among other factors, seem likely to result in a policy that pursues Theater Missile Defense (TMD), seeks to undermine the North Korean regime, and pushes South Korea on trade issues.

US POLICY ON THE KOREAN PENINSULA SINCE 1945

In 1945 Korea was liberated from Japanese domination. A communist government was established in the North, while in the South a republic was established. The natural conflict between the North and South erupted in the Korean War of 1950-53, which was the first of two in the twentieth century that the US did not win (Vietnam, of course, is the other). The Korean War began on June 25, 1950, when North Korea invaded the South. US involvement began almost immediately after the invasion by the North, and by September the Northern forces were in retreat. While victory may have appeared imminent, this perception changed quickly when China joined the fray on the side of the North in October 1950. Truce talks began in mid-1951, with quick agreement on the 38th parallel as the dividing line between the Koreas. The war continued until 1953, however, when an armistice was signed by North Korea, China, and the United Nations. Neither South Korea nor the US signed the armistice. The US military lost nearly 35,000 lives during the Korean War.

The US had almost no contact with North Korea in the decades after the war, and North and South Korea had no diplomatic relations until 1971—although both sides asserted that they desired reunification. While the North lived in secrecy under a communist dictatorship, things were a bit different in the South. In 1961 Park Chung Hee led a military coup, and he remained in power until his assassination in 1979. This assassination occurred during one of the must tumultuous periods of relations between South Korea and the US.[2] Jimmy Carter campaigned in 1976 on a promise to remove US troops from South Korea, which he began while president, but suspended the removal due to pressure on the Park government by student and labor groups that resulted in repression.

With the elimination of Park and the eventual ascent to power of General Chun Doo Hwan, the Carter administration's main interest in South Korea became the saving the life of Kim Dae Jung, who had nearly defeated Park in the 1971 presidential election and had been sentenced to death in 1980 by the Chun government for treason. After his election in 1980, President Ronald Reagan invited Chun to the White House in exchange for commuting Kim's death sentence and lifting martial law.

From the end of the Korean War until the mid-1970s, the US was fairly generous with direct economic aid to South Korea. In that period the US gave South Korea $4 billion, with 75 percent of that coming before 1968.[3] In 1969 President Richard Nixon announced that US allies would have to defend themselves against invasion, and in 1970 the US announced plans to withdraw much of its ground forces from South Korea.[4]

By the late 1980s South Korea was considered one of the most successful economic development stories in the world, and its per capita GDP is now 13 times that of the North.[5] This success was achieved with close cooperation between the government and the private sector, and without much movement toward democratization and economic reform, especially with regard to openness to imports. In the late 1990s economic crisis hit Asia, and in 1997 South Korea signed a $58 billion loan package arranged by the US, the IMF, and the World Bank. North and South Korea signed a nonaggression treaty in 1992, but a summit was canceled in 1994 following the death of North Korean leader Kim Il Sung. In 1997, former dissident Kim Dae Jung was elected president of South Korea, and he commuted the sentences of former Korean presidents/dictators Chun Doo Hwan and Roh Tae Woo.

The Clinton administration signed the US-North Korea Agreed Framework in 1994 and afterwards pushed for its full implementation. The agreement resolved a potentially volatile situation in the early 1990s. At this time forces on both sides of the demilitarized zone were placed on alert, while North Korea flirted with withdrawal from the Nuclear Nonproliferation Treaty (NPT) and refused to cooperate with the International Atomic Energy Agency (IAEA). Since the Agreed Framework was signed, North Korea appears to have shelved its indigenous nuclear program at Yongbyon, has allowed the IAEA access, and has remained a party to the NPT.[6] North Korea is also emerging from diplomatic isolation and is seeking to diminish the US role in peninsular relations.[7]

Fulfilling its part of the bargain, the US has been organizing the construction by South Korea and Japan of two proliferation-resistant light-water reactors

(LWRs) for North Korean use as part of the Korean Peninsula Energy Development Organization (KEDO).[8] The US has also agreed to supply North Korea with 500,000 metric tons of fuel oil annually until the reactors are built. South Korea and Japan have agreed to pay most of the LWR cost, while the US and the European Union (EU) have pledged funding to the overall Agreed Framework effort.[9]

Before the LWRs are to come on-line, North Korea must be in compliance with IAEA NPT protocol. Should additional international donors not be forthcoming, it remains to be seen if Congress will make funding available to fully implement the Agreed Framework. Congress spent $53 million on KEDO in FY 1999 and the Clinton administration asked for an increase for FY 2001.[10]

While nuclear programs seem to be on hold since 1994, the North Korean regime is actively furthering its ballistic missile capabilities. Since 1994, leadership has changed hands in both Koreas. Kim Jong Il has taken control in the North while Kim Dae Jung has assumed power in the South. President Kim has sought engagement and has pledged not to attempt to undermine the North. In 1998 North Korea tested its three-staged Taepo Dong-2 missile. This test troubled governments in the US, Japan, and South Korea, and jeopardized the 1994 Agreement. The proliferation of North Korean Medium-Range Ballistic Missiles (MRBMs) in the Middle East and Asia is perceived as a growing threat to US security[11]

The agreement opened the door for four-way talks between the Koreas, the US, and China. These talks tie in broader US-Chinese trade and strategic considerations. One of the issues China is concerned about is the potential US implementation of TMD in the region. Indeed, some estimates predict China could multiply its nuclear arsenal by tenfold if the US activates TMD.[12] China appears to recognize that North Korean missile development pushes the US ever closer to deploying some sort of missile defense system.[13] The Republican-controlled 106th Congress passed legislation in the FY 1999 National Defense Authorization Act requiring the administration to study the requirements for building a TMD that would protect Japan, Taiwan, and South Korea.[14]

China would also like to continue the move towards fully normalized trade with the US begun by President Bill Clinton. In March 2000 Clinton tied US interests to permanent normal trading status with China. The president asserted that free trade would gradually open China to democratic reform and stabilize the country, and thus the region. Based on this, some contend that China does not condone North Korean nuclear or ballistic missile activities.[15] The US House voted to grant China permanent normal trade relations status (PNTR) in May 2000.

US and South Korean security policies are tightly interconnected.[16] Economic policy coordination, however, is less apparent. South Korea, responding to US calls for trade liberalization, would like the US to better recognize the realities of the weakened South Korean economy. These economic problems have focused the attention of South Korean decision makers inward at the expense of bilateral relations with the US. South Korea has an interest in improving relations with North Korea and has urged the US to be patient with its northern neighbor.[17]

In late 1999 the US government released four important reports concerning the peninsula. The North Korea Policy Review Team (led by former Secretary of Defense William Perry) report explored several options. It recommended that the US negotiate verifiable steps by North Korea to end its missile development and export and nuclear programs.[18]

These steps would be built around the Agreed Framework. The Perry report also recommended that the US ease sanctions and move toward normalizing diplomatic relations. An agreement reached between the US and North Korea in Berlin in September 1999 opened the door for this plan to take effect. A second report to the Speaker of the House concluded that the Agreed Framework has not precluded a potential threat to the US from North Korean weapons of mass destruction (WMD).[19]

The General Accounting Office (GAO) also issued two reports. The GAO, acting upon a request from the chair of the House International Relations Committee, Benjamin Gilman (R-NY), reported that a small portion of the oil sent to North Korea under the terms of the Agreed Framework had been used for "unauthorized purposes".[20] A separate GAO report concluded that some of the food sent by the US was being diverted. US Representative Tony Hall (D-OH) critiqued the reports as partisan attacks on the Clinton administration's policy.[21]

The Clinton administration had several goals for its Korean Peninsula policy.[22] The primary goal was to ensure that there was no strategic threat to the US from the region. The US wanted the peninsula to be a stable part of a regional security balance. As a sign of its hopes for continued thawing of relations on the peninsula, near the end of the Clinton administration US Secretary of State Madeleine Albright visited North Korea. This was the first such high-level contact since the war.[23] This contact illustrates the importance of the security "basket" (in terms of North Korean missile technology and nuclear aspirations).

US policy was also geared toward maintaining regional stability so that economic development and democratization could take place. According to then-Acting Assistant Secretary for East Asian and Pacific Affairs Rust Deming, in testimony before Congress, "the American strategic, political, and economic stake in East Asia has only increased" since the end of the Cold War. Second, it would have liked more balanced trade with South Korea.[24] For instance, it would have liked South Korea to allow in more US beef and for South Korea to slow the export of steel to the US.[25] This falls into the economic "basket," as US policymakers must address these issues to the satisfaction of domestic constituencies. The US also would have liked South Korea to bear more of the cost of the US forces in the post-Cold War era. This again is largely a political issue for US policymakers.

Now, we turn to the present and future US policy for the Korean Peninsula. First, we discuss the linkages between politics and foreign policy. As a subset of this discussion, we explore the 2000 US elections and the implications for the Koreas. Next, we develop several (not necessarily mutually exclusive) policy options for the US. We conclude by developing the point that the peninsular security and economic baskets should be merged.

DOMESTIC POLITICS AND US FOREIGN POLICY

President Clinton endured a Republican Congress that second-guessed his policy for the peninsula. For example, the president was harshly criticized from the right on the deployment of TMD. In 1999 Congress passed the Missile Defense Act by a wide margin. The act said that US missile policy was to deploy a national missile defense system as soon as feasibly possible. According to his critics, the president's plan to methodically assess the feasibility of missile defense over the course of 2000 defied the duly passed legislative intent of the act, and ignored the immediate threat posed by the three-stage North Korean Taepo Dong-2 missile.[26]

Indeed, in August 2000, President Clinton postponed making any decision on implementation of missile defense before leaving office. This decision was made easier by the failed test of a prototype system earlier in the summer. More significant, it left this very controversial decision to his successor.

In 2000 the US narrowly elected George W. Bush as president. For only the second time in history, the US elected, through the electoral college, a president who had received fewer popular votes than his main opponent. Foreign policy issues, such as the North Korean missile threat, impact vote choice in the general election—particularly among those voters with little or no party allegiance. The growing class of nonaligned voters was especially pivotal in that year's elections. Al Gore and George W. Bush, having appealed to ideologues while winning their respective nominations, set their sights on the centrist voters during the fall campaign. Gore used security issues such as TMD and North Korean missile proliferation in his race to the middle of the political spectrum. Bush staked out a more aggressive position. He pledged to increase defense spending and push hard for space-, land- and sea-based missile defense systems.[27]

In May 2000, Bush said that the US should develop "all options" for missile defense and should even be able to protect allies. Gore adhered to a solely land-based system that would protect the US.[28] With opinion polls revealing that approximately 70 percent of Americans supported some form of missile defense, Gore grew gradually warmer toward the policy.[29] Missile defense entered the electoral cycle, because security issues such as these were within the few areas that differentiated these two moderate candidates.

Republicans in general have strongly favored TMD. Former Republican foreign policy appointees were eagerly awaiting an opportunity to resurrect TMD in earnest when their party took over the White House in January 2001. Many of Bush's campaign advisers were drawn from the administrations of Reagan and the senior George Bush.[30] Many of Bush's top foreign policy appointees were from the administrations of Bush, Reagan, Gerald Ford and Nixon. These include Secretary of State Colin Powell, Secretary of Defense Donald Rumsfeld, National Security Advisor Condoleeza Rice, and, of course, Vice President Dick Cheney.

Domestic politics figures into NMD and TMD as well. Defense industry political action committees (PACs) were very friendly toward Republicans in the 2000 elections. Defense-related PACs donated a total of $5,691,769 during the 2000 elections.[31] Of this, $3,722,754, or 65 percent, went to Republicans. Guided missile and space vehicle manufacturers donated $1,518,650, or 64 percent of their total, to Republicans. The aerospace industry donated $1,536,928 to Republicans, which amounted to 69 percent of their total contributions. Moreover, four of the largest defense-industry contributors (Boeing, Lockheed Martin, Raytheon, and TRW) are also among the largest recipients of Pentagon missile defense contracts.[32] What do these figures mean? The Bush administration and congressional Republicans may have more than global strategic concerns in mind when advancing plans for a multibillion-dollar missile shield.

THE FUTURE OF US FOREIGN POLICY ON THE KOREAN PENINSULA

As mentioned, there are two broad Korean policy options for the US. The first is the status quo. The US can also change its tack, making TMD a reality and pursuing a tougher stance on trade with South Korea. These policies could also be cross-matched for a third option. For example, President Bush could push South Korea on trade and continue to delay TMD. Below, we discuss three main options. This discussion draws in part from the recommendations and considerations of President Clinton's Policy Review Team.[33] An important distinction is that, while the Policy Review Team did not link peace in the region to economic policy, we posit that trade and aid issues are integral to the long-term success of US policy for the peninsula.

The Status Quo Option

The status quo option entails a strong element of military deterrence, the Agreed Framework, food aid to North Korea, four-way talks, a loose stance on trade with South Korea, and normalization of trade with China.[34] If there is an overarching consideration behind the status quo, it is the US' stated desire for stability in the region. The Clinton administration Policy Review Team which toured the region in 2000, concluded that the best policy for the peninsula is to work to end North Korea's nuclear program and long-range missile activities.[35]

The idea behind this two-pronged approach is that a nuclear-capable North Korea could upset the stable deterrence in place since 1953. The US is also wary of North Korean missile exports and the potential for a peninsular arms race. The Agreed Framework addresses these issues. LWR nuclear fission is less likely to be used for weapons. A House amendment to the Foreign Operations Appropriations Bill for FY 2000 put new conditions on the appropriations for the light-water reactor. These conditions meant the US must certify progress in arms control and missile deployment. The Agreed Framework makes for stable conditions so that a permanent peace can be pursued on other tracks.

As with each of the options, there are implications for US foreign policy toward China. As of March 2000, President Clinton urged Congress and the nation to get behind full normalization of trade with China, which the House then approved in May. However, some members of Congress are reluctant to cooperate with China because, as recently as 1999, that nation has allegedly sold North Korea specialty steel to be used in its missile program. Some in Congress also criticize China because of that country's threats during the recent Taiwanese election, ongoing human rights abuses, and potential ability to lure away jobs from US workers by offering corporations a less expensive option.

There are several positive benefits to be had from the status quo. First, the status quo has worked well for the last few years. The North Korean nuclear program is stalled, some aid is reaching the people of North Korea, and there is some degree of engagement. This option also has the support of key allies South Korea and Japan. The status quo option does not require the US to reduce its force level in South Korea.

The downside to the status quo is that it might not be amenable to unexpected events. According to the North Korea Policy Review Committee report, the status quo has served the US well for the past five years, but it could prove unsustainable in the face of a successful long-range North Korean missile launch.[36] A key point regarding the status quo option needs to be made. The US can require North Korea to offer verifiable assurances on its missile and nuclear programs before relations are normalized and sanctions are reduced. This is the recommendation made in the Perry report. The alternative is to offer inducements to North Korea before that country agrees to cease missile testing and exports.

The Hard-Line Option

A hard-line approach to the peninsula could entail efforts to undermine the North Korean regime, introduce TMD into the region, and pressure South Korea on trade and the costs of the US military presence.[37] The drawbacks to such an aggressive stance are abundant. First, there is currently no domestic opposition in North Korea that could be targeted by US destabilization efforts. Any US attempt to dislodge the present regime would probably take many years, if it succeeded at all. This is incommensurate with the time frame in which North Korea could develop its nuclear and ballistic programs. The destabilization plan could also lead to war and could hurt the people of North Korea more than the regime.[38]

Second, TMD could destabilize the region. China is opposed to TMD and it is likely that a missile defense system in the region would lead China to deploy additional missiles.[39] As the US is currently working with China on trade and other issues, TMD could be counterproductive. Finally, most analysts agree that missile defense systems would undermine the tenets of the 1972 Anti-Ballistic Missile (ABM) Treaty between the US and Russia.[40]

Third, pushing South Korea to open its economy and pay more for US defense efforts does not recognize the severe economic crisis from which the country is recovering. An aggressive American stance at this time could lead to resentment in South Korea. It could also lead to instability in the face of the North Korean threat and the competing political factions in South Korea.[41] Such moves by the US could jeopardize South Korea's transition toward democracy.

Compromise

A third option involves components of the previous two. This modified approach is built upon the assumption that the economic and strategic baskets must be merged. The Clinton administration demonstrated its willingness to combine these two policy areas by restructuring the foreign policy apparatus. For instance, the administration created a National Economic Advisor tantamount to the National Security Advisor. The administration also increased participation of economic policymakers within the National Security Council (NSC) and the State Department.

To these ends the US can continue working to help stabilize the nascent democracy in South Korea, as economic growth in that country climbs back to pre-crisis levels. Once the South Korean recovery is complete and democratization has taken further root, the US can continue its pursuit of a more liberalized South Korean market. This is the safest way to ensure a peaceful transition to democracy, as South Korea maintains its policy of engagement with North Korea.

Continued food aid and talks aimed at normalization and further easing of sanctions with North Korea seem to be another prudent policy choice. Normalized relations could decrease the incentives for North Korea to expect payment for "foregone" income from missile sales. Payments to North Korea in return for ending its missile program are politically unpopular in the US. Many in Congress consider it a form of blackmail.

In terms of the security basket, the Agreed Framework, which has worked well to date, could be modified to address ballistic weapons. This could reduce the sense of urgency surrounding the potentially destabilizing TMD. The hardline unilateral option of tough talk and action aimed directly at North Korea has the unintended result of cutting South Korea out of the process. Four-way talks aimed at dealing with North Korean issues maintains South Korea's rightful role as a key player and keeps South Korean-US relations warm.

This compromise approach is balanced and politically more neutral than the other two options. This policy could conceivably be sold to the divided Congress, with Republicans dominating the US House and Democrats in control of the Senate. It is a prudent policy that overcomes partisan politics and generates progress in the wider East Asian region at a pivotal time.

EARLY BUSH ADMINISTRATION POLICY

After taking office in January 2001, the Bush administration suspended talks with North Korea pending a complete review of US policy toward the nation.[42] It took a number of important steps with regard to policy toward the Koreas, however. First and most important, under the guidance of Defense Secretary Donald Rumsfeld, the administration decided to actively pursue aggressive NMD and potentially TMD plans due to the perceived threat from North Korea and other unfriendly states.[43] As Defense Secretary Rumsfeld put it, "Effective missile defense—not only homeland defense but also the ability to defend US allies abroad and our friends—must be achieved in the most cost-effective manner that modern technology offers."[44] While this may require abrogating the 1972 ABM Treaty, the administration has indicated a willingness to do so—in part because the treaty was negotiated with the Soviet Union, which no longer exists.

During an Oval Office visit in March 2001 by South Korean President Kim Dae Jung, President Bush also dampened expectations concerning President Kim's "sunshine" policy of rapprochement with the North by saying that he believed North Korea was a threat to the United States.[45] This comment embarrassed both the Korean president and Bush's own secretary of state, who had hoped for a quick resumption of talks. This smiting of Colin Powell is also telling of the conflict in the Bush administration foreign policy team, with moderates led by Powell on the one side and hawks led by Secretary of Defense Donald Rumsfeld on the other.[46]

The US also continued to pressure the South to purchase American military equipment, despite the economic crisis in the country. House Minority Leader Richard Gephardt and Senator Christopher S. Bond, both of Missouri where F-15 fighters are manufactured, traveled to South Korea in early 2001 to pressure President Kim to purchase the planes.[47] The administration was not clear in its support of or opposition to these purchases, however.

President Bush appeared to scuttle the Clinton policy on the Korean Peninsula in part to please Republican who controlled the US Congress. However, the defection of Vermont Republican's Senator James Jeffords tipped the balance of power in that chamber to the Democrats. This may have given the Democrats more power to pressure the president to become less belligerent with the North Koreans. North Carolina conservative Republican Jesse Helms was replaced as chairman of the Senate Foreign Relations Committee by Delaware moderate Democrat Joseph Biden, who has vowed to defeat NMD.[48] Also, President Bush's father cautioned him to reopen negotiations with North Korea, which Bush agreed to do in June 2001.[49] Moreover, at the same time, the administration appeared willing to deliver the light-water nuclear reactors South Korea and Japan are building for the North.[50] Moderation has replaced the hard-line rhetoric, yet it remains unclear if the administration is pursuing a hard-line approach, the status quo, or some as yet ill-defined third option.

CONCLUSION

East Asia will be the focus of much international attention for years to come. Whereas defense budgets are being cut in most of the world, Asian defense spending is climbing.[51] There are significant regional conflicts in Asia centering on territoriality, independence movements, religion, and resources. In terms of the Korean Peninsula, the US must choose whether to remain a force for stability or to push for change. The Bush administration must choose whether to continue to engage North Korea and assist in the warming of relations between the Koreas, or to raise a missile shield over itself and its allies and further isolate Pyongyang. By demonstrating support for both options in its early months, the Bush administration has left its true intentions wide open to interpretation.

One condition is fairly clear however. Implementation by the US of TMD would signal a new approach for the US in the region. China opposes the US' extending TMD protection to Taiwan. Angering China could diminish the prospects for successful four-way talks on peninsular issues. However, some argue that China is already upsetting the regional balance by increasing its missile arsenal. President Bush has said on several occasions that he supports missile defense in the region, and that he would offer the Russians the opportunity to modify the ABM Treaty to allow TMD.[52] However, in his first visit to Europe as president, Bush failed to convince the allies to take his position. Whether he can do so in the future remains unclear.

George W. Bush vilified the North Koreans during the 2000 presidential campaign. His administration continued to do so after he took the oath of office, with then-Secretary of State nominee Colin Powell referring to North Korean leader Kim Jong Il as a "dictator."[53] After suspending talks with North Korea, pressure from his father and the power shift in the Senate seem to have softened the President's position on the peninsula. Early flip-flops on foreign policy are common in new presidential administrations. On China, for example, the Clinton administration moved from the left to the center on the issue of linking trade and human rights. The Bush administration appears to have shifted from the right to the center on North Korea policy. With relatively few options on peninsular policy actually available, it seems the administration will continue to pursue NMD and TMD, but try to do so without antagonizing North Korea, China, Russia, and Western European allies. It will be a very impressive balancing act if it succeeds.

NOTES

1. Evidently this food aid was desperately needed. It is estimated that 1 million of North Korea's 23 million people died of hunger from 1995 through 1998. See Barbara Slavin, "Missiles Not The Focus of Bush's Korea Policy," *USA Today*, 6 March 2001.

2. William H. Gleysteen, *Massive Entanglement, Marginal Influence* (Washington, DC: Brookings Institution Press, 1999).

3. Library of Congress/Federal Research Division <http://memory.loc.gov>.

4. Gleysteen, *Massive Entanglement, Marginal Influence*.

5. *Korea Report 2000-2001*, CountryWatch, www.countrywatch.com.

6. Rust Deming, "US-North Korea Agreed Framework and KEDO," testimony before the Senate Foreign Relations Committee, Subcommittee on East Asian and Pacific Affairs, 14 July 1998. See also Suk Jung Lee and Michael Sheehan, "Building Confidence and Security on the Korean Peninsula," Contemporary Security Policy 16 (December 1995), pp. 267-98, for discussions of KEDO and the history of arms negotiations on the peninsula.

7. See Doug Struck, "The New North Korea Scrambles the Picture; US Influence in Region May be Reduced," International Herald Tribune, 29 July 2000; Charles Lee, "North Korea Urges South to Sever Ties with US," United Press International, 22 August 2000.

8. See Larry Niksch, "North Korea's Nuclear Weapons Program," Congressional Research Service Report No. 91141 (1999).

9. Deming, "US-North Korea Agreed Framework and KEDO."

10. Stanley Roth, "East Asia and the Pacific, Congressional Budget Justification for Foreign Operations, Fiscal Year 2001." submitted by the Office of the Secretary of State (2001). Roth is currently the State Department's Assistant Secretary for East Asian and Pacific Affairs.

11. See Robert Walpole, "The Ballistic Missile Threat to the United States," statement for the Record to the Senate Subcommittee on International Security, Proliferation, and Federal Services, 9 February 2000. Walpole is national intelligence officer for strategic and nuclear programs within the CIA.

12. "US Missile Shield Could Spur Arms Buildup by China, Russia," Agence France-Presse, 10 August 2000. See also Walter B. Slocombe (2000), "The Administration's Approach," The Washington Quarterly, 23, pp. 79-170. for a discussion of strategic issues surrounding missile defense deployment.

13. William Perry, "Review of United States Policy toward North Korea: Findings and Recommendations," unclassified report by US North Korea Policy Coordinator and Special Advisor to the President and Secretary of State, 12 October 1999.

14. There was a host of missile defense legislation introduced in the 106th Congress. Many of these bills refer specifically to East Asia. See Robert Shuey, "Theater Missile Defense: Issues for Congress," Congressional Research Service Report No. 98028 (1999); Robert Shuey, "Missile Defense Options for Japan, South Korea, and Taiwan: A Review of the Defense Department Report to Congress," Congressional Research Service Report No. RL30379 (1999); see also Richard L. Garwin (2000), "A Defense that will not Defend," The Washington Quarterly 23, pp. 79-170.

15. See Perry, "Review of United States Policy toward North Korea: Findings and Recommendations." However, the CIA reported in Summer 2000 that China has been increasing its support of the North Korean ballistic missile effort; see also "US Missile Shield Could Spur Arms Buildup By China, Russia," Agence France-Presse.

16. President Clinton and President Kim Dae Jung had several meetings over the past few years. These talks resulted in South Korea increasing its support payments for US forces. The talks also covered trade and North Korean issues. The four-way talks that have begun have enhanced US-South Korean relations because they allay fears of a bilateral agreement between the US and North Korea. See Larry Niksch, "Korea: US-South Korean Relations Issues for Congress," Congressional Research Service Report No. 98045 (1999); Lee and Sheehan, "Building Confidence and Security on the Korean Peninsula."

17. It is important to note that many in South Korea are beginning to question the utility of the US' paternalistic behavior. This is in part due to the revelation that the US may have killed South Korean civilians at the beginning of the Korean War. See Shuey, "Missile Defense Options for Japan, South Korea, and Taiwan: A Review of the Defense Department Report to Congress."

18. Perry, "Review of United States Policy toward North Korea: Findings and Recommendations."

19. See Niksch, "Korea: US-South Korean Relations Issues for Congress."

20. Ibid.

21. Steven Mufson, "North Korea Aid Hard to Trace, Reports Say," Washington Post, 10 October 1999.

22. See Rust Deming, "US Security Concerns in Asia," testimony Before the House International Relations Committee, Subcommittee on Asia and the Pacific, 8 March 2000; Roth, "East Asia and the Pacific."

23. Cuday Bhaskar, "Kimchi and Curry," The Times of India, 4 November 2000.

24. Deming, "US Security Concerns in Asia."

25. President Clinton complained to the World Trade Organization in February 1999 that South Korea was not open to US beef exports. See Niksch, "Korea: US-South Korean Relations Issues for Congress."

26. Frank Gaffney Jr., "Anti-Missile Defense Dawdling," Washington Times, 15 February 2000.

27. Ibid.

28. Robert Burns, "Pentagon Spending $7 Million to Study Sea-based Missile Defense Idea," Associated Press, 30 May 2000.

29. J. Michael Waller, "Candidates Lock on Missile Defense," Insight on the News, 31 July 2000. This support seemed to decline after the election. A June 2001 survey showed only 51 percent of Americans supported missile defense. See Joseph Boris, "Poll: 51 Percent Favor Missile Defense," United Press International, 11 June 2000.

30. David Sanger, "The 2000 Campaign: The Foreign Policy Issues," New York Times, 5 March 2000.

31. The Political Money Line <www.fecinfo.com>. This is a reputable organization when it comes to campaign finance information. The Federal Elections Commission directs inquiries to the site. Also, these figures closely match similar reports published by The Center for Responsive Politics <www.opensecrets.org>.

32. World Policy Institute <www.worldpolicy.org>.

33. See Perry, "Review of United States Policy toward North Korea: Findings and Recommendations."

34. See Roth, "East Asia and the Pacific."

35. See Perry, "Review of United States Policy toward North Korea: Findings and Recommendations."

36. Perry, "Review of United States Policy toward North Korea: Findings and Recommendations."

37. See Perry, "Review of United States Policy Toward North Korea: Findings and Recommendations"; Shuey, "Missile Defense Options for Japan, South Korea, and Taiwan: A Review of the Defense Department Report to Congress"; Niksch, "Korea: US-South Korean Relations Issues for Congress."

38. Perry, "Review of United States Policy toward North Korea: Findings and Recommendations."

39. Shuey, "Missile Defense Options for Japan, South Korea, and Taiwan: A Review of the Defense Department Report to Congress."

40. See Amy Woolf, "Arms Control and Disarmament: A Catalog of Recent Activities," Congressional Research Service Report No. 95-134F (1996), pp. 20-22.

41. Niksch, "Korea: US-South Korean Relations Issues for Congress"; Shuey, "Theater Missile Defense: Issues for Congress."

42. Howard W. French, "North Korea Rebuffs US on Troop Talks," New York Times, 19 June 2001.

43. Michael R. Gordon and Steven Lee Meyers, "Bush Team Vows to Speed Up Work on Missile Shield," New York Times, 30 April 2001.

44. Keiji Urakami, "Focus: Bush Likely to Pursue Tougher China, N. Korea Policy," Japan Economic Newswire, 20 January 2001.

45. William Douglas, "Bush: North Korea Still a Threat," Newsday, 8 March 2001.

46. Martin Kettle, "Powell Losing Policy Battle to Hardliners: From Korea to Kosovo, the Pragmatic Secretary of State Is Being Forced into Increasing Isolation," The Guardian, 12 March 2001.

47. Steven Mufson, "Bush to Pick Up Talks on North Korean Missiles," Washington Post, 7 March 2001.

48. Bill Nichols, "Del. Senator to Lead Charge Against Missile-Defense Plan," USA Today, 13 June 2001.

49. Jane Perlez, "Fatherly Advice to the President on North Korea," *The New York Times*, 10 June 2001.

50. Jim Mann, "US is Seen as Ready to Fulfill 1994 North Korea Reactor Deal," *Los Angeles Times*, 10 June 2001.

51. See Uk Heo and Karl DeRouen Jr. (1998), "Military Expenditures, Technological Change, and Growth in the East Asian NICs," *Journal of Politics*, 60, pp. 830-46.

52. George W. Bush, "A Distinctly American Internationalism," speech given at the Ronald Reagan Presidential Library, 19 November 1999 <georgewbush.com/speeches/foreignpolicy/foreignpolicy.asp>. In a September 1999 campaign speech at the Citadel, Bush said that he would have a "solemn obligation to protect the American people *and our allies*, not to protect arms control agreements signed almost thirty years ago" [italics added]. In the same speech, Bush pledged $20 billion in military R&D in his first term. See George W. Bush, "A Period of Consequences," speech given at the Citadel, 23 September 1999 <georgewbush.com/speeches/defense/citadel.asp>.

53. Charles Lee, "South Korea Welcomes Bush's North Korea Policy," *United Press International*, 19 January 2001.

8

In India's Shadow: The Evolution of Pakistan's Security Policy

Kanishkan Sathasivam and Sahar Shafqat

Since independence in 1947, Pakistan and India have fought three wars and engaged in countless border skirmishes. The two countries have always been at odds with each other, leading one to think almost of siblings who cannot break out of their rivalry. How did this happen? Will the situation remain so that Pakistan and India remain hostile rivals, unable to break out of a cycle of suspicion and violence, and unable to forge a durable peace? In this chapter we attempt to provide some context for these questions. First, we examine the domestic context of Pakistan's security policy; then we turn to its strategic concerns.

THE DOMESTIC DETERMINANTS OF PAKISTAN'S SECURITY POLICY

As with most countries, Pakistan's security policy is heavily influenced by domestic factors. At base, Pakistan, like many postcolonial societies, has struggled to define its national identity. This struggle to define itself, and the attendant uncertainties, have cast a long shadow on Pakistan's relations with its neighbors, especially India. In addition, some critical events have affected how Pakistan defines itself, and consequently how it perceives its neighbors and its own security needs.

The Formation of Pakistan

Pakistan was created in 1947 when British India was partitioned into the majority-Hindu state of India and the majority-Muslim state of Pakistan. But Pakistani independence was by no means inevitable. The struggle for independence from British India was initially dominated by Hindus and led by the Indian National Congress, and the movement focused on the independence of a united India; the division of India never occurred to leaders such as Jawaharlal Nehru and Mahatma Gandhi. But Muslims, who had not been very politically active in British India, especially after the uprising in 1857, began to feel increasingly alienated from the independence movement. In 1906, the All-India Muslim League was formed. Slowly, Muslim members of the independence movement, feeling increasingly marginalized, joined the Muslim League. Eventually the League came to be led by secular and Western-educated activists such as Muhammad Ali Jinnah.

The idea of Pakistan as an independent country was first articulated by Muhammad Iqbal in his "Two Nation Theory," which argued that the Muslim and Hindu communities in India were two separate and distinct nations. It was only in 1940 that the first explicit demand for an independent Pakistan was made, in the Lahore Resolution. The group at the helm of the Pakistan movement lacked the overtly religious component that one associates with Pakistan today, and it was committed to a secular state. Indeed, as Hamza Alavi has put it, "the Pakistan movement was not a movement of Islam but of Muslims."[1] Within the Muslim community in India, groups that were overtly religious (Islamic) in nature—such as the Jama'at-i-Islami party, or those associated with the Deobandi movement—distanced themselves from the Pakistan movement. Indeed, somewhat ironically, the Islamists in India were fiercely opposed to the division of British India. Thus, the Pakistan movement remained dominated by a group that has been called the "salariat": secular, urban professionals in the Muslim community.[2] The movement's leaders were eager to attract members of the *ulema*—roughly equivalent to the Western clergy, but much less formalized in the Islamic context. Some of the *ulema* eventually joined the movement, but the consequence was a struggle over whether the new state was to be secular or Islamist.

Most Hindu Indians (and the British) remained strongly opposed to the idea of Partition, but massive civil disobedience campaigns eventually forced the hands of the leaders. It became clear that independence from the British would come only with Partition. When Pakistan did become independent, it inherited a state that was geographically divided. West Pakistan, consisting of the Muslim-majority regions of the northwest of British India, and East Pakistan, consisting of the Muslim-majority portion of Bengal, were separated by almost 1,000 miles, with newly independent India lying between them. The new country was not only difficult to maintain and defend militarily, but faced considerable logistical challenges. The geographical divide also did little to help existing ethnic tensions between East and West Pakistan. These would eventually worsen, leading to a civil war and the secession of East Pakistan to form Bangladesh in 1971. The new Pakistani nation was born feeling besieged by the larger and more powerful India. And many Pakistanis continue to believe that most Indians have never reconciled themselves to the reality of Partition, which leads to even greater suspicion between the two countries.

Apart from the secular-Islamist tension in Pakistani identity, Pakistan has always been obliged to explain its identity vis-à-vis that of India. And since the Indian self-proclaimed identity, from the very start, was that of a secular and modern nation, Pakistan found it increasingly difficult to justify its existence as anything except an Islamist nation, especially after the massive migration of

Hindus and Sikhs from the newly created Pakistan in 1947-48 left Pakistan even more heavily dominated by Muslims.[3]

A critical issue for Pakistan, which has its roots in the founding of the country, is the status of Kashmir. Kashmir is officially a state of India, but the territory has been contested between India and Pakistan since independence. According to the plan for Partition, Muslim-majority areas were to go to Pakistan, while Hindu-majority areas were to go to India. But princely states, of which Kashmir was one, were technically allowed to decide their own fate. Kashmir was the largest princely state, and moreover was in a unique position in that it was Muslim-majority but ruled by a Hindu king. The king, under considerable pressure from India, eventually acceded to India, and Pakistan reacted immediately, leading to an armed confrontation between the two young nations. The cease-fire line in that war, brokered by the United Nations, remains the de facto border in Kashmir, leaving approximately one-third of Kashmir under Pakistani control and two-thirds under Indian control.

Kashmir has been the flashpoint for tensions between the two countries, serving as the focus for two of the three wars that Pakistan and India have fought. The most recent confrontation between the two, in the spring of 1999, was in Kashmir. Most Kashmiris are unhappy with Indian rule, and many have engaged in an armed uprising over the last decade, a movement that is heavily supported by Pakistan in both political and military terms.[4] For Pakistan, Kashmir is primarily a territorial issue. But Kashmir is also intimately related to the country's self-perception and national identity. Kashmir is a Muslim-majority region that is contiguous and perceived to be a natural addition to Pakistan. Kashmir has also proved a useful tool for Pakistan to criticize India for its human rights abuses, and Kashmir also offers some limited geostrategic advantages.

The Ethnic Dimension within Pakistan

Although the new nation had successfully gained independence both from the British and from India, it was by no means a united entity. In fact, Pakistan was composed of various ethnic groups, which supported the new country to varying degrees. The Muslim salariat, which was the vanguard of the Pakistan movement, was drawn most heavily from two ethnic groups: the Punjabis, and the Urdu-speaking Muslims in the United Provinces (UP). Additionally, support for Pakistan was strongest in these regions as well. These were the two groups that came to dominate independent Pakistan. This in turn led to increased resentments and tensions between the various ethnic groups that constituted Pakistan. There were six primary ethnic groups in Pakistan:

1. Punjabis, which dominated the political and economic systems, as well as the military;
2. Pashtuns,[5] who were also well represented in the military; Baluchis, who were perhaps the least enthusiastic supporters of Pakistan; Sindhis, who were also aligned with a Sindhi nationalist movement;
3. Muhajirs, who were refugees from India who had migrated to Pakistan at Partition; Bengalis, who historically had a very strong sense of Bengali (as opposed to Muslim) nationalism.

The biggest challenge to Pakistani nationhood was from Bengali nationalism. Bengalis dominated East Pakistan and continued the biggest ethnic group in terms of population in all of Pakistan. But Punjabis and Muhajirs dominated the administrative, political, and military arms of the country; and Bengalis were marginalized in the new country. Their sense of alienation was only underscored by the fact that their wing of the country was literally on the other end of the subcontinent from West Pakistan, the nucleus of the country. Emblematic of the ethnic tensions were the political struggles over declaring a national language for Pakistan. The language chosen was Urdu, which was spoken natively only by the Muhajirs, but was widely spoken by many other Pakistanis. However, Urdu was not spoken widely by the Bengalis. The conflict over the institution of Urdu as the exclusive national language in 1952 was an early sign of the tensions between East and West Pakistan that were eventually to result in civil war.

Another important event that complicated the ethnic dimension of Pakistani politics was the 1979 Soviet invasion of Afghanistan. The Afghanistan war has had tremendous fallout for Pakistan to the present day. Most notably, Pakistan was faced with a humanitarian crisis, as millions of Afghan refugees streamed into Pakistan after the Soviet invasion. This humanitarian crisis was coupled with a more delicate political one, since the presence of the refugees stirred the complicated stew that is Pakistani ethnic politics. The majority of the Afghan refugees were Pashtuns, an ethnic group that is about equally divided across both sides of the Afghan-Pakistan border. The border itself is based on the British-era Durand Line, which Afghanistan has never officially accepted as the international boundary between Pakistan and Afghanistan. Additionally, Pashtuns are an important ethnic minority group within Pakistan, being well represented in the military, for example. But there is also a strong Pashtun nationalist movement that has posed threats to the Punjabidominated central government. The threat such a nationalist movement poses becomes even greater if the movement spreads across international boundaries, leading to calls for an independent Pashtunistan.[6]

The threat that Bengalis and other internal nationalisms posed to Pakistan's political and territorial integrity led the military to emerge as the only de facto guarantor of national unity. These ethnic tensions have also allowed successive generations of Pakistani leaders to manipulate Islam for political ends, by arguing (explicitly or implicitly) that Islam was the only common bond that could transcend particularistic ethnic ties.

Soldiers in Mufti: The Military in Pakistani Politics

Another critical factor in determining Pakistan's security policy has been the dominant role that the military has played in Pakistani politics throughout its history. Pakistan has been under military rule for approximately half of its history. As was the case with many postcolonial countries, Pakistan inherited weak civilian political institutions from British colonialism. The military, dominated by the Punjabis, has styled itself as the only real guarantor of Pakistani national unity. The military has stepped in to take control in response to many crises in Pakistani history. Even when the military has not been in direct control, it has exerted enormous influence. Consequently, the Pakistani military has not only seen itself as being charged with *external* security, but also with *internal* security.

The military has responded most significantly—but not exclusively—to threats from ethnic nationalist movements. For example, in 1970, when civil unrest in East Pakistan was at its peak, General Yahya Khan declared martial law.[7] But, in 1977, when Islamist parties were leading the civil unrest in opposition to alleged electoral rigging by the Bhutto administration, General Zia ul Haq declared martial law yet again. During periods of military rule, some of the most brutal acts of repression of ethnic nationalist movements have occurred. For example, the civil war in East Pakistan in 1971 was marked by widespread raping and killing of local Bengalis by Pakistani military personnel. During the Zia government, the military forcefully suppressed uprisings by Baluchi and Sindhi nationalists.[8] This resulted in a greater degree of militarization of Pakistani society, and the military has been able to acquire more space in the public arena to make a case for its special role in Pakistani society. One consequence was that the military remains unaccountable for its actions—in domestic affairs and especially in external security matters.

The Islamization of Pakistani Society

One important trend in Pakistani politics has been the growing "Islamization" of the society. While Islam has always been an important part of Pakistan's culture and society, Islamization refers specifically to explicit imposition of laws and practices in accordance with Islamic law. As mentioned, Pakistan was not envisioned as a theocratic state by its founders. But many Pakistani leaders since then have found it politically expedient to manipulate Islam for their own ends.

The politically expedient use of Islam reached a new high under the government of Zulfikar Ali Bhutto. Bhutto was the first popularly elected prime minister of Pakistan, coming to power in 1973 (after the civil war and the secession of Bangladesh). His main constituency consisted of the landed rural classes, peasants, and the laboring classes, and he had to find a way to reach out to other groups. According to Anita Weiss:

Bhutto adopted Islamic slogans, particularly those stressing egalitarianism and social justice as a means of legitimating his economic policies, thereby increasing his popularity. There was no attempt to include specific Islamic laws in the legal system until it became politically expedient to do so in early 1977 when drinking, gambling, and night clubs were banned. This was soon followed by the replacement of Friday for Sunday as the weekly holiday.[9]

Besides trying to appeal to a broader cross-section of society, Bhutto and others introduced such measures in response to Islamist activists. One of the truisms of Pakistani politics has been that Islamist parties control no more than 10 to 15 percent of popular support. However, it is also true that Islamists have generally been successful and efficient at mobilizing popular support and organizing civil unrest. This was very much the case during the Bhutto administration. In fact, it was the civil unrest generated by Islamists (and others) that became the pretext for the military to move in again, in 1977, under General Zia. The most dramatic imposition of Islam in public life occurred under Zia's Islamization program.

Islamization has certainly changed the national identity of Pakistan decisively in the direction of an Islamic as opposed to a Muslim state. But there were security consequences of this trend as well. Most important, perhaps, it was with the Bhutto administration that Pakistan first began to seek closer relations and cooperation with actors in the Muslim and Arab world. Pakistan had been traditionally more aligned with the United States, with India leaning more toward the Soviet Union. But Bhutto was a proponent of a more independent, nonaligned foreign policy. After the sound defeat of Pakistani forces in East Pakistan in 1971 and the nuclear test by India in 1974, Pakistan's security establishment was in a major crisis. Bhutto and others saw the Middle East connection as an extremely useful counterforce to India—one that could be more dependable than either the US or the Soviet Union. (The Soviet Union in any case was partial to India, despite Bhutto's ostensible socialist credentials.)[10]

India's nuclear test in 1974 gave urgency to Pakistan's plans for a nuclear weapons program. The ultimate motivation was that Pakistani policymakers believed that India had overwhelming superiority in conventional military terms (as had been evidenced by the 1971 war), so a nonconventional nuclear weapons capability was the only means of regaining some measure of equilibrium vis-a-vis India. Bhutto sought assistance from the Middle East for this project, and certainly common religious and cultural ties helped the effort. For example, Pakistan hosted the Islamic Conference in Lahore in 1972, and began providing some technical assistance to some countries in the Gulf, such as training in the field of military aviation.[11] To this day, many Pakistani military pilots fly combat aircraft for the air forces of several Arab states, in particular Saudi Arabia and the United Arab Emirates, thus raising questions about whether or not these pilots would return to Pakistan with their Arab aircraft in the event of war with India. Notably too, many Gulf countries were flush with petrodollars during the 1970s and 1980s, and were in a position to provide significant financial assistance to Pakistan's nuclear program. In particular, Saudi Arabia emerged as a crucial ally in terms of material support.[12] The process of growing closer to countries in the Middle East and the Gulf continued under General Zia after 1977. Indeed, it has remained one of the cornerstones of Pakistani foreign policy since the 1970s.

Ties with the Arab world grew even closer after the Soviet invasion of Afghanistan in 1979. For General Zia, the invasion was fortuitous. He was able to strengthen his tenuous position in power with US and other external support for the fight against the Soviets in Afghanistan. The episode also served to strengthen pan-Islamic ties, both at the elite and mass level. Certain elements of Islamic ideology were easily adapted to the new cause in Afghanistan. For example, the Islamic notion of *ummah*, meaning the community of Muslims worldwide, was used to persuade Muslim countries that their fortunes were linked to the fate of the mujahideen in Afghanistan.[13]

The Chinese Connection

The Islamic connection cannot be exaggerated, though, because certainly cultural and religious differences have not prevented Pakistan from allying closely with China. Whereas Arab countries provided financial support for Pakistan's nuclear program, China almost certainly provided technical and scientific support. This is the outcome of the dual game that is played on the subcontinent: Pakistan fears India, and India fears Pakistan but also (and increasingly more so) China, so Pakistan allies with China to counter the threat from India. The relationship with China goes back to the 1960s—especially after the 1965 war with India, with China having fought a war with India in 1962. China has applied diplomatic pressure on behalf of Pakistan, and has also provided conventional military assistance and limited economic assistance. More symbolically, China did not recognize Bangladesh (the erstwhile East Pakistan) until India had released Pakistani prisoners of war.[14] More recently, General Pervez Musharraf, after taking power in a military coup in October 1999, made one of his first international trips to China, in January 2000. General Musharraf was greeted warmly by the Chinese government. Referring to the coup, Beijing declared that "what happens in Pakistan is its internal affair."[15]

The Chinese connection is a powerful counterweight to India, since China has considerable superiority over India in both conventional and unconventional military assets. The Chinese alliance has also been useful for Pakistan because Beijing has tended to ask few questions about internal matters in Pakistan. With the heavy involvement of the military in Pakistani politics, Pakistan has always had to make excuses for its domestic politics in the international arena, particularly with Western countries. China, by contrast, does not demand democracy and human rights from its allies. Nearly every Pakistani leader, whether elected or not, has visited Beijing, and has sought to maintain close ties with China.

THE PERCEIVED THREAT FROM INDIA AND PAKISTAN'S STRATEGIC VULNERABILITY

Pakistan's threat perception, and therefore its security policy, is driven almost entirely by its understanding of Indian strategic doctrine. As discussed, many Pakistanis are convinced that India has never truly accepted the partition of the subcontinent along largely sectarian lines. The inflammatory statements of some Indian political leaders over the years, coupled with similar expressions within Indian popular sentiment, have often reinforced this belief among Pakistanis. India's brutal suppression of the ongoing rebellion in predominantly Muslim Kashmir with massive use of force and heavy loss of noncombatant lives is, in the eyes of Pakistanis, damning evidence for this perception.

The Historical Roots of Pakistan's Threat Perception

Pakistan sees India, in the best case, as a nation obsessed with a grandiose vision of regional domination, and willing to employ military force to attain this strategic goal. Frequent displays of military might and coercive diplomacy are considered to be India's preferred instruments for getting whatever it wishes from its smaller neighbors in the region. In the worst case, Pakistan perceives an

Indian inclination for a decisive preemptive military strike against Pakistan, the aims of which would be twofold. First, India would seek to destroy completely Pakistan's nuclear capability—including Pakistan's ability to produce nuclear weapons in the future. Second, India would very seriously consider the possibility of eliminating Pakistan as a regional strategic competitor once and for all, by dismembering Pakistan along its internal ethnic fault lines. This would turn Pakistan into a motley collection of small, weak states forever locked in tribal feuding with one another.

The Pakistani perceptions of Indian strategic motives detailed above are founded in the post-Partition military history shared by the two antagonistic neighbors. The disorganized and hurried British withdrawal from the subcontinent in 1947 left several critical issues unresolved. With respect to the strategic concerns of the newly created state of Pakistan, two issues in particular stood out: the equitable division of military and financial assets inherited from the departing British Empire; and the integration of the nominally independent princely states of Junagadh, Hyderabad, and Kashmir into either India or Pakistan under a mutually acceptable formula. Pakistan's fear that Indian strategic doctrine was centered on the eventual (forcible) reunification of the subcontinent, with the destabilization of Pakistan as an interim step in accomplishing this goal, was significantly strengthened by India's subsequent actions. India blatantly engaged in stalling tactics in response to Pakistan's desperate pleas for a just and timely resolution of the issue of the division of military and financial assets, thereby contributing greatly to continued political, social, and economic chaos within the newborn Muslim state. Worse still, India proceeded to unilaterally and violently annex the princely states of Junagadh and Hyderabad, and engineered the accession of Kashmir into the Indian union.

The continuing dispute over Kashmir, having sparked wars between the two neighbors in 1947 and 1965, remains the single biggest contributor to mutual suspicion, bitterness, and hostility between Pakistan and India. However, two other major events dating back to the early 1970s served significantly to shape Pakistan's sense of profound insecurity vis-à-vis India. The first event was Pakistan's decisive defeat in the third India-Pakistan War in 1971. That war resulted in the dismembering of Pakistan by the Indian armed forces, with what was then "East" Pakistan becoming the independent state of Bangladesh. The loss of East Pakistan, especially as the result of Indian military intervention, was a crippling blow to Pakistan's sense of nationhood and identity. Physically, the loss of East Pakistan translated to a 15 percent reduction in Pakistan's territory and, more importantly, a nearly 60 percent reduction in Pakistan's population. Additionally, over 90,000 Pakistani troops were taken prisoner by the Indians.[16] In and of themselves, these losses in population, economic resources, and military capability were devastating indeed. The defeat made Pakistan intensely fearful of further dismemberment by India in the future.

Pakistan's principal policy response to its loss of East Pakistan was a "bunker" mentality and a single-minded pursuit of a nuclear weapons capability. Pakistan has pursued this capability not only as a deterrent against potential Indian "adventurism," but also as a relatively cost-effective means of blunting India's conventional superiority. This reality is enunciated in a recent assessment of the Carnegie Endowment for International Peace: "Pakistan's quest for a nuclear deterrent has been motivated principally by fears of domination by India, whose population, economy, and military resources dwarf those of its western neighbor .... Since the 1971 India-Pakistan War, relations between Islamabad and New Delhi have alternated between periods of relative peace and periods of considerable tension, punctuated with crises that nearly erupted into war during the winter of 1986-87 and the spring of 1990."[17] Pakistan initiated its nuclear weapons program in 1972 in the aftermath of that disastrous 1971 war with India. The fledgling Pakistani nuclear weapons program gained panicked urgency but also political strength from a second major event that took place in 1974. On May 18, India detonated what is believed to have been a 12-15 kiloton nuclear device at its Pokhran test site in the Rajasthan desert.[18] India termed the detonation a "peaceful nuclear explosion." This characterization went essentially unchallenged by the international community, although Canada and the United States, which had hitherto assisted India in pursuing peaceful uses for nuclear technology, formally suspended all further nuclear cooperation.

The dual events of the 1971 war and the 1974 Indian nuclear test led Pakistan's political and military leadership to the unshakable conclusion that Pakistan's sovereignty, perhaps even its very existence, would be at stake in the future if India's strategic superiority over Pakistan went unchecked.[19] This firm belief is reflected in the oft-quoted words of the prime minister of Pakistan in the mid-1970s, Zulfikar Ali Bhutto: "If India developed an atomic bomb, we too will develop one 'even if we have to eat grass or leaves or to remain hungry' because there is no conventional alternative to the atomic bomb."[20]

In the light of these Pakistani sensitivities, it is not hard to understand Pakistan's contribution to the events of 1998. On May 11, 1998, Indian Prime Minister Atal Behari Vajpayee stunned the world by announcing that India had carried out three nuclear tests at its underground test facility at Pokhran, 550 kilometers southwest of New Delhi. Indian nuclear scientists even claimed that one of the tests was of a thermonuclear device, i.e. , a hydrogen bomb. Two days later, a distraught international community was informed of two additional Indian underground nuclear tests.

A few weeks later, Pakistan responded with its own series of underground nuclear tests. It claimed to have conducted five tests on May 28, followed by a single additional test on May 30. Why did Pakistan opt to test the bomb, even in the face of strong opposition from the international community and the attendant potential for grave diplomatic and economic consequences? It appears that the hawks within Pakistan's military establishment and the defense and foreign ministries could have been persuaded that giving up Pakistan's nuclear deterrent force was not necessarily detrimental to Pakistan's security interests. Unlike other cases of nuclear weapons proliferation, actual and potential, the Pakistani case seems centered more on strategic and operational military considerations than on politics, jingoistic ultranationalism, or misplaced national pride. For example, Pakistan may well have foregone a nuclear capability in exchange for a US guarantee to support Pakistan's territorial integrity and interests in Kashmir against India's massive conventional superiority. These Pakistani sentiments are well reflected in the words of Pakistan's then-foreign minister Gohar Ayub Khan, who stated in a local television interview that Pakistan would be willing to forego nuclear testing only if it were given conventional weapon systems advanced enough to take on India's conventional military forces. He went on to say that these weapons should be given to Pakistan at no cost, and that they should be transferred immediately.[21]

The Strategic Determinants of Pakistan's Insecurity Dilemma

Pakistan's insecurity dilemma, and thus by extension its desire to acquire a nuclear capability, is centered on two sets of vital strategic factors: military geography, and the extent and availability of resources for the conduct of conventional military operations. Geography, along with topography, has played a key role in military strategy throughout the history of warfare, and the case of India and Pakistan is no exception. The issue of limited Pakistani resources for conventional warfare encompasses not only the limits that follow from having a smaller population and a smaller economy, but also the limits resulting from the lack of access to modern conventional weapons. These strategic factors, taken together, contribute to two primary security policy issues of critical importance and concern for Pakistan. First, Pakistan is faced with having to find a way to resolve the inherent contradiction between maintaining a peacetime defense posture that is as inexpensive as possible, while also ensuring that this defense posture can blunt and stall an Indian attack launched with little or no advance warning. Second, with respect to its decisions regarding force structure, equipment, deployment, and operational doctrine, Pakistan is by necessity forced into being reactive to and restricted by the analogous Indian decisions. This Pakistani dilemma is well described by Ross Masood Husain:

The overriding national objective of India goes beyond ensuring its national security to attaining regional hegemony, and India appears to have devised a strategy whereby it seeks to accomplish that objective through military means. The military strategy of India seems to involve a mix of continental and maritime approaches, an emphasis on war-fighting rather than deterrence, a rapid reinforcement posture and an emphasis on tactical and operational initiative. This strategic choice sets the parameters within which [Pakistan's] choices about force structure and decisions on military doctrine are made.[22]

The strategic factors that have generated these security concerns require some elaboration.

In very general terms, Pakistan is a country of 803,943 square kilometers, in comparison with India's 3,166,829 square kilometers. But this in and of itself does not tell the whole story. Unfortunately for Pakistan, it faces India, geographically speaking, along the length of its long axis, thereby leaving it without any strategic depth. As a result, most of Pakistan's population, industry, and arable land are located within 300 to 400 kilometers from the India-Pakistan border. This places all of Pakistan's major population centers, as well as all of its conventional military assets, well within the strike range of India's combat aircraft and ballistic missile forces.

The absence of strategic depth affects Pakistan's insecurity dilemma in three ways. First, classical military doctrine dictates that a country ought to give up ground initially in the face of an enemy offensive, withdrawing into the depths of its own territory. Such a strategy makes it possible for the defender to absorb that first heavy blow of the attacker even while preserving the bulk of its own strength; to identify the primary offensive axes of the attacker so that defending forces may be more efficiently allocated to the task of halting the attacker's offensive; and to force the attacker to operate far from its sources of logistical support, thus rendering the continuation of the offensive that much harder. Simply put, trading away "geographic space" for "reaction time" is a sound military strategy for the defender. This has been well illustrated by the Russians, first against Napoleon and then against Hitler. The absence of strategic depth strips Pakistan of this classic defensive strategy.[23]

Second, the geography of Pakistan leaves its major cities and lines of communication vulnerable to India as well. The capital city of Islamabad and the adjacent city of Rawalpindi are just 80 kilometers or so from the India-Pakistan border. Hyderabad is about 130 kilometers from the frontier, and the invaluable port city of Karachi is about 160 kilometers away.[24] The eastern outskirts of the large Pakistani city of Lahore are a mere 15 kilometers from the border, making it highly likely that it would be encircled by the Indian army within hours of the initiation of hostilities. Furthermore, most of Pakistan's critical highways and rail lines also run close to and parallel to the border. The only terrain feature that could have provided Pakistan with some protection, the Indus River, runs to the west of all major Pakistani cities, with Karachi being the only significant exception. According to a Pakistani assessment of its own strategic weaknesses, "Pakistan feels exposed because its lines of communication and the highly developed canal system that irrigates the fertile areas of Pakistan that are critical to its economic survival run close to the Indo-Pakistani border. . . . India's capture of just [40 kilometers] would wipe out Pakistan because its communications, irrigation, industry, and population are all together within that depth."[25] An additional complicating factor for Pakistan is the fact that Karachi is the only deepwater seaport available to Pakistan, making it very easy for India to enforce a naval blockade of Pakistan and thereby cut off Pakistan's access to international commerce.[26]

Third, all of Pakistan's airbases,[27] including those from which Pakistan's very small force of nuclear-capable US-supplied F-16 aircraft would operate, are extremely vulnerable to massive Indian preemptive air strikes[28] with smart-bomb technology supplied to India by none other than the United States.[29] All of Pakistan's nuclear and ballistic missile research and deployment sites are similarly vulnerable to Indian air strikes. This is a particularly troublesome problem for Pakistani defense planners, because air support is a crucial element of an effective defensive combat strategy. Even more troubling for Pakistan, however, is the reality that it could lose its entire arsenal of aircraft and ballistic missiles capable of delivering nuclear warheads very early on in any war with India. Instead of being able to wait to see if the use of tactical nuclear weapons is its only remaining option for breaking up India's offensive military formations and reversing Indian battlefield gains, Pakistan would be faced with an immediate decision regarding the use of tactical nuclear weapons as soon as hostilities are initiated—perhaps even before they are initiated. In other words, Pakistan would face the classic dilemma vis-à-vis its nuclear arsenal in the event of war with India: "Use them or lose them."

Things are no better for Pakistan on the Indian side of the 1,300-kilometer-long common border. Of the four Indian states bordering Pakistan, only Rajasthan offers good terrain conditions for large, mechanized offensive forces. The border area in Gujarat state is composed of marshlands, Punjab state is covered with rice paddies, and Kashmir is mountainous. But precisely because the vast desert and plains of Rajasthan state offer the best conditions for the large-scale operation of mechanized forces, Rajasthan is very likely to be the springboard for any Indian offensive into Pakistan,[30] leaving little if any possibility for significant Pakistani territorial gains along that sector of the border.[31] Furthermore, even if Pakistan were to seriously entertain the notion of staging a significant ground offensive of its own deep into Indian territory, major strategic objectives such as the critical Indian cities of New Delhi and Mumbai (formerly Bombay) are over 320 kilometers and 640 kilometers, respectively, from the Indo-Pakistani frontier.[32]

The second major strategic factor affecting Pakistan's insecurity dilemma is the massive quantitative and qualitative advantage enjoyed by the Indian armed forces relative to Pakistan's. India's significant advantage over Pakistan in terms of its population size and gross domestic product (GDP) translate directly into a major advantage in conventional military forces. According to 1999 data provided by the International Institute for Strategic Studies,[33] India had a population of about 1,016,242,000 and a GDP of $440 billion, in comparison with Pakistan's population of about 148,012,000 and GDP of $61.6 billion. The national debts of India and Pakistan were $99 billion and $34.5 billion, respectively. India spent about $14.2 billion on its armed forces, comprising about 1,303,000 active-duty and 535,000 reserve military personnel. Its major military equipment holdings included about 3,400 main battle tanks, about 4,450 artillery pieces and rocket launchers, more than 800 combat aircraft, 16 submarines, and 26 major warships (including one aircraft carrier). In comparison, Pakistan spent about $3.5 billion on about 612,000 active-duty and 513,000 reserve military personnel. Its major military equipment holdings included about 2,250 main battle tanks, about 1,750 artillery pieces and rocket launchers, some 400 combat aircraft, 7 submarines, and 8 major warships (but no aircraft carriers). India has more than a two-to-one conventional superiority over Pakistan. India also enjoys a significant superiority over Pakistan in equipment quality. For example, while Pakistan has been able to procure and deploy a mere 40 modern combat aircraft over the past two decades, India has placed or anticipates placing into service over 650 modern aircraft within that same time frame.[34] Tables 8.1 and 8.2 provide a breakdown of the Indian and Pakistani offensive land forces and the Indian and Pakistani air forces, respectively.

Ballistic missiles are one type of weapon system where Pakistan currently has a significant edge over India. This is not surprising, since ballistic missile systems are relatively inexpensive to develop, deploy, and maintain. They are considerably less vulnerable to preemptive strikes (particularly if they are small and mobile systems), and they have a much higher probability of successfully delivering their nuclear payloads on target than manned aircraft. The corresponding disadvantage, though, is that ballistic missiles do not offer the broad range of mission capability or operational flexibility that manned aircraft are able to offer military planners. Pakistan has around 130 ballistic missile launchers in its

Table 8.1
Orders of Battle for Indian and Pakistani Offensive Land Forces, 2000-2001

Offensive combat formations: Formation Type	Number	
	India	Pakistan
Armored divisions	3	2
Armored brigades	5	6
Armored reconnaissance regiments	0	3
Mechanized infantry divisions	4	1
Mechanized infantry brigades	0	6
Airborne, commando, and special forces brigades/regiments	4	4
Amphibious brigades/regiments	2	0

Offensive combat equipment: Equipment Category (excluding equipment in storage)	Inventory	
	India	Pakistan
Main battle tanks	2,654	2,325
Light tanks and armored infantry fighting vehicles	890	100
Reconnaissance vehicles and armored personnel carriers	110	1,215
Self-propelled artillery	80+	202
Attack helicopters	31	19

inventory at present, while India has about 30 launchers.[35] The technical characteristics of Pakistan's inventory of ballistic missile systems are to be found in Table 8.3.

There are two reasons for Pakistan's inability to compete with India on the qualitative level. On the one hand, Pakistan's considerably smaller GDP and considerably larger foreign debt (relative to GDP) make it virtually impossible for Pakistan to spend a significant amount of its very limited hard currency resources on buying sophisticated weapon systems from abroad. Resources that can be spared are better spent on nuclear and ballistic missile systems because

Table 8.2
Orders of Battle for the Indian and Pakistani Air Forces, 2000-2001

INDIAN AIR FORCE (Bharatiya Vayu Sena)			
Aircraft Type	Number of Squadrons	Inventory	
Fighters			
MiG-29 S/SE/UB	3	74	
MiG-23 MF/UB	1	26	
MiG-21 bis,/U	10	168	
MiG-21 FL/U/UM	4	66	
Fighter-bombers			
Su-30 K/MK/MKI	1	18	
Jaguar S(I)/M(I)/B(I)	5	122	
Mirage 2000 H/TH	2	44	
MiG-27 ML	7	135	
MiG-23 BN/UB	3	50	
MiG-21 M/MF	4	69	

PAKISTANI AIR FORCE (Pakistan Fiza'ya)		
Aircraft Type	Number of Squadrons	Inventory
Fighters		
Mirage III EA	1	38
F-7 P, FT-7 P (Chi.)	5	129
F-6, FT-6 (Chi.)	1	65
Fighter-bombers		
F-16 A/B	2	32
Mirage V PA/DPA/EF/DF,	5	87
Mirage III DA/DP		
Mirage III EP/RP	1	24
A-5-III (Chi.)	2	42

they provide a bigger bang for the buck. This arming strategy is clearly visible
in Pakistan's significant numerical advantage over India with respect to ballistic
missile launchers. Serious efforts have been undertaken by Pakistan to establish
a domestic industrial base for military production, and domestic industry does
contribute substantially to the maintenance of military hardware and the production of some weapon systems and munitions.[36]

Table 8.3
Pakistan's Ballistic Missile Systems

System Name	Range (km)	Warhead (kg)	Fuel Type
Hatf-1/1A	80/100	500	Solid
Hatf-2	300	500	Solid
Hatf-3 Tarmuk	550	600	Solid
Hatf-4 Shaheen 1	750	320	Solid
Hatf-5 Ghauri 1	1,100 to 1,500	700	Liquid
Hatf-6 Ghauri 2	2,000 or 2,300	1,000 or 700	Liquid

On the other hand, geopolitics also plays a role in limiting Pakistan's ability to acquire high-technology conventional weapon systems. Because of Pakistan's clandestine nuclear weapons program, and congressionally mandated sanctions that have followed from that program, the US has refused to sell to Pakistan the high-technology weapons that it wishes to possess. Ironically, this US
arms transfer ban has forced Pakistan to move even further toward reliance on
nuclear weapons for deterrence and defense.[37] The United Kingdom and France
have been quite willing to sell modern arms to Pakistan. However, these countries exact market prices and demand complete payment in hard currency for
their hardware, making it incredibly expensive for a country like Pakistan to buy
European high-technology military equipment in any reasonable quantities.
Russia would appear to be a good potential source of high-technology weapons,
given that it has actively courted buyers around the world for its weapon systems since the collapse of the former Soviet Union. Unfortunately for Pakistan,
Russia's long-standing relationship with India as India's primary supplier of
military hardware, and India's position as one of Russia's largest and most reliable clients, has made Pakistan one of only a handful of countries in the world
with which Russia has pointedly refused to conduct any military commerce.[38]
Given these geopolitical and fiscal conditions, China has been the only major
arms supplier with which Pakistan has been able to build a durable patron-client
relationship. Chinese conventional weapon systems, however, do not compare
favorably, in terms of quality, with equivalent Western or even Russian weapon
systems.[39]

CONCLUSION: THE CENTRAL ROLE OF NUCLEAR WEAPONS IN PAKISTAN'S SECURITY POLICY

From the discussion above it should be rather clear that India's overwhelming superiority in conventional military forces is a cause for great concern in Islamabad. Because of Pakistan's strategic weaknesses vis-à-vis India, successive Pakistani governments of all stripes have been wedded to the goal of obtaining a nuclear deterrent force since the mid-1970s. Pakistan's fears about India are at the core of its doctrine for the use of nuclear weapons:

Pakistan's nuclear arsenal is India-specific and designed to counter the perceived conventional and nuclear superiority of its larger neighbor. It has an implicit first-use doctrine. . . . [Given] India's conventional superiority, nuclear weapons are seen as equalizing the imbalance. They are to be used at the appropriate moment of Pakistan's choosing to preserve the existence of Pakistan. . . . This [implies] that there [is] scope for limited military engagements as long as they [are] confined to a localized area . . . and did not escalate into either hot pursuit or a fully fledged conventional war. Either one of the latter eventualities would signal a break-out as far as Pakistan [is] concerned, carrying the prospect of the conflict expanding to threaten the state of Pakistan and, therefore, eventually escalating to the nuclear level.[40]

Pakistan's military strategy is therefore one of forward deployment of mechanized and light infantry units in interlocking, layered defensive positions that begin right at the border with India, with its limited number of armored units being held far behind the front lines in strategic reserve to help seal breaches in the front lines or to counterattack if opportunities present themselves. A large number of highly mobile ballistic missile systems armed with tactical nuclear warheads are also to be held in strategic reserve, so that they may be employed to break up Indian strike formations effecting a major Pakistani collapse on any sector of the battlefront. Given the 1,300-kilometerlong border that Pakistan must defend, and the significant Indian quantitative and qualitative advantage in conventional military forces, a major Indian offensive is quite likely to produce such a breakthrough. Thus, any future India-Pakistan conflict going beyond a limited clash of forces along a small sector of the common border to a fullblown war is very likely to escalate to the use of tactical nuclear weapons.

NOTES

1. Hamza Alavi, "Ethnicity, Muslim Society, and the Pakistan Ideology," in Anita Weiss (ed.), *Islamic Reassertion in Pakistan: The Application of Islamic Laws in a Modern State* (Syracuse, NY: Syracuse University Press, 1986), p. 22.
2. Alavi, "Ethnicity, Muslim Society, and the Pakistan Ideology."
3. According to many estimates, approximately 7-8 million people moved across the newly created India-Pakistan border at Partition (in both directions). There were violent riots associated with this movement of people, resulting in massive dislocation, injuries, rapes, and the death of as many as 1 million people. Today, Pakistan is approximately 95 percent Muslim.

4. Not all factions within the movement in Kashmir support union with Pakistan. Some groups have complete independence as their goal, while some factions want greater autonomy within the framework of Indian federalism.

5. This community is referred to variously as Pashtuns, Pathans, and Pakhtuns.

6. Greater ethnic tensions were not the only fallout of the Afghan war. The effort against the Soviets also led to a huge arms buildup within Pakistan, which served to further militarize Pakistani society in what has been called the "Kalashnikov culture." In addition, the Afghan war led to an increase in the narcotics trade.

7. The Pakistani Supreme Court later declared this imposition of martial law illegal.

8. For more details, see Selig S. Harrison, "Baluch Nationalism and Superpower Rivalry," *International Security* 5, 3 (1980-81), pp. 152-63; Selig S. Harrison, *In Afghanistan's Shadow: Baluch Nationalism and Soviet Temptations* (New York: Carnegie Endowment for International Peace, 1981); C.G.P. Rakisits, "Centre-Province Relations in Pakistan under President Zia: The Government's and the Opposition's Approaches," *Pacific Affairs* 61, 1 (1998), pp. 78-97.

9. Anita Weiss, "The Historical Debate on Islam and the State in South Asia," in Anita Weiss (ed.), *Islamic Reassertion in Pakistan: The Application of Islamic Laws in a Modern State* (Syracuse, NY: Syracuse University Press, 1986), p. 9.

10. W. Howard Wriggins writes that many in the Pakistani foreign policy establishment felt that the US had "let them down" in the 1965 and 1971 wars with India, and could not be considered a reliable ally. See "Pakistan's Foreign Policy after the Invasion of Afghanistan," *Pacific Affairs* 57, 2 (1984), p. 290.

11. Wriggins, "Pakistan's Foreign Policy after the Invasion of Afghanistan," pp. 285-6.

12. See Shirin Tahir-Kheli and W.O. Staudenmaier, "The Saudi-Pakistan Military Relationship: Implications for U.S. Policy," *Orbis* 26, 1 (1982), pp. 155-71. In some circles, the proposed product of a Pakistani nuclear program even came to be known as the "Islamic" bomb. See also Hasan-Askari Rizvi, "Pakistan: Ideology and Foreign Policy," *Asian Affairs*, Spring 1983, pp. 48-59.

13. The Afghanistan war's dramatic effects continue to the present day. Most notably, Pakistan was faced with a humanitarian crisis, as millions of Afghan refugees streamed into Pakistan. Again, this humanitarian crisis was coupled with a more delicate political one, since the presence of the refugees complicated the ethnic dimension of Pakistani politics.

14. Wriggins, "Pakistan's Foreign Policy after the Invasion of Afghanistan," p. 286. See also Y. Vertzberger, *The Enduring Entente. Sino-Pakistan Relations, 1960-1980* (New York: Praeger, 1983).

15. Ajay Singh, "The General's Tactic: In Beijing, Musharraf Makes a Few Points," *Asiaweek* 26, 3 (28 January 2000), p. 18.

16. International Institute for Strategic Studies, *The Military Balance: 1971-1972* (London: IISS, 1971).

17. Carnegie Endowment for International Peace (1998), "Non-Proliferation—Tracking Nuclear Proliferation, 1998: Pakistan," from the Internet web site of the CEIP <http://www.ceip.org>.

18. David Albright, "The Shots Heard 'Round the World,'" *Bulletin of the Atomic Scientists*, July/August 1998; M.A. Khan and Ezio Bonsignore, "India and Pakistan Towards Nuclear Power Status," *Military Technology*, July 1998; and Andrew Koch, "Report: Nuclear Testing in South Asia and the CTBT," *Nonproliferation Review* 3, 3 (1996).

19. Pervaiz Iqbal Cheema, "Arms Procurement in Pakistan: Balancing the Needs for Quality, Self-reliance and Diversity of Supply," in Eric Arnett (ed.), *Military Capacity and the Risk of War: China, India, Pakistan and Iran* (Oxford: Oxford University Press, 1997), pp. 152-3.

20. As quoted by Zafar Iqbal Cheema, "Pakistan's Nuclear Policies: Attitudes and Posture," in P. R. Chari, Pervaiz Iqbal Cheema, and Iftekharuzzaman (eds.), *Nuclear Non-Proliferation in India and Pakistan: South Asian Perspectives* (New Delhi: Monohar, 1996), p. 105.

21. As quoted in "Pakistan to Restrain Nuclear Test if Aided to Bring It in Balance with India," *India Daily*, 25 May 1998.

22. Ross Masood Husain, "Threat Perception and Military Planning in Pakistan: the Impact of Technology, Doctrine and Arms Control," in Eric Arnett (ed.), *Military Capacity and the Risk of War: China, India, Pakistan and Iran* (Oxford: Oxford University Press, 1997), p. 133.

23. Geoffrey Kemp and Robert E. Harkavy, *Strategic Geography and the Changing Middle East* (Washington, DC: Brookings Institution Press, 1997), p. 161.

24. Kemp and Harkavy, *Strategic Geography and the Changing Middle East*, p. 163.

25. As quoted by Shirin Tahir-Kheli, "Defense Planning in Pakistan," in Stephanie Neuman (ed.), *Defense Planning in Less-Industrialized States* (Lexington, MA: D.C. Heath, 1984), p. 212.

26. See Eric Grove, "Maritime Forces and Stability in Southern Asia," in Eric Arnett (ed.), *Military Capacity and the Risk of War: China, India, Pakistan and Iran* (Oxford: Oxford University Press, 1997), pp. 299-301, for a brief discussion of Indian and Pakistani naval strategy.

27. The combat aircraft of the Pakistani air force operate from just seven primary air bases: Masroor, Mianwali, Minhas/Kamra, Peshawar, Rafiqui-Shorkot, Sargodha, and Sumungli. The F-16 force and some of the ballistic missile force are located at the modern Sargodha complex.

28. The Indian air force has six squadrons of highly capable Su-30 and Jaguar aircraft dedicated to the deep strike role, backed up by nine and a half squadrons of Mirage 2000 and MiG-27 fighter-bombers.

29. Carnegie Endowment for International Peace (1998).

30. Two of India's three "strike" corps, I Corps headquartered at Mathura in Uttar Pradesh state and XXI Corps headquartered at Bhopal in Madhya Pradesh state, are part of India's strategic reserve and are oriented toward the Rajasthan sector of the India-Pakistan border. The third "strike" corps formation, II Corps headquartered at Chandimandir in Punjab state, is deployed forward on the border.

31. In the last two wars, most of the fighting has taken place on the Punjab-Kashmir sector of the border between Sialkot to the north and Lahore to the south. There was also some fighting in the Rann of Kutch area on the Gujarat border. The Rajasthan desert frontier area was relatively quiet. Many military analysts suggest, however, that the next war between India and Pakistan might see India attempting to employ concentrated combined-arms forces on a very large scale to drive deep into Pakistan from the Great Indian Desert in Rajasthan. See Kemp and Harkavy, *Strategic Geography and the Changing Middle East*, pp. 402-9; and Husain, "Threat Perception and Military Planning in Pakistan: the Impact of Technology, Doctrine and Arms Control," pp. 133-6.

32. D.K. Palit, *The Lightning Campaign: The Indo-Pakistan War, 1971* (Salisbury, UK: Compton Press, 1972), p. 77, asserts that "the Pakistani High Command

has for a number of years nursed a pipedream about launching a massive, surprise offensive deep into Indian territory spearheaded by armored formations, a la Moshe Dayan."

33. International Institute for Strategic Studies, *The Military Balance: 2000-2001* (London: Oxford University Press, 2000).

34. Pakistan took delivery of 40 US-supplied F-16 fighters in the mid-1980s. An additional 71 F-16s were ordered in the late 1980s, but their delivery was blocked in 1990 on account of the provisions of the Pressler Amendment barring US arms transfers to Pakistan. It was 28 of these aircraft, manufactured before the order was canceled but held in storage in the US since the early 1990s despite Pakistan having paid for them, that the US offered to deliver to Pakistan as a "reward" for not conducting tit-for-tat nuclear tests in 1998. Deliveries or anticipated deliveries of modern combat aircraft to India include some 165 Jaguars from the UK, 59 Mirage 2000s from France, and 165 MiG-27s, 80 MiG-29s, and 190 Su-30s aircraft from Russia.

35. Pakistan's ballistic missile force consists of some 100 indigenously developed Hatf-1/1A, Hatf-4 (Shaheen 1), and Hatf-5 (Ghauri 1) launchers, and perhaps 30 Chinese-supplied M11 launchers (labeled Hatf-3 Tarmuk). All of Pakistan's launchers are mobile systems. India deploys around 30 indigenously developed SS-150 Prithvi mobile systems. Both countries are developing more advanced and longer-range ballistic and cruise missile systems.

36. Yezid Sayigh, "Arms Production in Pakistan and Iran: the Limits of Self-reliance," in Eric Arnett (ed.), *Military Capacity and the Risk of War: China, India, Pakistan and Iran* (Oxford: Oxford University Press, 1997), pp. 161-77.

37. P.I. Cheema, "Arms Procurement in Pakistan: Balancing the Needs for Quality, Self-reliance and Diversity of Supply," p. 153; L.S. Spector, *Nuclear Ambitions* (Boulder, CO: Westview Press, 1990), pp. 63-117.

38. Ian Anthony, "Arms Exports to Southern Asia: Policies of Technology Transfer and Denial in the Supplier Countries," in Eric Arnett (ed.), *Military Capacity and the Risk of War: China, India, Pakistan and Iran* (Oxford: Oxford University Press, 1997), pp. 277-98.

39. P.I. Cheema, "Arms Procurement in Pakistan: Balancing the Needs for Quality, Self-reliance and Diversity of Supply," pp. 154-60.

40. W.P.S. Sidhu, "Pakistan Puts Its Nuclear Cards on the Table," *Jane's Intelligence Review*, July 1998, p. 27.

9

Shades of Realism: The Impact of Personality, Ideology, and Systemic Pressure on Indian Foreign Policy

Timothy D. Hoyt

For generations, theorists and analysts of international relations have sought to understand the motivations of actors in the international system. The sources of policy have been defined from a number of perspectives, each possessing particular strengths and, sometimes, weaknesses. This chapter will apply the concepts of *levels of analysis*[1] and three key approaches to explaining international relations—*realism*, *liberalism*, and *idealism*[2]—to the examination of Indian foreign policy in the twentieth century. India represents a particularly interesting case for study, as each of these levels and approaches provides particular insight into Indian policy.

In an effort to limit, and better illuminate, important aspects of Indian foreign policy, this chapter will focus on three elements of policy related to security—a driving force in international relations. India's approach to alignment, both during and after the Cold War, is a defining characteristic of Indian foreign policy, but one which was subject to shifts and reinterpretation. Similarly, India's strong stance on disarmament and arms control was based on moral assumptions apparently at odds with its decision to test and deploy nuclear weapons. Finally, Indian willingness to use military force for political objectives has varied widely since independence.

This chapter, therefore, will examine the key factors influencing Indian foreign policy in each of these three areas. It will also suggest several competing themes in Indian foreign policy which continue to emerge in current political debate. Particular emphasis will be placed on the roles of ideas, individuals, institutions, and structural pressures on Indian perceptions and security responses. The conclusion will detail the tensions inherent in India's policymaking apparatus, and suggest areas for future study.

THREE VISIONS OF INDIA

Modern Indian history is dominated by three charismatic and influential leaders—Mahatma Gandhi, Jawaharlal Nehru, and Nehru's daughter Indira Gandhi. Each had different visions of India and its role in the world. Each supported significantly different policies on the legitimacy of military force, the relationship between India and Pakistan, and the proper role of India in the international community.[3]

Mahatma Gandhi is best known for his long campaign of nonviolent protest and civil disobedience, which created a model for the pursuit of civil and human rights in the United States and elsewhere. Gandhi was the spiritual leader of the Indian National Congress, the political organization which led the movement for Indian independence. His political views rejected violence, except if necessary to oppose evil, and called for an insular India based on autarkic policies and a return to traditional cottage industries. Gandhi did not believe in the political division of India and Pakistan, and in fact went on a hunger strike to protest India's refusal to abide by financial elements of the partition agreement. He was eventually killed by a member of a militant Hindu organization because of his sympathy for Muslim victims of the partition crisis.

Nehru was the political mastermind of the Indian independence movement. His vision of India's role in the world was one of broad engagement and as a moral example.[4] He viewed Indian civilization as a potentially powerful force in international affairs, a leader of the anticolonial movement, a voice for civil and human rights, and a "third way" between the antagonistic forces of communism and the capitalist West. Nehru supported a policy of nonalignment and *panchsheel* (nonintervention), opposed the growing arms race between the US and the Soviet Union, and hoped to use international organizations like the United Nations to mediate conflict and achieve a more just international society. Nehru supported the use of force within what he considered India's boundaries, and resorted to force on a number of occasions—not only in the Indo-Pakistani dispute over Kashmir, but also in then-Portuguese Goa, Muslim Hyderabad, and on the border of India and China.

Nehru's daughter, Indira Gandhi, inherited the mantle of leadership in the late 1960s—contributing to a legacy of Nehru family involvement in Indian politics that continues today with her daughter-in-law, Italian-born Sonia Gandhi, who remains a leader in the Indian Congress Party. Indira Gandhi's political focus was more regional, responding to the disastrous war of 1962 against China and the 1965 clashes with Pakistan. Under her leadership, India took a more pro-Soviet view of nonalignment, and became firmly dependent on Soviet arms and political support. She took advantage of grave errors and atrocious human rights violations by Pakistan to liberate the eastern half of that country and help establish Bangladesh. Her autocratic leadership and efforts to firmly assert central control from Delhi over India's chaotic federal politics eventually prompted her to test nuclear weapons—a decision driven at least in part by the need to increase domestic support—but also to declare a state of national emergency and impose the functional equivalent of martial law. Voted out of office in 1977, she reemerged as the elected leader in 1980, just in time to take a public noncon-frontational position with the Soviet Union over its invasion of Afghanistan.[5] Under Indira and her son Rajiv Gandhi, Indian foreign policy became more militarized, including a series of provocative military exercises in 1986-87 and a disastrous intervention in Sri Lanka from 1987-90.

Indian foreign policy, therefore, has spanned a wide range of options, re-flecting both the judgments of individual leaders and also the perceptions of systemic pressures and historical factors under which decisions were made. The next sections will briefly analyze three key elements of Indian foreign pol-icy—the role of the military, the role of alliances, and the issue of nuclear weap-ons and disarmament. Each area provides important insights into how Indian foreign policy is created and changes over time.

Military Policy[6]

The variations in Indian military policy can best be discerned by focusing on three areas—civil-military relations, defense budgeting, and the use of force. Each of these areas defines and constrains a state's diplomatic and military op-tions. India's preferences have varied widely over time, and cannot be ex-plained by a single methodological approach. For example, India—like many other democracies and other states—thinks of itself as a peace-loving nation, and is closely linked to the pacifist ideology of Mahatma Gandhi and the nonin-terventionist ideology of Nehru. It has, however, resorted to the use of military force outside its borders on at least five occasions, and has suffered harsh inter-national criticism for the use of military forces for counterinsurgency purposes within Indian territory.

It should hardly be surprising that India has a history of complicated and sometimes contradictory civil-military relations. The Indian independence movement, led by Mahatma Gandhi, relied on nonviolent demonstrations to undermine the legitimacy of British imperial rule. The Indian army's function as the primary instrument through which Britain enforced its colonial policy con-tributed to hostility between the Indian National Congress (INC) and the mili-tary. As early as 1942, the INC refused to state its support for the Allied mili-tary effort against Germany and Japan.

The Indian independence movement actually exhibited at least three differ-ent approaches toward the military. The most idealistic, exemplified by Gandhi, saw the military as unnecessary in post-independence India. He said, "Today, they must plough the land, dig wells, clean latrines and do every constructive work that they can, and thus turn the peoples' hatred of them into love."[7] A sec-ond approach was that of Jawaharlal Nehru, India's first prime minister and leading intellectual. Nehru accepted the need for conventional military forces, but he preferred to minimize defense expenditure and rely on diplomacy to en-sure national security. A third approach, discredited by World War II, was rep-resented by Subhas Chandra Bose, who led an Indian National Army which supported the forces of Imperial Japan, in hopes that a war of national liberation would lead to Indian independence through military force.[8]

Early Indian civil-military relations, therefore, were confused. The army—the dominant service, was distrusted by Nehru and the INC, and was symbolically degraded in official status. The small air force and navy, on the other hand, received more official support, partly as a counterbalance to the institutional strength of the army and partly because they had mutinied in support of independence.[9] The military also suffered from an absence of trained higher-level officers, relying initially on British volunteers for leadership, and from the division of the military between India and Pakistan under the terms of the partition agreement.[10] Military leadership was carefully isolated from key decision-making bodies and was allowed only limited input even in security affairs. Basic preparations for predictable problems were rejected by political leadership—Nehru vetoed preparation of a manual for mountain fighting for fear of alienating China.[11]

Under Nehru, India regularly used military force to secure what it considered its "natural borders." This included the 1947-48 Kashmir dispute with Pakistan and the invasion and occupation of Hyderabad. It also included a series of border clashes with China and the invasion and conquest of Portuguese Goa—an act which risked war with a NATO ally of the US. However, Nehru refused to intervene to help Tibet, offered to mediate the Korean War rather than choose sides or send troops, and otherwise stayed removed from military involvements outside India's immediate periphery. This was a period of low military budgets, when procurement and research and development (R&D) were focused on prestige projects or used for economic development, and when the civilian minister of defense—V. K. Krishna Menon—interfered in army promotion and almost caused a political crisis.[12]

Nehru's ill-fated policy of probing the Sino-Indian border led to the disastrous Himalayan War of 1962. After this conflict, Indian military policy changed substantially. The defense budget and number of men under arms virtually doubled. From 1962 until the mid-1970s, the military leadership's opinions regarding defense acquisition began to be taken more seriously, and the leadership gained a voice in purely professional issues of military science and operational deployment. India's military requirements for high-technology equipment influenced policies on non-alignment. India's political leaders also showed a greater willingness to use military force—Indira Gandhi's decision to use force to liberate Bangladesh in 1971 severely hurt Pakistan and assured Indian regional hegemony.

In the 1980s, for a brief period, the military abruptly gained substantial influence in determining Indian foreign policy. The combination of an inexperienced prime minister (Rajiv Gandhi), a charismatic and intellectual chief of army staff (General K. Sundarji), and a quiet but brilliant civilian administrator and planner (Arun Singh) led to a far more aggressive use of military coercion and much higher defense budgets. Responding to Pakistan's emerging nuclear capability, India staged a massive, highly provocative military exercise on the border between the two countries which led to a political crisis.[13] This demonstration of Indian military capability, larger than any previous military exercise and including virtually all of India's mechanized units, could easily have been expanded into an actual invasion. Virtually simultaneous maneuvers and exercises were held on the Chinese border, with similar results. For the first time, military officers were included in nuclear planning.[14]

During this period, defense budgets increased to record percentages of gross national product and government expenditure. Vast shipments of weapons were purchased from the Soviet Union, and all three services began to implement grandiose expansions in force posture and capability. Indian intelligence services actively encouraged insurgencies in neighboring Sri Lanka and elsewhere. India's foreign policy, exemplified by the "Indira Doctrine" and the "Rajiv Doctrine," used India's military preponderance to justify a more proactive interventionist policy within the South Asian region, including inserting an Indian peacekeeping force into Sri Lanka and responding to an attempted coup in the Maldives. This period ended with another potential nuclear crisis in 1990, as both India and Pakistan misinterpreted one another's actions over winter military exercises.[15]

The assassination of Rajiv Gandhi on May 21, 1991, ended India's brief flirtation with assertive, militarist foreign policies. The 1990-91 economic crisis, and the collapse of the Soviet Union and its arms industries, crippled the military expansion originally planned in the late 1980s. The threat and use of force were downplayed by a series of vulnerable coalition governments more concerned with economic revival than asserting Indian regional predominance. The election of a more nationalist government, led by the Bharatiya Janata Party (BJP), in 1998 increased the militancy of government rhetoric—the minister of defense publicly identified China as India's greatest enemy. The nuclear tests in May 1998, and more important Pakistan's limited invasion of Kargil the following spring, contributed to increasing military input in certain aspects of foreign policy—a position similar to that of the 1962-75 period. India has created a National Security Council and a joint service command, and has given the military more influence in the creation of nuclear doctrine and command and control. After the nuclear tests, the defense budget increased substantially, primarily in nuclear-related areas. After Kargil, however, an additional large supplement was provided.[16]

Throughout the past two decades, however, the military has also been asked to take a large role in internal security—a role that many analysts and officers fear undermines professionalism and conventional capabilities. Insurgencies in Jammu and Kashmir and also in Punjab, states which border Pakistan, have strained military forces since 1984, and a simmering insurgency also continues in the Northeast. Indian forces have been accused of grave human rights violations. In an effort to resolve the dilemma, India has increased the role and numbers of various paramilitary and federal police organizations, effectively creating a parallel military structure for internal security. Efforts to reform the intelligence structure have also accelerated after the Kargil conflict. Cooperation between the military, intelligence bodies, and civilians could clearly still be improved.[17]

Ultimately, Indian military policy can only be adequately explained by a number of different approaches. Civil-military relations, dominated by political

leadership, have clearly been influenced by the ideas of Nehru and Gandhi and
the legacy of imperialism. Indian military capability grew substantially in response to the rise of legitimate external threats, particularly the attacks by Pakistan in 1965 and the disastrous war with China in 1962. Kargil is apparently
having a similar stimulating effect. Use of military coercion as a political instrument, however, is associated with individuals, rather than structural forces,
particularly Indira and Rajiv Gandhi and General Sundarji.

Indian Foreign Policy—Visions of Non-Alignment[18]

Like its military policy, Indian foreign policy is a product of the Indian nationalist movement, as well as the more structural factors of India's size, location, and potential role in global and regional politics. For much of the Cold
War, India pursued a policy of nonalignment with the superpowers. In practice,
however, India tilted to one side or the other depending on circumstances and
perceptions of strategic advantage. Similarly, while India attempted to create
and lead the nonaligned movement (NAM) based on the noninterventionist principles of *panchsheel,*[19] it proved more than willing to modify its principles for
short-term gains or other advantage under the right circumstances. Tension
between idealism and *realpolitik,* and the crucial roles of ideas and individuals,
help to explain the complexities of Indian foreign policy.

Nonalignment, as originally conceived by Nehru, was a response to the
emerging Cold War. As a Fabian Socialist, Nehru lacked the visceral dislike for
Communism found among most American and some British elites. Nehru also
distrusted the US, which he perceived as heir to and defender of Europe's bank-
rupt colonial policies. He perceived the US as a racist society which supported
the most malignant and oppressive capitalist ideas. Given these predispositions,
rejecting alliance with Joseph Stalin and Harry Truman, and later Dwight
Eisenhower, was entirely reasonable.

Nonalignment under Nehru was more than just a national policy. It was
intended to foster a new world order, based on a combination of principles not
unlike those espoused by Woodrow Wilson. Nehru hoped to use the weight of
India's moral strength to undermine colonialism, and then use the power of
emerging postcolonial states to balance the superpowers and arrange for a
peaceful redistribution of power in the international system. Crucial normative
concepts included the principle of nonintervention, as well as some faith in the
potential role of multinational (NAM) and international (UN) institutions. These
institutions would provide alternatives to the use of military force or economic
coercion as a means of settling disputes, and they might encourage a redistribution of resources from the wealthy developed states to the developing world.
India's role as the leading postcolonial state and as a powerful moral force
would provide it with a stronger global role than its large, impoverished status
would otherwise merit in a bipolar system.

Nehru never realized his dream of non-alignment. The Bandung Conference in 1955 that first articulated multinational commitments to *panchsheel* was
led by India, Yugoslavia, Indonesia, China, and Egypt. The latter three were

already drifting into the Soviet bloc in some form. Egypt supported irredentist policies toward Israel that compromised its commitment to nonintervention, and China and Indonesia supported national liberation movements that frightened their neighbors. Finally, despite their mutual declarations of *panchsheel*, China and India were already moving toward conflict based on mutually unacceptable definitions of their Himalayan border.

Nehruvian visions of postcolonial, pan-Asian, and African nonalignment collapsed in 1962, with the Himalayan War disaster. Even before this time, however, cracks had been occurring in the Nehru vision, and non-alignment policies were already contributing to Indian *insecurity*. Nehru's decision to submit the Kashmir dispute to UN arbitration kept the issue in the forefront of UN debates throughout the 1950s—publicity not always to India's advantage. India's refusal to join an anti-Soviet alliance with the US or UK led to Pakistan's entrance into collective security agreements with the US—an act that Eisenhower later lamented as a terrible mistake. The result, however, was a much more heavily armed and economically robust Pakistan with US diplomatic support on the Kashmir issue.

Nonalignment took a decidedly more pragmatic, India-centric focus over the next twenty years. After 1962, Nehru turned to the US for assistance, including joint exercises on Indian territory and negotiations for a substantial military assistance pact. This growing cooperation faltered in 1965, when Pakistan invaded India with US weapons, and the US imposed sanctions on both states. In addition, President Lyndon Johnson deliberately micro-managed food assistance to India in the midst of a serious famine in an effort to lessen corruption and terrible inefficiencies in the Indian distribution system. However, this intervention offended Indian leaders and the public, and it did little for Indo-US relations.[20]

Instead, India turned to the Soviet Union for support. Under Khrushchev, the USSR had taken steps to improve relations with the developing world and had emphasized anti-colonialist rhetoric. In addition, the Soviets agreed to provide India with first-line military equipment—something the West was reluctant to do—at lower cost and on far better terms of payment. This relationship became formal with the signature of the Treaty of Peace and Friendship between India and the USSR in 1971. This treaty was signed shortly before India began military operations against Pakistan to liberate what is now Bangladesh. This new relationship assured India of a veto on the UN Security Council—vital for postponing UN intervention—and some form of nuclear umbrella against US or Chinese nuclear threats. This relationship did *not* equate, however, to India joining the Warsaw Pact or other Soviet organizations, nor did India provide the Soviets with bases or other facilities. US-Indian relations reached their nadir when President Richard Nixon sent the aircraft carrier USS *Enterprise* into the Bay of Bengal during the 1971 war.

India maintained its leadership position in NAM, which was taking a decidedly anti-American tilt at this time. However, it suffered two important defeats in its effort to maintain a dominant position among postcolonial states. First, Pakistan was allowed to join NAM—something India opposed but could not

prevent. Second, India's application to join the Organization of Islamic Conference (OIC) was rejected under Pakistani pressure, despite the fact that India has
one of the largest Muslim populations in the world. The need to maintain good
relations with the increasingly powerful and influential Arab bloc also prevented
India from recognizing Israel.

Under Indira Gandhi, nonalignment became much more closely affiliated
with the Soviet bloc than previous Indian governments. Her domestic difficulties eventually undermined her authority, and a disparate coalition led by the
Janata Party was elected in 1977. In an effort to reassert a more neutral form of
nonalignment, India began negotiations with the Carter administration and with
Western European suppliers for military equipment. This short-lived tilt toward
the US ended abruptly, with the collapse of the Janata coalition and the re-
election of Indira Gandhi in early 1980. This election coincided with the Soviet
invasion of Afghanistan, which Janata criticized as one of its last acts in power.
Indira Gandhi's initial statements refused to condemn the Soviet invasion of a
non-aligned power, reflecting poorly on the depth of India's commitment to
nonintervention and nonalignment.

Indian nonalignment policy in the 1980s did move toward some accommodation with the US, even though both Indira Gandhi and Rajiv Gandhi continued
to rely heavily on massive infusions of Soviet arms. The renewed US alliance
with Pakistan, prompted by the Afghanistan crisis, drew condemnation from
India, but also prompted Indira Gandhi to strengthen India's ties with the new
Reagan administration. Rajiv Gandhi, a great believer in technology, also encouraged better relations with the US, including negotiations for cooperation on
the Indian Light Combat Aircraft, and the sale of sophisticated supercomputers.
The improving US-Indian relationship facilitated US efforts in 1990 to defuse a
potential nuclear crisis between India and Pakistan.

Since the end of the Cold War, nonalignment has become virtually obsolete.
India has reluctantly been forced to engage in a far more unipolar world, led if
not dominated by the US. During the 1990 run-up to Desert Storm, India allowed US transport aircraft to refuel at Indian airports. Faced with substantial
opposition once this news became public, India withdrew permission. The collapse of the Soviet Union coincided with a major Indian economic crisis, forcing
the heavily socialized Indian economy to gradually open to the market. This led
to major protests by opposition parties, as competition forced many firms to shut
down. Reform efforts have proceeded gradually but with significant effect, and
the US is now India's largest trading partner. India's expertise in computers and
software has linked the two economies in very important ways. President Bill
Clinton's visit to India in the spring of 2000 ended with both countries signing a
joint vision statement acknowledging the changing relationship and the opportunities both perceived in closer ties.[21] India quickly volunteered the use of air
bases and facilities for the US war against terrorism in 2001, recognizing an
important shared interest between the two countries.[22]

ARMS CONTROL AND NUCLEAR WEAPONS[23]

India's policy on arms control and nuclear weapons can best be described as convoluted. Since independence, India has frequently been an articulate and impassioned spokesman for disarmament and arms control. At the same time, it vigorously pursued a nuclear "option" by instituting a nuclear research program in 1946, under the direction of Homi Bhabha, a brilliant young scientist. Bhabha and Nehru both agreed that nuclear technology offered great possibilities for India—for example, the ambitious civilian nuclear power program intended to put India on a self-sufficient energy path utilizing local deposits of thorium as a fuel source.[24] Using nuclear technology, India would not be dependent on foreign sources for energy. Dependence of any sort, but particularly technological dependence, was very threatening to India.

This concern over technological dependence also colored India's views on arms control—it was, after all, a more technologically developed Britain which had destroyed the last vestiges of the Indian Empires in the eighteenth and nineteenth centuries, leading to 150 years of colonialism. India therefore supported disarmament, but not at the cost of depriving itself of access to weapons that it might need for self-defense.

Nehru himself, in a crucial debate held on April 6, 1948, admitted that India's failure to keep pace with technology—particularly steam power—had made her a backward country. He also conceded that nuclear energy had both civil and military uses, and that a civilian nuclear program could be used for weapons, although he hoped this would not be necessary.[25] Therefore efforts to control nuclear materials would be fiercely resisted, if they did not apply to all states equally. This dominated India's position on the Nonproliferation Treaty (NPT), which it refused to sign in 1968, and the Comprehensive Test Ban Treaty (CTBT), which it refused to sign in 1995. Nehru had originally proposed a test ban treaty in 1954, and had hailed the signature of the Partial Test Ban Treaty by the US, USSR, and UK in 1963—so the rejection of the latter seems particularly contradictory.

In fact, from the beginning both Nehru and Bhabha viewed the nuclear program as a dual-use project—one which could leapfrog India into the ranks of the most sophisticated technological states, provide for India's future energy needs, *and* provide India, if necessary, with the most modern and decisive military instruments. Nuclear energy, in its civilian and weaponized forms, was a repudiation of colonialism and a demonstration of Indian scientific and military prowess. The nuclear program was kept under Nehru's direct authority, and Bhabha assembled a team of highly capable scientists with virtually no parliamentary oversight. This nuclear enclave would keep the weapons option open in future decades, even when standing prime ministers directly opposed it.

Since the national nuclear program had a security component, Indian arms control policies could not be entirely idealistic, despite Nehru's opposition to the superpower arms race. Indian opposition to the creation of nuclear "haves" and "have-nots" resulted in significant modifications to the International Atomic Energy Agency (IAEA) and to the NPT, which India later refused to sign. India's objection to these treaties can, perhaps, best be summed up by the slogan "nuclear apartheid," coined in rejection of non-universal disarmament proposals.[26] The CTBT debate was even more heated, taking place shortly after the 1995 indefinite extension of NPT. India was particularly offended by the "entry into force" provision, which implied that any state not signing it within three years might be exposed to sanctions from the rest of the international community.

This was already a sore point with India, which had been under various sanctions since 1974. The NPT recognized five "nuclear weapons states"—the US, UK, USSR, China, and France—which had tested weapons before the treaty was submitted in 1968. Bhabha claimed to have been ready for a test, if necessary, in the mid-1960s, but India did not pursue that option. In 1974, however, partly to draw attention away from internal difficulties, Indira Gandhi approved a test explosion of a "Peaceful Nuclear Explosive."[27] The plutonium used in the device was obtained from facilities in the US and Canada, in violation of the original sales agreement. As a result, both Canada and the US began to constrain supplies of nuclear equipment and fuel to India. During the winter of 1995, under a coalition government, India prepared the Pokhran test facilities for another nuclear detonation. This was detected by the US, which threatened to impose sanctions that would endanger India's economic recovery. The idea that India could face further sanctions simply for refusing to sign another treaty was, therefore, a matter of great resentment. India refused to sign the CTBT, despite its history of supporting a test ban.

Interestingly enough, however, none of India's nuclear tests appear to have been driven primarily by security threats—the obvious driver, according to realism, of increased military efforts. India's most vulnerable moment was in 1962, after the crushing defeat by China. When China tested its first nuclear device in 1964, this prompted a long debate in the *Lok Sabha* (Parliament).[28] Still, India declined to develop its own capabilities or to detonate a device, despite continued Chinese testing and the emerging nonproliferation regime. Security concerns were insufficient to persuade either of Nehru's successors—Lal Bahadur Shastri and Indira Gandhi—that nuclear weapons were a priority. Shastri was opposed to nuclear weapons in principle, while Gandhi and the new head of the Indian Atomic Energy Commission (Vikram Sarabhai) both would accept continued work on a Peaceful Nuclear Explosive (permitted by the IAEA), but not a nuclear weapons project.

India's nuclear test, in 1974, also occurred at an unusual point, in terms of security concerns. India's crushing defeat of Pakistan in 1971 created the state of Bangladesh, effectively halving Pakistan's population and resources and reducing the threat of war with Pakistan from two fronts (East and West Pakistan) to one. India's victory cemented its regional hegemony, and Pakistan was in the process of desperately rebuilding. India's treaty with Russia provided it with a nuclear-armed supporter and a veto in the UN Security Council, and the Chinese threat had decreased significantly given India's expanded conventional capability. The nuclear test, therefore, took place at a time when India was actually very secure.

India's nuclear environment changed during the 1980s, as Pakistan developed its own nuclear capability and the US, Pakistan, and China all became more engaged in the region through the Afghanistan conflict. In 1983, Indira Gandhi briefly approved a second nuclear test, but then rescinded the order. In 1987, Rajiv proposed a phased timeline for global disarmament—a proposal that was never seriously considered by the US. Shortly thereafter, he authorized research on the development of thermonuclear weapons. The failure of an idealistic arms control effort led him to the realist alternative—within limits.

Still, India failed to test at a time when, arguably, the security environment was unstable. Instead, support for testing increased during the NPT extension negotiations, including the previously mentioned effort to test in 1995, and a decision by the BJP-led coalition to test in mid-1996, which was forestalled by the collapse of the government. The May 1998 tests were staged by another BJP coalition. Again, it is difficult to argue that India was less secure in 1998 than, say, in 1990. There were concerns from the scientific community, however, that if India did not test soon, it would lose much of its weapons expertise to retirement. Official arguments stated that India was growing increasingly vulnerable to China,[29] but China had been providing the uranium which fueled India's nuclear reactors (and weapons production facilities), while Pakistan's conventional weapons capabilities were atrophied by almost a decade of US sanctions. The result of the tests, at least initially, was a series of American sanctions which damaged India's military capabilities, delaying the Light Combat Aircraft project and cutting off repairs and spare parts for Sea King helicopters.

Security does not adequately explain India's convoluted history of nuclear tests, but idealism cannot explain the failure to support nonproliferation and arms control measures. Clearly, as with other issues, some portion of the explanation must be sought elsewhere—in the role of personalities, of ideas, and of organizations and institutions.

Nehru's dedication to disarmament and simultaneous commitment to national security remains an important tradition, and creates a marked tension in Indian analysis and policy. Indian strategic analysts have turned this around into a policy of "build the bomb to ban the bomb"—only through acquisition of nuclear weapons will India gain the reputation necessary to encourage the five nuclear powers to disarm. Proponents of the nuclear arsenal go even further, trying deliberately to destroy the vision of India as a Gandhian or nonviolent state through deployment of nuclear weapons.[30] This effort was taken to its logical conclusion by India's foremost strategic thinker, K. Subrahmanyam, in an article claiming that Gandhi would have supported India's nuclear weapons, published shortly after the May 1998 tests.[31]

And yet, despite these pressures for a more *realpolitik* approach to the nuclear issue, the Indian government remains wedded to the ideals of Nehru and Gandhi. Prime Minister Vajpayee's statement to the *Lok Sabha* on May 27, 1998, carefully and deliberately refers to Nehru's legacy and to the importance of global disarmament.[32] India's Draft Nuclear Doctrine, released in 1999, is a remarkably passive and confusing document.[33] More recently, India's unexpected support for President George W. Bush's national missile defense plans appear to be tied both to efforts to improve the Indo-US relationship and to Bush's commitment to attempt to reduce the number of nuclear weapons in the US and on a global level.

CONCLUSION

Realists argue that the foreign policy of states can be encapsulated by the study of power and security. Thucydides believed that honor, fear, and self-interest explained the behavior of states.[34] Traditional realists, like Morgenthau and Liska, believe that the pursuit of power explains state behavior, while more modern neo-realists focus on the pursuit of security.[35] It appears, however, that none of these realist methodologies adequately explains Indian foreign policy behavior.

Another approach is the concept of "levels of analysis"—examining the role of individuals, organizations and institutions within the state, and pressures from an anarchic international system to explain state behavior. Using these levels or lenses explains some of the apparently contradictory aspects of Indian policy.

As we have seen, people matter enormously in Indian foreign policy. Nehru dominated Indian politics for over a decade, and he left a family legacy that remains a political power even today. The impact of his personality, and of his policies, cannot be overestimated. The re-election of Indira Gandhi fundamentally changed India's response to the Afghan crisis. Homi Bhabha single-handedly created an Indian nuclear industry that led, fifty years later, to India's nuclear weapons tests. The combination of General Sundarji, Arun Singh, and an inexperienced Rajiv Gandhi set the stage for a significantly more militarized Indian foreign policy in the late 1980s, marked by threats, provocations, and regional interventions.

Individuals alone, however, do not explain some Indian actions. Lal Bahadur Shastri was the single most anti-nuclear politician ever elected prime minister. He attempted to reforge the Indian nuclear program, but his effort was forestalled by Homi Bhabha and by the unfortunate timing of the Chinese nuclear tests in the autumn of 1964. The efforts by Vikram Sarabhai, Bhabha's successor, to suppress the design of peaceful nuclear explosives failed in the face of determined opposition by the rest of the scientists in the nuclear enclave. Efforts by Defense Minister V.K. Krishna Menon to dominate the promotion process in the late 1950s failed in the face of military objections.

The role of institutions and organizations offers further explanatory power into Indian policy. The unique role of the Indian army—a veteran force of long and proud tradition—and its consistent subservience to and, in some cases, humiliation by Indian civilian leaders stands in stark contrast to the Pakistani army, with its long history of political interference. Even when India's political leaders floundered or created disaster, the Indian military has remained subordinate. As a result, the military has until recently had little input into nuclear force issues—a clear area of professional expertise, but one categorically denied to India's military leaders until the mid-1980s.

The role of India's nuclear establishment has also been fundamental in determining India's nuclear policy. Perkovich argues that the scientists have played a major role in keeping the nuclear weapons option alive. As a body, they were able to undermine the efforts of Sarabhai to cut off the nuclear option. India's nuclear option, until recently, relied on the ability of the scientists to maintain the program and persuade each successive prime minister of its value and importance. The scientists maintained a unique and highly secret relationship with a series of successive Indian prime ministers, including at least two (Shastri and Morarji Desai) who were personally opposed to the nuclear option.

Another institution with a unique role is the *Lok Sabha*. Indian parliamentarians play little role in national security or foreign policy. The occasional major debate, such as the nuclear debate in late 1964, stands out as a major exception to the rule. Indian politicians have little oversight or expertise in defense issues, although this may be changing. Even budget approval, to date, has been pro forma, rather than vigorously debated.

Structural issues mattered as well. The balance of power in the region and in the international system has profoundly affected Indian policy. It is difficult to remain nonaligned when one of the two superpowers in the global system collapses, for example. Nehru's inability to keep China friendly and nonaligned led to increased tension and eventually war. Nixon's rapprochement with Pakistan as an entrée to China fundamentally changed India's perception of the balance of power, contributing to the decision to align itself closely with the Soviet Union. China's economic growth, military and nuclear assistance to Pakistan, and increased ambitions in East Asia and the subcontinent contributed to Indian nuclear aspirations. The apparent willingness of the international system to adopt the CTBT, with possibly deleterious results for India, helped create the conditions for a nuclear test *before* the "entry into force" provision could be applied. The US war on terrorism led India to welcome an American presence in the region, even if it required a temporary rapprochement with Pakistan in the interests of crushing Afghan terrorist camps which threaten both the US and India.

What are we to make of this conglomeration of factors? At first glance, it is not apparent what ties them all together. On closer study, however, the apparent eccentricity of Indian policy bears distinct traces of consistency. The most important link between these various facets is India's vision of itself—the idea that India represents a unique culture of great strength and vitality and an important moral force deriving from thousands of years of history.

Indian policy cannot be adequately explained without looking at the power of ideas. These ideas are personified in the work of Gandhi and Nehru, who skillfully crafted a political movement that could appeal broadly to many different sectors of Indian society. Its unique Indian-ness helps explain both its tactics (nonviolent protest, drawn both from religious tradition and from relative social and economic weakness) and its strategic success—boycotts and imprisonment achieved freedom from Britain long before an armed uprising or fanciful "liberation" by the Japanese Empire could have succeeded.

In creating a domestic political movement that achieved national liberation by moral force, Gandhi and Nehru also created the basis for India's engagement with the world after independence. The Cold War was already beginning when India moved onto the world stage. Nehru perceived two inexperienced superpowers with histories of racism or inhumanity, armed with weapons of incredible destructiveness, vying for power over the remnants of the colonial empires. Only a large and ancient civilization like India could offer an alternative, based in this case on moral leadership, nonalignment, liberation, and nonintervention. Moral leadership also maximized India's strengths, given its terrible poverty and weakness in all other traditional aspects of power. But most important, Nehru's policies reflected the same values and ideas that India had rallied behind in the independence struggle.

History also played a role. India was more inclined to work with the Soviet Union than with the West, despite the obvious common factors of democratization, the English language, and (at least in the case of the militaries) joint operation in World War II. India's leaders at independence advocated socialist domestic policies and rejected the colonial powers and their perceived heirs. They found it easier to work with the USSR, whose actions were fairly predictable, than with the US, whose actions were affected by problems common to all democracies—the vicissitudes of public opinion, the occasional change of administration or power in the legislature, and the difficulties of maintaining consistent policies over time. This played on the US side as well—Richard Nixon was poorly received in India in a visit in the 1950s, and this reportedly affected his policies when he became president.

Nehru's policies appealed to the Indian people and tried to provide an alternative path in the international system. The moral element demonstrates the power of ideas and the novelty of the Indian independence experience. The effort to coordinate the power of weak and until recently disenfranchised postcolonial states demonstrates the liberal tendencies in his thought, and the value he placed on multi- or international institutions to counteract global inequities in the distribution of traditional measures of power. His concern to maintain access—both for India and for other states—to the dual-use technologies which apparently defined modern economic and military power demonstrates a concern for security and a realist approach to power and influence.

Nehru has been condemned after his death by a series of analysts, politicians, and scholars who seek to make India a greater and more traditional power. None has been able to purge his influence from Indian foreign policy. India has become a nuclear power, but it has adopted a unique and non-aggressive nuclear doctrine and force posture, and maintains its rhetorical commitment to global disarmament. It maintains a reluctance to escalate crises and engage in external wars—even during the Kargil conflict, the option of attacking over the line of control to cut off Pakistani supply lines was rejected.

Indian international influence was never higher than in the 1950s, when it appealed to the weak and loftily ignored its Pakistani neighbor. In this, Nehru was fortunate—for most of his rule, Pakistan was poor, weak, and ridden with internal strife. Nehru was able to ignore regional tensions and focus India's policies on the international system. In the absence of hard threats, India's weakness in the traditional measures of power did not matter. Nehru could convert India's moral vision into a platform for global leadership. Despite India's weakness—it was desperately dependent on external economic aid—it has never been more influential on the global scene.

Nehru's failure occurred when India was forced, partly through Nehru's own actions, to compete in the traditional forms of power—with military force over territorial boundaries. Critics have condemned his idealism, and successors have narrowed their vision and focused on more concrete issues like regional hegemony, nuclear weapons, and military coercion. As a result, India has become stronger in the traditional forms of power—although it remains sharply limited in power projection capabilities and economic influence—but it has lost its position of leadership and influence on global issues. Playing by traditional rules, Indian influence will be tied to its economic and military growth—areas of great potential which may not be recognized for decades.

Indian strategists have sought to conceptually remove Pakistan from India's security equation by measuring themselves against China. The nuclear issue has played a role in this. Until India can again reach some sort of accommodation with Pakistan it will forever be frustrated in its efforts to redefine itself as an extra-regional power. Modern India cannot simply define the Pakistani threat away—it is real, it is active, it has claims on India which many credit as legitimate, and it is nuclear.

India has now reached an apparent accommodation with China which Nehru would have approved of, despite the fact that the current government has openly identified China as a threat. The border issue remains unsettled, but neither side appears willing to fight over it. China has accepted India's nuclear status, albeit reluctantly, and the two states are engaging in various diplomatic and economic activities. Indians are right to think that China doesn't accept India as an equal—but it does have concerns about India's trajectory as an emerging power.

Similarly, India must now reconsider its relationship with the US. Many of the issues Nehru disapproved of have changed—America's domestic racism, institutionalized in the Jim Crow laws, has disappeared, although discrimination still exists. India's need to reform its economy, and the failure of state control as an economic model, helps bridge the gulf between American capitalism and India's need for modernization. Finally, the recognition that both India and the US represent multiethnic democracies, in an age of fierce nationalism and ethnic strife, raises the possibility of close cooperation between the two states.

The power of shared ideas, combined with patience, carefully crafted policies, and a willingness to work out modest differences, can change the world. Britain's careful management of its relationship with the United States in the nineteenth century represents a model for the emerging Indo-US relationship.[36] In both the Anglo-American and the US-Indian cases, the stronger power had the opportunity to forge a relationship with an emerging power that required compromise but was facilitated by shared values. The Indo-US agreement over NMD suggests a framework—both states concede the necessity for greater limits on arsenals, India does not protest a potentially destabilizing weapon, and the US tacitly accepts India's irreversible possession of nuclear weapons.

For the power of ideas to encourage change, there must be willing partners. While India may be well positioned to prosper in a market-based international system strongly inclined toward democracy, the South Asian region is an entirely different matter. India and Pakistan do not share common ideas or visions of the future. Pakistan continues to perceive of itself as "not India," to define itself in religious terms as a haven for South Asian Muslims, and to harbor irredentist ambitions in Kashmir. Efforts to bridge the gap include the famous Lahore Agreement in 1999 and a wide range of unofficial contacts and Track II diplomacy. These efforts have been undermined by the Kargil War and Pakistani support for the Kashmir insurgency. No early solution to this deep-rooted dilemma appears possible, and this will drain Indian resources and attention from its global agenda. When ideas and institutions cannot provide security, nations must fall back on more traditional means—one reason realism remains a compelling methodology for explaining international relations. Indian policy will, for the present, remain a combination of realism and idealism, constrained by the actions of India's neighbors. It will represent, as so many previous Indian administrations' policies, one of the many shades of realism—an unfortunate reality in a conflicted world.

NOTES

1. Kenneth Waltz, *Man, the State, and War: A Theoretical Analysis* (Newyork: Columbia University Press, 1954).

2. Stephen M. Walt, "International Relations: One World, Many Theories," *Foreign Policy* (Spring 1998), pp. 29-43.

3. A basic history of India is Stanley Wolpert, *A New History of India,* sixth Edition (Oxford: Oxford University Press, 2000). Another useful text is Vernon Hewitt, *The New International Politics of South Asia* (Manchester: Manchester University Press, 1997). An outstanding study of Indo-Pakistani relations is *India & Pakistan: The First Fifty Years,* ed. Selig S. Harrison, Paul H. Kreisberg, and Dennis Kux (Cambridge: Cambridge University Press for Woodrow Wilson International Center for Scholars, 1999). The most recent book on India is Stephen P. Cohen, *India: Emerging Power* (Washington, DC: Brookings Institution Press, 2001).

4. See, for example, Jawaharlal Nehru, *The Discovery of India,* Centenary Edition (New Delhi: Oxford University Press, 1985); Jawaharlal Nehru, *Glimpses of World History* (New York: The John Day Company, 1942).

5. See S. Nihal Singh, *Indira's India* (Bombay: Nachiketa Publications, 1978); Surjit Mansingh, *India's Search for Power: Indira Gandhi's Foreign Policy 1966-1982* (New Delhi: Sage Publications, 1984).

6. Studies of Indian military policy include Lorne J. Kavic, *India's Quest for Security: Defence Policies 1947-1965* (Berkeley: University of California Press, 1967); Stephen P. Cohen, *The Indian Army: Its Contribution to the Development of a Nation* (Berkeley: University of California Press, 1971); Raju G.C. Thomas, *Indian Security Policy* (Princeton: Princeton University Press, 1986); *Securing India: Strategic Thought and Practice—Essays by George K. Tanham with Commentaries,* ed. Kanti P. Bajpai and

Amitabh Mattoo (New Delhi: Manohar Publishers & Distributors, 1996); Timothy D. Hoyt, *Rising Regional Powers* (Ph. D. Dissertation, Johns Hopkins University, 1997); Jaswant Singh, *Defending India* (New York: St. Martin's Press, 1999).

7. Mahatma Gandhi, cited in Herbert Wulf, "India: the unfulfilled quest for self-sufficiency," in *Arms Production in the Third World,* ed. Michael Brzoska and Thomas Ohlson (London: Taylor & Francis, 1986), p. 125.

8. Gerhard L. Weinberg, *A World At Arms: A Global History of World War II* (Cambridge: Cambridge University Press, 1994), p. 198; Cohen, *the Indian Army*, pp. 99-114, 149-161.

9. Kavic, *India's Quest for Security*, pp. 141-63 discusses early civil-military relations, as does Cohen, *The Indian Army*, pp. 114-80. An interesting analysis of the changing national view of the military is Ragini Gujral, *The Military, War, and National Integration: Symbolic Treatment of the Military and War for Purposes of National Integration* (Ph.D. dissertation, University of Illinois at Urbana-Champaign, 1984).

10. Cohen, *The Indian Army*, pp.169-80.

11. Kavic, *India's Quest for Security*, p. 95.

12. Hoyt, *Rising Regional Powers*, pp. 84-95; Kavic, *India's Quest for Security*, pp. 141-63.

13. *Brasstacks and Beyond: Perception and Management of Crisis in South Asia*, ed. Kanti P. Bajpai, P.R. Chari, Pervaiz Iqbal Cheema, Stephen P. Cohen, and Sumit Ganguly (Urbana: University of Illinois at Urbana-Champaign, 1995).

14. George Perkovich, *India's Nuclear Bomb: The Impact on Global Proliferation* (Berkeley, University of California Press, 1999), pp. 273-276.

15. *Conflict Prevention and Confidence-Building Measures in South Asia: The 1990 Crisis,* Occasional Paper No. 17, ed. Michael Krepon and Mishi Faruqee (Washington, DC: Henry L. Stimson Center, April 1994).

16. Timothy D. Hoyt, "Modernizing the Indian Armed Forces," *Joint Force Quarterly 25* (Summer 2000), pp. 17-23.

17. For example, India's Research and Analysis Wing trained the Tamil guerrilla forces which caused such difficulties for Indian peacekeepers in Sri Lanka and who were, eventually, responsible for the assassination of Rajiv Gandhi. Cohen, *India: Emerging Power,* p. 149.

18. Useful studies, in addition to those already cited, include Robert J. McMahon, *The Cold War on the Periphery* (New York: Columbia University Press, 1994); Dennis Kux, *Estranged Democracies: India and the United States* (Washington, DC: National Defense University Press, 1992). On Indo-Pakistani relations, see Robert G. Wirsing, *India, Pakistan, and the Kashmir Dispute* (New York: St. Martin's Press, 1998); Robert Jackson, *South Asian Crisis: India-Pakistan-Bangla Desh*[sic] (London: Chatto & Windus for the International Institute for Strategic Studies, 1975); Richard Sisson and Leo E. Rose, *War and Secession: Pakistan, India, and the Creation of Bangladesh* (Berkeley: University of California Press, 1990); Sumit Ganguly, *The Crisis in Kashmir: Portents of War, Hopes of Peace* (Cambridge: Cambridge University Press, 1997).

19. The five principles of *panchsheel* are mutual respect for territorial integrity and sovereignty, mutual nonaggression, mutual noninterference in the internal affairs of other states, equality and mutual benefit, and peaceful coexistence. Jawaharlal Nehru, *India's Foreign Policy: Selected Speeches September 1946—April 1961* (New Delhi: Government of India, 1961), p. 99.

20. Kux, *Estranged Democracies*, pp. 247-61.

21. The text of the Joint Vision Statement can be found at http://www.acronym.org.uk/spvisit.htm (accessed December 7, 2001).

22. "India to consider fresh military aid to US," *The Times of India,* November 19, 2001.

23. Definitive books on India's nuclear program include Perkovich, *India's Nuclear Bomb*; Rear Admiral Raja Menon, *A Nuclear Strategy for India* (New Delhi: Sage Publications, 2000); Itty Abraham, *The Making of the Indian Atomic Bomb: Science, Secrecy and the Postcolonial State* (London: Zed Books, 1998); Ashley J. Tellis, *India's Emerging Nuclear Posture* (Santa Monica, CA: Rand, 2001); Raj Chengappa, *Weapons of Peace* (New Delhi: HarperCollins, 2000).

24. Perkovich, *India's Nuclear Bomb*, pp. 26-34.

25. *Constituent Assembly of India (Legislative Debates)*, vol. 5, April 6, 1948, p. 3333-4, cited in Perkovich, *India's Nuclear Bomb*, p. 20.

26. For example, Jaswant Singh (the current Foreign Minister of India) wrote an article after India's nuclear tests in 1998 entitled "Against Nuclear Apartheid," *Foreign Affairs* 77 5 (September/October 1998), pp. 41-52.

27. Since this first test, some Indian scientists have admitted that this device was actually an effort to produce a nuclear *weapon.*

28. This debate is explored exhaustively in Perkovich, *India's Nuclear Bomb*, pp. 65-85.

29. See, for instance, "Evolution of India's Nuclear Policy" http://www.meadev.nic.in/govt/evolution.htm

30. Cohen *India: Emerging Power,* pp. 168-70, 195.

31. K. Subrahmanyam, "Hedging Against Hegemony: Gandhi's Logic in the Nuclear Age," *Times of India,* June 6, 1998, http://www.meadev.nic.in/govt/evolution.htm

32. "Suo Motu Statement by Prime Minister Shri Atal Bihari Vajpayee in Parliament on twenty-seventh May 1998," http://www.meadev.nic.in/govt/statement-parliament.htm

33. See http://www.indianembassy.org/policy/CTBT/nuclear_doctrine_aug_17_1999.html for a copy of the Draft Nuclear Doctrine.

34. Thucydides, *History of the Peleponnesian War,* translated by Rex Warner with introduction and notes by M.I. Finley (London: Penguin Press, 1954), p. 80.

35. Waltz, *Theory of International Politics*; Hans J. Morgenthau, *Politics Among Nations: The Struggle for Power and Peace,* 6th edition, revised by Kenneth W. Thompson (New York: Alfred A. Knopf, 1985); George Liska, *The Ways of Power* (Cambridge, MA: Basil Blackwell, 1990).

36. For a rare analysis of Anglo-US relations, see Stephen R. Rock, "Anglo-U.S. Relations, 1845-1930: Did Shared Liberal Values and Democratic Institutions Keep the Peace?" in *Paths to Peace: Is Democracy the Answer?* ed. Miriam Fendius Elman (Cambridge, MA: MIT Press, 1997), pp. 101-49.

10

The United States and the India-Pakistan Rivalry: Assistance and Condemnation

Christopher Sprecher and Sungho Park

Since India and Pakistan gained independence in 1947, the United States has felt compelled to play a major role as a peacemaker in the region. During the Cold War, the US invested vast amounts of foreign aid in an effort to contain the Soviet Union and develop amicable relations with India and Pakistan. Additionally, the US encouraged the spread of democracy to promote peaceful relations between India and Pakistan. Through the use of cooperative and coercive measures, the Unites States sought to ensure Indian and Pakistani compliance with its containment policy.

To understand the difficulty of obtaining peace between India and Pakistan, the roots of the rivalry must be explored. Then US efforts to alleviate tensions between the two rivals can be examined. The US continues to adjust to the responses of these warring rivals, especially as both states acquired and tested nuclear devices. Yet future US policies will most likely mirror previous ones.

INTRODUCTION

Since India and Pakistan gained independence from Great Britain in 1947, their relations have been marred by constant hostility. Over the last 50 years, the rivalry has erupted into three wars and numerous disputes. Due to the proximity of the countries to the Soviet Union and China, the US made various attempts during the Cold War to utilize their locale to contain the communist threat. US involvement in the region helped promote peaceful relations between the two adversaries, and provided the US with the opportunity to maintain a presence on the borders of its major rivals.

In approaching the explosive India-Pakistan rivalry, the goals of the US have been threefold. First, during the Cold War, the US tried to maintain cordial relationships with both India and Pakistan in order to contain communism.

Second, the US used its influence to promote democracy in the region, again as a bulwark to keep communism at bay. Third, and potentially most important, the US has worked to establish relationships with the two states to prevent nuclear proliferation in South Asia.

The US used both aid and sanctions to shape the behavior of India and Pakistan, primarily to keep them out of the Soviet orbit. American policy promoted cooperative relations with India and Pakistan, while never becoming embroiled militarily within the rivalry. However, the US did not treat both countries as equals. Instead, the US practiced a policy of oscillation, sometimes favoring India, and at other times favoring Pakistan.

As the international political environment changed with the collapse of the Soviet Union in 1991, the US adapted its policies in the region accordingly. US policy shifting from containment to preventing a nuclear conflagration between the two belligerent foes. Instead of containing communism, the US concerned itself with nuclear proliferation and the establishment of democratic norms within South Asia and the successor states of the Soviet Union.

The first section of this chapter examines the roots of the Indo-Pakistani rivalry and the power relationships that govern these two hostile states. The second section analyzes US relations with both states during the Cold War, emphasizing the policy of containment as the driving force behind US policy in the region. In the third section, implications of the end of the Cold War for the rivalry between India and Pakistan are scrutinized within the context of the new American emphasis on nonproliferation. Finally, the chapter concludes with some possible scenarios for US policy in the region in the aftermath of the September 11, 2001, terrorist attacks on New York and Washington, DC.

THE INDO-PAKISTANI RIVALRY

As part of the independence agreement with Great Britain in 1947, the former British colony of India was divided into two separate states based on religious orientation. (Indians are predominantly Hindus, whereas Pakistanis are predominantly Muslims). Cultural differences between the two were so deep that they could not peacefully coexist within one state. Since this division, relations between the two have been characterized by enduring military rivalry and hostility.

India and Pakistan are two of the small number of states responsible for the majority of conflict that occurs within the international system.[1] Since 1816, more than 45 percent of all militarized disputes have been the result of enduring rivalries, and 53 percent of all wars have occurred within the context of enduring rivalries.[2] Because enduring rivalries possess numerous features that make them unique, this paper focuses on two elements that are especially important in the India-Pakistan relationship: the notion of recurring conflict and the stability that shapes these long-term relations.

According to Gary Goertz and Paul Diehl, an enduring rivalry is an antagonistic relationship between two states that engenders a military component and witnesses at least six militarized disputes in twenty years. The rivalry terminates if it goes for ten years without a dispute.[3] This definition of recurring tension between rivals is an empirical one, based upon patterns of behavior, rather than a theoretically driven one. However, it helps to demonstrate that certain pairs of states are overwhelmingly more hostile than others.

India and Pakistan have experienced forty disputes between 1947 and 1992, and in the decade after the Cold War have experienced an average of one dispute a year.[4] This continued bellicosity has erupted in three major wars between these states during their short history, and at least two disputes in the 1990s have nearly escalated to armed warfare. India and Pakistan have emerged as one of the most bellicose set of enduring rivals of the post-1945 era. Both of them have laid claim to territory that the other desires, and both have been willing to use military force to alter the territorial status quo in their favor. Both India and Pakistan during their short lifetimes have been driven by power considerations and the desire to use their military might to gain their objectives.[5]

In order to send hostile signals and challenge one another, India and Pakistan have developed both conventional and nuclear military capabilities. Many of their actions are deterrence-based in nature. Attempts at deterrence have driven the foreign policies of both states, especially when it comes to the pursuit of nuclear weapons technology.

Deterrence at its most basic level refers to a policy of using threats to persuade an adversary that the political costs of using military force will be greater than the benefits reaped from using the military force.[6] Deterrence in this regard is a strategy of attempting to deny an adversary any advantage that may come from initiating some form of crisis. A nation keeps forces ready and makes it clear to an adversary that, if threatened, it will respond in kind.

Deterrence assumes two distinct forms. The first is general deterrence. Such a scenario implies that an adversarial relationship exists between two states, in which (1) leaders in at least one state would consider resorting to force to gain a demand, and (2) the opponent would be willing to resort to arms and makes threats of its own in order to prevent such a demand from being made.[7]

The second type of deterrence scenario that involves a pair of states is that of immediate deterrence. In such a case three conditions must be met: (1) officials in at least one state are actively considering an attack on the other; (2) the leaders of the second state are aware of this threat; (3) the leaders in the second state issue threats to retaliate if the first state goes through with its intentions.[8]

Within the context of enduring rivals, it has been noted that "regional rivalries are characterized by high levels of animosity between neighboring states and the potential for intervention by outside states that are militarily stronger than any of the regional powers."[9] General deterrence among enduring rivals is a common security issue for such states, because they are continually preparing for hostilities with one another. This is especially so in the two most prominent enduring rivalries of the post-Cold War era, that between Israel and its Arab neighbors and between India and Pakistan. Both of these rivalries have deep rooted animosities based upon territorial and ideological issues that are not readily resolved.

Throughout their rivalry, India and Pakistan have experienced both general and immediate deterrence failures. Because both sides view the stakes in their rivalry as being so high, both have sought throughout their history to deter one another by developing military technology and by posturing on the diplomatic stage. Below we discuss the crises and wars that have emerged out of deterrence failures between the two states, and then discuss how each state has attempted to develop nuclear weapons as a guarantee of its sovereignty. We then examine the US role in this enduring rivalry, and discuss why the US has felt it to be so imperative to maintain a presence in this area of the world.

Crises and Wars: The Pursuit of a New Status Quo

When India gained its independence in 1947, it was divided into two separate states. India was predominantly Hindu, while Pakistan was predominantly Muslim. The ethnic and religious differences between India and Pakistan fueled the hatred of each state, and the desire to gain territory at the expense of the other. This was especially so due to the fact that East and West Pakistan were separated from each other by over a thousand miles of hostile Indian territory. Almost immediately, Indian Prime Minister Jawaharlal Nehru declared his intention to reunify these two successor states. Pakistan responded by proclaiming its staunch commitment to remain independent.[10] While reunification has been and remains India's official policy, it has gradually diminished. In the aftermath of the 1971 Bangladesh War, both sides strove to preserve the status quo and prevent the recurrence of another war.[11]

Despite their short history as nation states, there have been four major military conflicts between the two rivals: the first Kashmir crisis in 1947; the Rann of Kutch Crisis in 1965; the second Kashmir war in 1965; and the Bangladesh war in 1971. The first three were territorial conflicts aiming to expand control of strategically important disputed regions. In contrast, the Bangladesh war was escalated by India's intervention in response to domestic unrest in East Pakistan. It resulted in the birth of a new independent state of Bangladesh.

All of these conflicts were triggered by attempts to establish a new status quo in the region. While both India and Pakistan used coercive measures in their attempts to gain territory, these clashes were not designed as total wars meant to destroy each other. Instead, they were limited by clearly defined territorial issues and were aimed at attacking the legitimacy of the rival's government.

The following section demonstrates that these military conflicts occurred mainly due to deterrence failures. The key argument advanced suggests that both sides have failed to build up a sufficient military capacity and reputation for resolve. These failures signal weakness on both sides. Neither state was able to convince its opponent that the cost of using military forces would be greater than the benefits reaped from the use of force. The continuous failure of deterrence, along with threats from China, eventually led India to develop nuclear weapons.

The initial conflict between India and Pakistan broke out in the very year of independence, 1947, over the status of Kashmir. At the time of independence, the British allowed the hundreds of former princely states to choose their own political futures. The majority of them chose to accede to either India or Pakistan, but three states opted for independence: Junagah, Hyderabad and Kashmir. Of these three, Kashmir was the most important region in a strategic sense. In particular, Pakistan viewed Kashmir as being intrinsically linked to the survival of the Pakistani state.[12] India also laid claim to Kashmir, and on October 22, clashes began between Pathen tribesmen, supported by Pakistan, and the Kashmir military. Bloody fighting erupted as India intervened to assist the Kashmir government in the battle against Pakistan.

At this time, early in their nationhood, both states did not have a clear understanding of the overall capacity of its opponent. India appeared to be in a superior position, at least in relation to the Kashmir issue. Prime Minister Nehru was on friendly terms with the top leaders in Kashmir, and many of them were seeking to join with India. This was a substantial diplomatic advantage,[13] especially when combined with the fact that India had 200,000 soldiers in comparison to Pakistan's 55,000 soldiers. Pakistan, however, had a logistical advantage due to its proximity to the area of contention. India was forced to cross vast mountain ranges in order to reach Kashmir. This made the war especially costly, and when winter set in India suffered greatly.[14] This situation created considerable uncertainty in gauging the other side's relative capabilities. The war ended with a United Nations-brokered cease-fire that left Kashmir a disputed territorial entity, claimed by both India and Pakistan, but parititoned between the two.[15]

After the first Kashmir crisis, Pakistan realized that it would not be able to defend itself from India based upon its own capabilities. It eagerly began to court and obtain military assistance from the West, especially the US. This coincided with the first priority of US foreign policy at that time, the containment of the Soviet Union. The US decided to enlist Pakistan as a bulwark against communism in Southwest Asia, and induced Pakistan to enter the Southeast Asian Treaty Organization (SEATO) in 1954. The decision by Pakistan to formally ally with the US forced India to develop a closer relationship with the Soviet Union.

Even though American foreign policy in the region emphasized Pakistan during this early Cold War period, the US also had an interest in supporting India. This is due to the rivalry that the US had with China. This set of circumstances forced the US to provide 'direct' military aid to Pakistan and 'indirect' military aid to India.[16]

While American assistance was indispensable to Pakistan's military development, it was not sufficient to reduce the gap in military capacity between India and Pakistan. The period from 1948-1965 was an era fraught with tension and distrust between India and Pakistan. India was also embroiled in a rivalry with China at the time. This led to a war between the two states in 1961, and a turn from total US support of Pakistan to one in which the US aided both states.[17] This caused both sides to reassess and reevaluate their positions.

Pakistan, feeling that its security had been compromised by US relations with India, was forced to seek another partner. It turned to China in an attempt to balance India's influence in the region. The Rann of Kutch Crisis and the second Kashmir war in 1965 occurred in this complex new environment, which altered the balance of power between India and Pakistan. Tensions culminated in another territorial dispute, this time over the Rann of Kutch. While this crisis did not escalate to a full-scale war, the cease-fire that prevailed set the stage for future conflict between India and Pakistan, as neither were satisfied with the settlement.

The Rann of Kutch Crisis began in April 1965, when small skirmishes between Indian and Pakistani patrols escalated. The Rann of Kutch had been dispute-prone since 1947, but its strategic significance was not very high when compared to Kashmir. The Rann is largely a desert area during dry season and becomes flooded during rainy season.[18] It is virtually uninhabited, except for a few high plains occupied by Pakistani forces. In spite of this unlikely setting, it has been widely accepted that conflict within the Rann of Kutch offered Pakistan a cheap opportunity to test India's resolve. India responded militarily in order to protect its reputation and credibility with its Pakistani adversary. Pakistan viewed the crisis as an opportunity to demonstrate its improved military power.[19]

At the onset of the crisis, Pakistan's leaders believed that their increased military capacity would grant them a high probability of winning a limited local war with India. India's defeat in the Indo-China border disputes of 1961 strengthened this view. Furthermore, Pakistan had a logistical advantage in this area, since it held dry highlands while India's territory was full of swamps and marshes.

Despite Pakistan's perceived strategic advantage, India still possessed overwhelming numbers. Its army numbered 800,000 soldiers, while Pakistan's was comprised of only 250,000 soldiers.[20] Additional support from the Soviet Union had increased the Indian military capability far beyond that of Pakistan. All these factors increased uncertainty about relative military capacities, which made military conflict more likely. In spite of India's overwhelming numbers, the Rann of Kutch Crisis ended as a military success for Pakistan. Although small in scope, this victory reinforced the confidence of Pakistan's leaders in their military capability and immediately led them to militarily challenge India again. Once more, Kashmir was the flashpoint.[21]

Increased distrust and Pakistan's feelings of superiority in a limited war quickly evolved into the second Kashmir War in 1965. In this instance, religious tensions within Kashmir forced the Indian government to crack down on Kashmir, and the simultaneous conflict within the Rann of Kutch merely exacerbated the situation. The second Kashmir War also had direct roots in India's declaration of President's Rule in 1964, which denied the independent status of Kashmir and allowed the federal government to dismiss the state government of Kashmir.

In the aftermath of the 1964 declaration of Presidents' Rule, violent protests continued in Kashmir. Pakistan decided to intervene in Kashmir to support the independence movements and to extend its control in the region. Again India appeared, logistically at least, to be in a superior position, but again neither side was able to mobilize enough strength to gain a decisive victory. For the second time in 20 years, India and Pakistan fought to a standstill in Kashmir.[22] Once again a United Nations cease-fire brought about an end to armed hostilities, but tensions still existed between the two states as they sought superiority on the subcontinent.

The period between 1965 and 1971 was a contentious one, with numerous disputes breaking out between India and Pakistan over Kashmir. The division of Pakistan into East and West came to a head in 1971, during the Bangladesh War. This war grew out of a conflict between Bengali revolutionaries and West Pakistan. India intervened to assist the rebels, and a bloody conflict broke out. India defeated Pakistan convincingly, and the state of Bangladesh was born.

The Bangladesh War in 1971 was different from the first three conflicts between India and Pakistan. In this case, the war was conducted wholly within Pakistani territory. Independence movements in East Pakistan, coercive repression by the West Pakistan government, and India's support for the independence movements, resulted in a major war between India and Pakistan.

Since the second Kashmir War, the independence movement in East Pakistan had attracted increased political support. Its growth emerged directly out of the 1965 war, which made the Pakistani government seem weak and indecisive. Once warfare erupted, India was able to sever all lines of communication between East Pakistan and West Pakistan. India was prevented from invading East Pakistan only because China threatened military intervention. However, this experience provided East Pakistan's people with a clear awareness of insecurity and vulnerability, and provided greater legitimacy for the independence movement.[23]

During the war, the Indian army was able to dominate Pakistan's for a variety of reasons. First, Pakistani soldiers had to travel 1000 miles to get from West Pakistan to East Pakistan. In addition to this logistical disadvantage, Pakistan was also suffering from a six-year US embargo on arms sales, while India was still receiving military aid from the Soviet Union.[24] The most critical issue, however, was China's role in this war. Contrary to India's fear, China's support for Pakistan in this war turned out to be limited to political rhetoric.[25] This enabled Indian soldiers to enter the territory of East Pakistan without fear of Chinese invasion. India defeated Pakistan convincingly, and the state of Bangladesh was born.

During the war, Pakistan's leaders experienced serious insecurity. They found that, in spite of US assistance, their military was not able to preserve Pakistan's territorial integrity. They also realized once again that the US strategic interest in the region was to contain China, and not necessarily to assist Pakistan against India. In the meantime, Indian leaders learned how important the role of China was in regional politics. China, even though its role at this conflict remained political and diplomatic, threatened India if it continued to pursue the war against Pakistan.[26]

In the aftermath of the Bangladesh war numerous crises erupted over the state of Kashmir, but open war never again broke out. Although China chose to publicly voice concern and threaten intervention over events in the region, neither the US nor the Soviet Union intervened militarily in any of these wars and crises. Instead, they worked to reduce the level of hostilities through United Nations procedures, while continuing to alternately support and condemn the participants.

The continued warfare between India and Pakistan saw challenges made by Islamabad toward the government in New Delhi on a regular basis. Both states realized that they could not wholly defeat one another through conventional warfare, and India also had to worry about China's actions. The inability of either state to convincingly emerge victorious from these three wars contributed to the onset of a nuclear arms race within South Asia.

The decision to test a nuclear device in India in 1974 was one of the most monumental foreign policy decisions made by the Indian government since its independence. India knew that it risked international condemnation, and that it could spark an arms race with Pakistan.[27] However, due to both military and domestic pressure, the Indian government decided to develop and weaponize its nuclear program.

Reaction to the 1974 test was critical. Pakistan in particular was incensed and fearful. Having fought a war with India in 1971, Pakistan was in no position to engage in a long, expensive arms race, and disliked the prospect of fighting with India again after such a brutal conflict only three years before.[28] In spite of these fears, Pakistan escalated its hostilities, verbally and rhetorically, in the months after May 1974, when the Indian test was conducted.

In the quarter of a century after the 1974 nuclear tests in the Indian desert, Pakistan began in earnest to develop nuclear weapons technology, despite American objections and coercive tactics. During this time, India and Pakistan continued to struggle over control of Kashmir, leading to numerous bloody disputes and attempts to gain the upper hand in the ongoing hostilities. Both parties continued to refine their nuclear capabilities, and almost escalated their hostilities to war in 1990.[29]

Bowing to domestic political pressures, on May 13, 1998, India detonated a nuclear device at its desert test site at Pokhran, its first test in 24 years. The test sent shock waves through the international community, as nuclear proliferation and its consequences were debated.

Scarcely two weeks later, on May 28, Pakistan tested a nuclear device of its own. This sequence of events heralded the possibility of a nuclear arms race in South Asia between two bitter rivals. In addition to reintroducing the specter of nuclear conflagration, thought to be a relic of the Cold War, this escalation presents an interesting theoretical puzzle. How can we explain increased hostile behavior in rival dyads in the aftermath of nuclear testing, when the goal of the test is supposed to inhibit rather than exacerbate conflictual behavior?

It can be argued that the Indian test was an attempt to deter future Pakistani aggression, and a means of pacifying both domestic constituencies and signaling military prowess to the international community. Pakistan's response was predictable under the theories of deterrence and enduring rivalry. Pakistan needed to demonstrate that it was able to compete with India, and that it had the wherewithal to withstand Indian threats against its sovereignty. The 1998 tests forced both India and Pakistan to endure global condemnation and sanctions, and limited the amount of weaponry they received from their patron states. But the hostile relationship that the rival states had developed inhibited any other course of action.

The specter of nuclear proliferation on the Indian Subcontinent, coupled with the ever present hostilities between India and Pakistan, led the US to remain involved in South Asian politics. During the Cold War, the goal was to contain the communist threat. After the Cold War, the US hoped to prevent the spread of nuclear weapons technology. The next section discusses how the second goal emerges directly from US concerns in the region.

US CONCERNS IN SOUTH ASIA DURING THE COLD WAR

US foreign policy during the Cold War was largely driven by power considerations, particularly by the desire to contain the communist threat. US attitudes toward India and Pakistan were no exception to this general policy. US fears within South Asia were heightened with the outbreak of the Korean War in 1950, and the fear of Soviet and Chinese expansion into the region.[30] American policy in South Asia was comprised of two interconnected strategies.

First, the US sought to create a stable alliance and alignment in the region to gain geo-strategic advantages in confronting the Soviet Union and China. Second, the US sought to stop the proliferation of nuclear weapons in the region. The first was more important during the Cold War, while the second goal has become more pressing after the Cold War and the nuclear tests of 1998. Underlying both of these goals was a desire to promote democracy and normalization of relations between India and Pakistan. The US intervened in the region actively in both cooperative and coercive fashion. Pakistan and India were rewarded with aid when their behavior coincided with US grand strategy, and punished with sanctions when Indian or Pakistani actions did not meet with US expectations.

US Alliance Policy in South Asia during the Cold War

During the Cold War, the US sought to contain communism wherever possible. Many have argued that containment was the driving policy behind American foreign policy during the Cold War.[31] One of the main ways the US approached containment was to form alliances with other states. This was true in South Asia just as it was in Western Europe.

The preeminent American military alliance during the Cold War was NATO, as it reflected American security concerns within Europe. As tensions between the US and the Soviet Union began to increase after World War II, occupied Germany became the symbol of a European continent divided by ideology. With the establishment of two German states in 1949, a Soviet blockade of Berlin in 1948, and US concern about communist expansion after the Korean War, the US decided to bring West Germany into the NATO alliance. West German entry into NATO guaranteed a US presence in Europe. In return, the West German state was guaranteed security from its eastern neighbors.[32]

In 1947 the goal of the US was to form an anti-Soviet alliance in South Asia that would include both India and Pakistan. However, this strategy was unsuccessful because India was not supportive of American goals within the region. India emerged as one of the cofounders of the Nonaligned Movement (NAM) and sought to realize the principle of self-determination outside of Cold War constraints. It was critical of the US, whom it accused of supporting colonialism. It implicitly supported the Soviet Union, even though it did not accept communism as an ideology.[33]

On the other hand, Pakistan enthusiastically responded to American overtures in order to obtain military and economic assistance. On his visit to the US in 1950, Pakistan Prime Minister Liaquat Ali Kahn declared his pro-America and anti-Soviet policy. When US Secretary of State John Foster Dulles visited Pakistan in 1953, Pakistani leaders exhibited great willingness to accede to a collective security pact suggested by the US.[34] Pakistan joined the Southeast Asian Treaty Organization (SEATO) in 1954 and the Central Treaty Organization in 1955, which allowed Pakistan access to American military and economic aid.

While membership in SEATO provided Pakistan with many benefits, notably military aid from the US, membership also exacerbated its tensions with India. India, as one of the leaders of the nonaligned movement, never desired to join SEATO or any other Cold War alliance, and sought to keep the subcontinent free of superpower entanglements. In 1972, angered by American support of Pakistan during the 1971 Bangladesh War, India signed a mutual defense treaty with the Soviet Union that remained in effect until the Cold War's eventual demise.

The US sought to emulate its success in Western Europe when it formed the Southeast Asian Treaty Organization (SEATO) in 1954. Pakistan, along with Thailand, the Philippines, Australia, New Zealand, France, and Great Britain joined together in a defensive pact. The US used SEATO as a means of basing troops in the region, to pursue the war in Vietnam and contain communist influence.

SEATO never ascended to the status of NATO. There was never a centralized command and control structure within the alliance, nor did the members conduct routine military exercises as the NATO allies did. Instead, SEATO was a vehicle for the US to pursue its interests in the region. The fall of South Vietnam in 1975 signaled the death knell of SEATO, for the rationale for the alliance perished along with the South Vietnamese regime.

During the 21 years that SEATO existed, Pakistan benefited greatly from US military assistance. Pakistan allowed the US to maintain listening posts within its borders, so that the US could monitor Soviet activity in the region. This led India to charge that the US and Pakistan were responsible for bringing the Cold War to the Indian Subcontinent.[35] From the mid-1950s to the mid-1960s, Pakistan was rewarded by the US with $650 million dollars in American military aid, making it one of the top recipients of American foreign aid at the time.[36]

In contrast to Western Europe and East Asia, where the US confronted a unified communist threat, South Asia presented a different scenario. In this region the US found communist powers fighting among themselves. Sometimes the US blocked the Soviets with implicit help from China, and sometimes it blocked China with implicit help from the Soviet Union. This strategy was effective in confronting communism, but it was not without cost. The inconsistent strategic stance of the US undermined the stability of alliances in this region, which was clear with Pakistan. This constrained not only the ability of India and Pakistan to calculate the military and diplomatic capacities of their opponents, but also limited the ability of the US to control their actions. Instead of seeking deterrence under the umbrella of superpowers, India and Pakistan tried complex alliance politics among the superpowers.[37] These manipulations perpetuated the insecurity in the region and led to continuous deterrence failures and, ultimately, development of nuclear weapons.

American aid to Pakistan played a crucial role in ensuring Pakistan's security, but China's entrance into the geopolitics of South Asia undermined the stability of these relations. China's involvement ultimately changed existing alliance patterns in the region. The India-China border conflict in 1962 was a crucial event. In fact, India's relations with China were very friendly in 1950s. They shared agreements on the problem of the Cold War system dominated by the US and the Soviet Union.[38] Furthermore, there had been official friendly relations since 1954, when they signed the Panchsheel treaty of friendship. However, this relationship was seriously challenged by emerging border tensions. These tensions finally escalated when Chinese troops attacked Indian soldiers in 1962. Fortunately, this conflict did not develop into a major war and ended quickly. However, the China's victory made her an important geopolitical actor and undermined India's reputation and military security.[39]

Equally important was the military conflict with the US. The US immediately provided military facilities and personnel to India in order to check the advance of the Chinese army.[40] After this conflict, the US began to seriously consider China when it developed its containment strategy in the region. The US began to seek improvement in its relations with India. It also began to take a cautious stance regarding unconditional aid for Pakistan, fearing that such aid would exacerbate India's military reaction.

The behavior of the US in the second Kashmir war illustrates this change of strategic perspective very clearly. When the war broke out, US leaders refused Pakistan's request for help and decided to impose an arms embargo on both sides. This decision weakened Pakistan's relative position in the war, because at the time Pakistan was heavily dependent on US arms. On the other hand, India had little difficulty in procuring arms from the Soviet Union. Pakistan tried to induce aid from China, but could not compensate for its inferior military capacity,[41] even though Chinese support for Pakistan prevented further Indian attacks on Pakistan's territory. It is also noteworthy that the US and the Soviet Union successfully coordinated their actions to end the war quickly.[42] Even though the Soviets provided weapons to India, they also understood that China might intervene if the war didn't end quickly. Fear of China enabled the two superpowers to work together for a peaceful settlement of the war under the flag of the United Nations.[43]

The entry of China onto the global stage changed the world from a clear bipolar confrontation in the 1950s to a more flexible multipolar international system. The US persuasively proved that it was ready to cooperate with India, in spite of India's relationship with the Soviet Union, in order to contain China. India and the Soviet Union responded favorably to this turn of events, and the loser was Pakistan. Pakistan could not retreat from its coalition with the US. But because it believed that the US was not trustworthy, it acted quickly to strengthen its friendly relationship with China. In fact, Pakistan's rapprochement with China began in 1962, after the India-China border conflicts.

Feeling betrayed by American support for India, many Pakistani political leaders called for a more equally balanced stance between the US and China. This exhortation led to a border agreement with China in 1963. Ayub Khan, the prime minister of Pakistan, further solidified relations with China by allowing the Pakistani national air carrier to fly to Chinese territory.[44] After the 1965 war, Pakistan fell deeper into China's orbit. In 1966 a Pakistani-Chinese economic agreement was signed, and in 1970, during Ayub Khan's visit to Beijing, the two countries announced their mutual agreement for liberation of Kashmir.

The US response to the increasing friendship between China and Pakistan was interesting. At first the US considered Pakistan's behavior as a betrayal, but as time progressed policy makers in the US began to think of a potential role for Pakistan in reconciling with China. They believed that reconciliation with China would reinforce the position of the US. It would show that only the US, of the three major powers, had the capability establish better relations with the other two.[45] In June 1971, Henry Kissinger's historic visit to Beijing was announced by the US government. Of course, intense reaction followed. In August 1971, the Soviet Union and India announced that they reached a 20-year Treaty of Friendship that prohibited support for any third party involved in a dispute with one of the two contracting countries. In November, supported by the Soviets, the Indian army entered the territory of East Pakistan to support the independence movements. This restored a bipolar confrontation in Southwest Asia, but the balance of power was more skewed in favor of the US because it now had Chinese support.

The story described above demonstrates three major phases in strategic relations among the major powers in Southwest Asia: a US-Soviet bipolar confrontation in the1950s; a flexible bipolar confrontation allowing limited cooperation between the US and the Soviet Union to contain China; and, finally, a strong bipolar confrontation where the US and China coordinated their actions against the Soviets. Through this complex maneuvering, the US sought to minimize communist influence in Asia, but could not succeed in normalizing relations between Pakistan and India. The complex and inconsistent behavior of the US created uncertainty in the military and diplomatic environments. This in turn widened the scope for the two dependent countries' deliberate maneuvering to maximize assistance from the major powers. The result of this process was repeated miscalculation and failure of deterrence.

Stable deterrence between India and Pakistan became possible after the early 1970s, when a stable bipolar confrontation was established. This was strengthened even more after the Soviet invasion of Afghanistan in 1979. The US immediately increased its military aid to Pakistan. India, threatened by the Soviet Union's offensive military campaign, did not condemn US actions. Furthermore, India was incorporated into the US security umbrella when it accepted an offer of technology transfers as a reward for normalization.[46] Here we see a gradual process of encirclement of the Soviet Union, based upon stable alliances with both major countries in Southwest Asia.

The US was successful to a degree in its pursuit of alliances in South Asia, as evidenced by the story described above. Its other goal, that of nuclear non-proliferation, was pursued with mixed results. While US assistance to India and Pakistan was beneficial at times, the aid did little to alleviate tensions between the states, and often exacerbated tensions. Additionally, US coercive attempts to prevent the proliferation of nuclear technology did not produce the desired effects, as evidenced by the nuclear tests of 1998.

Confronting Nuclear Proliferation in South Asia

In response to their continued rivalry, the Pakistanis and the Indians both endeavored to build a nuclear weapons arsenal for deterrent purposes. This ran counter to US policy, for the stated goal of the US under the Nuclear Non-Proliferation Treaty (NPT) of 1968 is, along with the other signatories, to prevent the spread of nuclear weapons technology.[47] Ironically, as has been noted, the US was the principle supplier of nuclear weapons technology to India.[48] Granted, most nuclear transfers the US made to India prior to its 1974 test were of a peaceful nature. But American controls were often lax, and India was able to finally detonate a nuclear device.

The non-proliferation issue emerged as an urgent concern of the US after India's nuclear explosion in 1974. In the last quarter of a century, it has gained more and more importance. India's desire to develop nuclear capabilities originated from its continuous military conflicts with Pakistan and the formidable threat posed by China. In addition, the superpowers' inability to create a stable security environment reinforced the need for a final guarantee of security.

The West responded to India's initial detonation by imposing economic sanctions against New Delhi. While Canada had enacted economic sanctions early on, in 1974, as a response to the Indian test, it wasn't until 1978 that the

US took any punitive actions against India.[49] The US concern was that India was using US nuclear fuel for weapons rather than for peaceful energy consumption. By 1982 an agreement had been reached between Washington and New Delhi to settle the disagreement. But India persisted in building up its nuclear weapons program, even under threat of increased sanctions by the US.

Not surprisingly, Pakistan's reaction to India's nuclear experiment was very strong. Immediately after the explosion, Pakistan began to negotiate the purchase of a plutonium reprocessing plant from France, even though this attempt was frustrated by US intervention. Pakistan's attempt to gain nuclear capabilities continued. Officially it pretended to look for capacities for reprocessing plutonium for peaceful use. However, in reality, its real purpose was to purchase equipment for uranium enrichment that could be used directly for military purposes.[50] In spite of US sanctions, Pakistan was successful in obtaining weapons grade nuclear material.[51]

The early 1990s saw the US switching its attention in the region toward India and away from Pakistan. Early in 1990, the US imposed sanctions on Pakistan due to its continued attempts to construct a viable nuclear weapons program. The stated goal of the US sanctions policy toward Pakistan at this time was to force Islamabad to forego its nuclear program. As has often been pointed out, the US stance on nonproliferation did not prevent Pakistan from seeking to acquire nuclear technology.[52] Instead, it tended to drive Pakistan into the arms of China, which was more than willing to supply Pakistan with nuclear technology. This shift in US-South Asian policy became more pronounced with the demise of the Cold War.

Why were these two countries so committed to developing nuclear weapons? If we think of the geopolitical situation of South Asia after the Cold War, the question becomes more puzzling. Since the Soviet invasion of Afghanistan in 1979, US interest in the region has increased. The Reagan Administration provided a stable military umbrella for both India and Pakistan. Furthermore, it continually linked foreign aid to a reduction in tensions. India gained high levels of technology to help with industrialization. US aid to Pakistan provided an increased defense capability.

In spite of all this aid from the US, both parties would not forego developing nuclear arms. This is because these external conditions, even though they were very favorable, could not overcome the fundamental distrust between Pakistan and India. Since India's first detonation in 1974, both sides have endeavored to develop greater nuclear capabilities in an attempt to gain supremacy in the region.[53] Such actions only served to heighten the distrust that existed between the rivals. This led to a nuclear arms race in South Asia, gravely threatening US interests.

AFTER THE COLD WAR

The end of the Cold War in 1991 caught the world by surprise, and South Asia was no exception. The US began to move away from its alignment with Pakistan shortly after the 1990 sanctions episode and to pursue a better relationship with India. While much of the 1945-91 era in US-Indian relations could be characterized as "the Cold Peace," the period after 1991 saw the US aligning itself with India.[54] The rationale behind this was twofold. First, with the Soviet Union's disappearance, the US became more concerned with China as a strategic and economic rival. Given the hostilities between India and China, it was in the US interest to contain China. Second, the US was concerned with the Pakistani tendency toward authoritarian rule and its continued attempts to develop a nuclear weapons arsenal.

The issue of China is one that has confronted American policymakers since the 1940s. It continued to confront them after the abatement of the Cold War. As Goldstein and Freeman have suggested, the relationship between the US, the Soviet Union, and China always depended upon a certain norm of reciprocity.[55] With the Soviet Union gone, the US began to search for a means to balance China's power and prestige within the Asian community. It has been suggested that the US needs to pay more attention to India if it desires to engage China constructively, given the proximity of India to China. There is also the possibility of open markets for US goods in the world's largest democracy.[56]

The second concern of the US after 1991 has been the slide toward authoritarian rule in Pakistan, coupled with an increase in Islamabad's attempts to acquire nuclear parity with India. Some have suggested that India and Pakistan nearly escalated their 1990 crisis to a nuclear exchange.[57] In spite of the sanctions placed by the US on Pakistan for its human rights record and its continued pursuit of nuclear weapons, Islamabad has been unwilling to accede to American demands.

In the decade after the Cold War, India and Pakistan have continued to engage in their rivalry, despite US attempts to mediate. As concerns over nuclear testing and proliferation continue to dominate the security agenda of major powers the world over, the US will most likely use its military and economic might to coerce and reward India and Pakistan toward resolving their longstanding rivalry and preventing a nuclear exchange. Such has been the US pattern over the past 50 years, and little will change as long as power considerations continue to dominate world affairs.

CONCLUSION

This chapter was begun shortly after the events of September 11, 2001, and had originally intended to examine India-Pakistani relations up to the nuclear tests of 1998. However, the events of September 11, 2001 brought the role of India and Pakistan back into public view. Concerns about Pakistani support of terrorism and Pakistan's fragile military dictatorship have worried US policymakers, especially since Pakistan has allowed the US to base operations within Pakistan as it strikes at Afghanistan's Taliban leadership and the Al Qaeda terrorist network. In the weeks following September 11, hostilities between India and Pakistan again escalated over the issue of Kashmir.

The turmoil in the region has a variety of implications for the US and its future policies toward India and Pakistan. First and foremost, the US will most likely continue its sanctions against Pakistan, albeit modified to some degree, to prevent further proliferation of nuclear weapons. The fear of nuclear exchange between India and Pakistan, especially in turbulent times, will most likely force the US to rethink its relations with both India and Pakistan, to ensure that neither side is tempted to strike the other with weapons of mass destruction.

Second, the US will most likely link lessening of sanctions against Pakistan to Pakistani government promises of democratic reforms and an end to all ties with suspected terrorist organizations. As much research in recent years has suggested, there is a "democratic peace" that suggests that democracies are not likely to go to war with one another.[58] The US hope is that Pakistan will democratize and then resolve its conflict with India without resorting to further violence.

The past 50 years of Indo-Pakistani relations have seen both sides attempt to revise the status quo, particularly by resorting to force to alter the situation in Kashmir. Both states have benefited from US assistance, and both have incurred the wrath of the US over the issues of nuclear weapons and human rights. As the twenty-first century begins, the US will be forced to continue its involvement in South Asia.

NOTES

1. Paul Diehl (ed.). *The Dynamics of Enduring Rivalries* (Urbana: University of Illinois Press, 1998). See also Paul Diehl and Gary Goertz. *War and Peace in International Rivalry* (Ann Arbor: University of Michigan Press, 2000).

2. Diehl, *The Dynamics of Enduring Rivalries*, p.7.

3. Diehl and Goertz, *War and Peace in International Rivalry*, p.146.

4. Diehl and Goertz, *War and Peace in International Rivalry*, p.146.

5. It should be recalled that India has an additional rival in the region, China. China's presence influences the foreign policy behavior of India, Pakistan and the US.

6. Paul Huth. *Extended Deterrence and the Prevention of War* (New Haven: Yale University Press, 1988) , p. 15.

7. Huth, Extended *Deterrence*, pp.15-18. See also Patrick Morgan. *Deterrence: A Conceptual Analysis, 2nd ed,* (Beverly Hills: Sage Publications, 1984), pp. 42-43.

8. Morgan, *Deterrence*, p. 38.

9. Gerald Sorokin 1994. "Alliance Formation and General Deterrence: A Game-Theoretic Model and the Case of Israel." *Journal of Conflict Resolution* 38 (2): 298-325.

10. Richard Sisson and Leo E. Rose, *War and Secession: Pakistan, India, and the Creation of Bangladesh* (Berkeley and Los Angeles: University of California Press, 1990), pp. 43-44.

11. Russell J. Leng, *Bargaining and Learning in Recurring Crises: The Soviet-American, Egyptian-Israeli, and Indo-Pakistani Rivalries* (Ann Arbor: The University of Michigan Press, 2000), p.265.

12. Alastair Lamb, *The Kashmir Problem: A Historical Survey* (New York and Washington: Frederick A. Praeger Publishers, 1967), pp.40-41.

13. Leng, *Bargaining and Learning in Recurring Crises*, p.198

14. G. W. Choudhury, *Pakistan's Relations with India 1947-1966* (New York and Washington: Frederick A. Praeger Publishers, 1968), pp. 67, 106.

15. Leng. *Bargaining and Learning in Recurring Crises,* pp. 197-209. Good discussions of the Indo-Pakistani crises and wars can also be found in Michael Brecher and Jonathan Wilkenfeld. *A Study of Crisis (*Ann Arbor: University of Michigan Press, 1997).

16. Sisson and Rose, *War and Secession,* pp. 50-52.

17. See Leng, *Bargaining and Learning in Recurring Crises*, p. 213.

18. William J. Barnds, *India, Pakistan, and the Great Powers* (New York: Praeger Publishers, 1972), p.197.

19. Leng, *Bargaining and Learning in Recurring Crises,* pp. 216-17.

20. Lt-Gen B. M. Kaul, *Confrontation with Pakistan* (Delhi: Vikas publications, 1971), p. 17.

21. Barnds, *India, Pakistan, and the Great Powers,* pp. 201-3. See also Altaf Gauhar, *Ayub Khan: Pakistan's First Military Ruler* (Oxford, New York and Delhi: Oxford University Press, 1996), pp. 211-12.

22. Lamb, *The Kashmir Problem,* p.123.

23. Leng, *Bargaining and Learning in Recurring Crises,* p.238.

24. Leng, *Bargaining and Learning in Recurring Crises,* p.243.

25. Sisson and Rose, *War and Secession,* p. 199.

26. Lamb, *The Kashmir Problem,* pp. 130-31.

27. See Sumit Ganguly. (1999). "India's Pathway to Pokhran II". *International Security.* 23 (4): 148-77.

28. Sumit Ganguly. *The Origins of War in South Asia.* (Boulder: Lynne Rienner, 1986).

29. See Devin Hagerty. (1995/1996). "Nuclear Deterrence in south Asia: The 1990 Indo-Pakistani Crisis." *International Security* 20 (3): 79-114.

30. Robert J. McMahon, *The Cold War on the Periphery: The US, India, and Pakistan,* (New York: Columbia University Press, 1994), pp. 123-24.

31. John Lewis Gaddis. *Strategies of Containment.* (New York: Oxford University Press, 1982).

32. Robert Osgood. *Alliances and the American Foreign Policy.* (Baltimore: Johns Hopkins University Press, 1968).

33. H. W. Brands, *India and The US: The Cold Peace,* (Boston: Twayne Publishers, 1990), pp. 58-64.

34. G. W. Choudhury, *India, Pakistan, Bangladesh, and the Major Powers: Politics of a Divided Subcontinent,* (New York: The Free Press, 1975), pp.78-83.

35. Shirin Tahir-Kheli. *India, Pakistan and the US: Breaking with the Past* (New York: Council on Foreign Relations Press, 1997), p. 5.

36. Ibid, p. 33.

37. Stephen M. Walt, "Testing Theories of Alliance Formation: The Case of Southwest Asia." *International Organization* 42, pp. 303, 307-8.

38. Ibid, p. 298.

39. Ido Oren, (1994), "The Indo-Pakistani Arms Competition: A Deductive and Statistical Analysis." *The Journal of Conflict Resolution* 38, pp. 202-3.

40. Brands, *India and the US,* pp. 103-4.

41. Gregory Sanjian, (1998), "Cold War Imperatives and Quarrelsome Clients: Modeling U.S. and USSR Arms Transfers to India and Pakistan." *The Journal of Conflict Resolution* 42, p. 119.

42. Choudhurry, *India, Pakistan, Bangladesh, and the Major Powers,* pp. 189-91.

43. McMahon, *The Cold War on the Periphery,* p. 334.

44. Tahir-Kheli, *India, Pakistan and the US,* pp. 34-35.

45. Leng, *Bargaining and Learning in Recurring Crises,* p. 241.

46. Tahir-Kheli, *India, Pakistan and the US.* pp. 38-43.

47. The other signatories to the NPT are Great Britain, France, the Soviet Union and China.

48. Milhollin (1987, 593)

49. Gary Hufbauer, Jeffrey Schott and Kimberly Elliott. *Economic Sanctions Reconsidered.* (Washington, DC: Institute for International Economics, 1985, pp. 598-602).

50. Onkar Marwah, (1981), "India and Pakistan: Nuclear Rivals in South Asia." *International Organization* 35, p.169.

51. See Hufbauer, Schott and Elliott, *Economic Sanctions Reconsidered*, p. 600.

52. Tahir-Kheli, *India, Pakistan and* the *US*, ch. 3.

53. Ibid, pp. 74-88.

54. Brands, India and the US.

55. Joshua Goldstein and John Freeman, *Three Way Street: Strategic Reciprocity in World Politics* (Chicago: University of Chicago Press, 1989).

56. Tahir-Kheli, *India, Pakistan and the US*, pp.125-41.

57. Hagerty, 1995/1996.

58. James Lee Ray. *Democracy and International Conflict.* (Columbia: University of South Carolina Press, 1995). See also Bruce Russett. *Grasping the Democratic Peace.* (Princeton: Princeton University Press, 1993).

Index

About the Contributors

Karl DeRouen Jr. is Lecturer in Political Science at the University of Canterbury, Christchurch, New Zealand. His interests are in conflict, U.S. foreign policy and international political economy. His work has appeared in the British Journal of Political Science, International Studies Quarterly, Journal of Conflict Resolution, Journal of Politics, Journal of Peace Research, Political Research Quarterly and other journals. He also has two books on U.S. use of force.

A. Cooper Drury is Assistant Professor of Political Science at the University of Missouri. He received his Ph.D. from Arizona State University. His research interests focus on American foreign policy, coercive diplomacy, economic sanctions, and political unrest. His research has been published in Journal of Communist Studies and Transitional Politics, Journal of Contingencies and Crisis Management, Journal of Peace Research, Political Research Quarterly, and Presidential Studies Quarterly. He is also co-editor of Sanctions as Economic Statecraft: Theory and Practice (Macmillan), and serves as an officer for the Foreign Policy Analysis Section of International Studies Association.

Uk Heo is Associate Professor of Political Science at the University of Wisconsin-Milwaukee. His work has appeared in American Politics Quarterly, Asian Survey, British Journal of Political Science, Comparative Political Studies, Comparative Politics, International Studies Quarterly, Journal of Politics, Journal of Conflict Resolution, Journal of Peace Research, International Interactions, Political Research Quarterly and others. His research focuses on the political economy of defense, Asian politics, democracy-growth nexus and international conflict.

Shale Horowitz is Assistant Professor of Political Science at the University of Wisconsin-Milwaukee. He has an MA in Economics and a Ph.D. in Political Science from UCLA, has taught for a year at Central European University in Budapest,

Hungary, and has done research in many countries of Eastern Europe and the former Soviet Union, and in China and Taiwan. He is co-editor of The Political Economy of International Financial Crisis (Rowman and Littlefield, 2001), and the author or co-author of articles in Comparative Studies in Society and History, European Security, International Migration, Journal of Peace Research, Journal of Public Policy, Nationalities Papers, Pacific Focus and Polish Review. He is also currently Co-Editor of the quarterly publication, Analysis of Current Events. His research focuses on ethnic conflict, the political economy of international trade and finance, the political economy of market transition and institutional change in the post-communist countries, and the politics of agricultural policy.

Timothy D. Hoyt is Professor of Strategy at the Naval War College's College of Continuing Education and is now visiting at Georgetown University. He received a Ph.D. in political science from Johns Hopkins University. He has authored many articles on international security and strategy. Recent articles on Indian security and strategy have appeared in National Security Studies Quarterly and Joint Force Quarterly.

Jing Huang is Associate Professor of Political Science and Co-Director of the Asian Studies Program at Utah State University. He received his Ph.D. in political science from Harvard University, and is also a faculty research associate at the John K. Fairbank Center for East Asian Research at Harvard University. His publications include Factionalism in Chinese Communist Politics (Cambridge University Press, 2000) and numerous articles on Chinese politics and security issues in the Asia-Pacific region. His research interests include Chinese politics and Asian security.

Chong-Min Hyun is Professor of Political Science and former Vice President of Kyonggi University, Korea. He received his Ph.D. in political science from George Washington University. He is the author of Multimedia in Information Age (1995), Korean Electoral Studies (1992), Women in Politics (1992), and Citizen's Attitude towards U.S.-Korea Relations (1991). Currently he is teaching at George Washington University and Long Island University. His research interests include Korean politics and security, democratization, and the political economy of Asian financial crisis.

David J. Jackson is Assistant Professor in Political Science at Bowling Green State University. He earned his Ph.D. in political science from Wayne State University. His research interests include popular culture and politics, political action committee behavior and American foreign policy. He has published an article in Political Research Quarterly, and Peter Lang will publish his book, Entertainment and Politics: The Influence of Pop Culture on Young Adult Political Socialization, in 2002.

Sungho Park is Ph.D. candidate of Political Science at Texas A&M University.

Terence Roehrig is Associate Professor of Political Science at Cardinal Stritch University. He received his Ph.D. in political science from the University of Wisconsin-Madison, and is the author of The Prosecution of Former Military Leaders in Newly Democratic Nations: The Cases of Argentina, Greece, and South Korea (McFarland, 2001). His research interests include Asian politics, political corruption, democratization, and security issues in East Asia.

Kanishkan Sathasivam is Assistant Professor of Political Science at Salem State College in Massachusetts. He received his Ph.D. in Political Science from Texas A&M University. His research interests include major power competition in Central Asia, multi-nation arms races, ethnic conflict, peacekeeping and humanitarian operations, the proliferation of weapons of mass destruction, and international terrorism.

Sahar Shafqat is Assistant Professor of Political Science at St. Mary's College of Maryland. She has a Ph.D. in Political Science from Texas A&M University. She has published articles in the American Journal of Political Science and the Journal of Communist and Post-Communist Studies. Her research interests are in democratization, nationalism and ethnic conflict, and social and political movements.

Christopher Sprecher is Assistant Professor of Political Science at Texas A&M University. He received his Ph.D. in political science from Michigan State University. His research interests focus on international relations, American foreign policy, alliance behavior, deterrence theory; crisis escalation in enduring rivalries, and empirical testing of formal models. His articles have appeared in Journal of Conflict Resolution, Journal of Peace Research and others.

Alexander C. Tan is Associate Professor of Political Science at the University of North Texas. He is the author of Members, Organization and Performance (Ashgate, 2000) and co-editor of Taiwan's National Security: Dilemmas and Opportunities (Ashgate, 2001). His research has also been published in journals such as the Journal of Politics, Political Research Quarterly, Comparative Politics, Comparative Political Studies, Party Politics, Electoral Studies, West European Politics, Issues and Studies, Journal of Asian and African Studies, and Journal of East Asian Affairs. He is currently an editorial board member of Electoral Studies and Political Research Quarterly.

Scott Walker is Ph.D Candidate in Political Science at the University of North Texas.

Tsung-chi Yu is Ph.D Candidate in Political Science at the University of North Texas.